Date Due

OC 05 '99			

A

Kiss and Tell

Kiss and Tell

SURVEYING SEX IN THE TWENTIETH CENTURY

JULIA A. ERICKSEN

WITH SALLY A. STEFFEN

HARVARD UNIVERSITY PRESS

CAMBRIDGE, MASSACHUSETTS, AND LONDON, ENGLAND   1999

Library of Congress Cataloging-in-Publication Data

Ericksen, Julia, A., 1941–
Kiss and tell : surveying sex in the twentieth century /
Julia A. Ericksen with Sally A. Steffen.
    p. cm.
Includes bibliographical references and index.
ISBN 0-674-50535-2 (alk. paper)
1. Sexual behavior surveys—United States.   2. Sexology—United
States—History—20th century.   3. Sex customs—United States.
I. Steffen, Sally A.   II. Title.
HQ18.U5E75   1999
306.7'0973'0904—dc21   98-38990

To the hundreds of men and women who undertook surveys
in the belief that the truth about sex can set us free

Acknowledgments

IN A BOOK which argues that researchers should acknowledge their histories and social positions, it seems appropriate for me to do the same. I was born in the North of England in a politically active, working-class family. My interest in the sociology of sexuality began in the late 1970s when I taught a course on the subject. I had read Howard Becker's book on social problems, with its insight that rather than trying to solve problems without questioning their origins we should examine the process of their creation. When I discovered John Gagnon and William Simon's book *Sexual Conduct*, I learned to ask the same questions of sexuality. Since the 1980s there has been an outpouring of work on the social construction of sexuality, most of which acknowledges Foucault as the intellectual parent, but for me the epiphany came earlier.

Two other intellectual genres also informed my work on *Kiss and Tell*. The first is survey research. As a graduate student at the University of Michigan, I participated in the Detroit Area Survey and first learned of fertility surveys. The second is feminist theory and practice. This also dates from Ann Arbor, where I joined a consciousness raising group in the late 1960s.

It was not until 1992, at the conclusion of twelve years in academic administration, that I brought these three topics together. My research had always been on women's work, but I had become increasingly curious about the way the social sciences produce knowledge, particularly in less easily investigated areas like sexuality. I remembered reading about a congressman who had persuaded the federal government not to fund the first large national survey of sexual behavior, intended to learn if the sexual practices of heterosexuals were leading to the spread of AIDS. I had wondered how this could be such a sensitive topic so many years after Kinsey. Along with Sally Steffen, my assistant in university administration and a law student, I decided to find out.

We began to trace the history of surveys that included questions about sexual behavior. We assumed there might be as many as 20 of these, excluding ones that only asked about sexual attitudes, but we found approximately 750 undertaken over a period of 100 years.

To locate surveys we traced those referred to by later ones. So as not to miss those which had rarely been cited, we also examined every issue of the five journals that reported the most surveys. These were the *Journal of Sex Research, Archives of Sexual Behavior, Family Planning Perspectives,* the *Journal of Marriage and the Family,* and the *American Journal of Public Health.* We think we found the large majority of surveys, including many which informed our analysis but which we were unable to discuss in the book because of space. We organized the material by date of data collection, when available, rather than by date of publication.

We also set about learning what had happened in the congressional debates on the survey of adults opposed by the congressman and on the American Teen Survey, which had met a similar fate. Our research quickly led us to Judy Auerbach at the Consortium of Social Science Associations. Along with others, she had been lobbying Congress to approve funding for both surveys. Without her help in describing the sequence of events and the key players on both sides of the debate, it would have been difficult to write Chapter 9. Sally and I interviewed many of those key players; we would like to thank the late Bill Baily, Maureen Burns, Lisa Kaeser, May Kennedy, Robert Knight, John Mashburn, Paul Mero, Victoria Otten, and Judith Reisman. Special appreciation goes to Wendy Baldwin, who was the deputy director of the National Institutes of Child Health and Human Development. She gave of her time most generously, and she brought her colleague Virginia Cain, who had been responsible for the adult survey, to a second meeting. In these meetings we learned not only the history of the two surveys but also how the federal government became involved in funding demographic research and later sex research.

We also interviewed a number of researchers, some of whom had worked on the two ill-fated surveys: Joseph Catania, Thomas Coates, William Darrow, Ronald Freedman, John Gagnon, Shere Hite, Morton Hunt, John Kantner, Edward Laumann, Robert Michael, Ira Reiss, Freya Sonenstein, William Simon, Tom Smith, Koray Tanfer, Ronald Rindfuss, and Richard Udry. Interviewing one's colleagues is a wonderful learning experience. All were generous with their time and willing to discuss the issues surrounding surveys dealing with sexual behavior and/or reproduction. And several went further, taking a profound interest in our work.

We received generous help from Temple University. I would like to thank Temple's president, Peter Liacouras, for granting me an administrative leave for the year 1992–1993 and the Center for Public Policy for granting Sally Steffen a research assistant's position for 1992–1994. A number of graduate and undergraduate students eased the way: Rich Alphonse, Sousan Barlow, Heather Broomhead, Carey Cawood, Kelly Feighan, Kristen Guzzetta, Bill Kaiser, Kelly Nelson, Kim Postgate, Bedelia Richards, and Peter Verrecchia. In addition, the staff of the Paley Library, particularly those in the Interlibrary Loan Department, helped us locate literally hundreds of survey reports, many in obscure and long-deceased journals.

From the beginning Joyce Seltzer of Harvard University Press believed in the book, and her editing skills, along with those of her assistant editor, Cherie Weitzner Acierno, made a great difference to the final product. Maurice Vogel read the book proposal in its early days and suggested that I send it to Joyce. The book was further improved by the style editing of Camille Smith, also of Harvard University Press, and by the comments of anonymous readers. These comments were particularly helpful. Because the book deals with so many living sociologists, I had been reluctant to ask colleagues to read the manuscript.

At the outset Sally and I envisioned a joint effort and coauthorship. The first two years—the research and conceptualization phases—were fully collaborative. Then Sally embarked on her legal career, and we reluctantly agreed that I would do most of the writing. Still, she wrote sections of Chapters 2 and 5 and edited many drafts of the manuscript. Without her enthusiasm and energy I doubt I could have returned from the wilderness of university administration and faced the no less daunting tasks and challenges of writing the book.

Finally, my children, Polly, Andrew, and Monica, and my grandchildren, Miles and Drew, reminded me that there are important things in the world besides scholarly publishing. And Gene Ericksen knows the numerous contributions he made, intellectual, financial, and emotional.

Contents

1   Asking Questions about Sex   1

2   In Urgent Need of the Facts   14

3   Sex in the Service of the Conjugal Bond   36

4   Sex before Marriage   67

5   Adolescent Fertility   87

6   Coupling and Uncoupling   110

7   Excising the Experts   135

8   Gay Men and AIDS   158

9   Politics and Sex Surveys   176

10   The Story Continues   209

11   Reforming Sex Research   219

Notes   231

Index   261

Kiss and Tell

Asking Questions about Sex

It is both surprising and disturbing how empirically ill informed we as a nation are about important aspects of sexual behavior.

—Edward Laumann, John Gagnon, Robert Michael, and Stuart Michaels, 1994

I N 1977, after reanalyzing findings from the Kinsey Reports of thirty years earlier, Bruce Voeller, the chair of the National Gay Task Force, declared that 10 percent of the U.S. population was gay.[1] The media accepted and promoted this as fact until the late 1980s, when the figure was challenged by conservative groups as inflated and self-serving, indeed as "Exhibit A in any discussion of media myths created by scientific research."[2] At a gay rights march in Washington, D.C., the Lesbian Avengers and Act Up, two politically militant groups, chanted "10 percent is not enough, Recruit! Recruit!" while Bob Knight of the conservative Family Research Council insisted that 10 percent was a gross exaggeration. Knight and other conservatives cast aspersions on a proposed national survey of sexual behavior designed to supply updated and more reliable data. They described this proposal as the result of pressure by "the homosexual activist community" to "gather evidence to buttress up the old claim; if not 10 percent, something close to it."

The controversy flared further when researchers at a Seattle-based think tank, the Battelle Research Center, concluded on the basis of a 1991 survey that only 1 percent of men were gay, a figure the press quoted widely.[3] This new finding stunned both gays and conservatives and became a new rallying point. Gay groups were concerned at the depletion of their numbers and suspicious of the survey's methodology; the sample was too small and the questions too few for an accurate measure. Conservatives were jubilant that gays were less than 10 percent of the population, but such a severely diminished adversary might compromise their anti-gay agenda altogether. Only forty years earlier McCarthyite senators had used Kinsey data to argue that the "homosexual menace" was considerably more serious than previously understood.[4]

To most observers, this disagreement about numbers could be easily resolved by a larger, more rigorous, and more comprehensive survey. Or could it? While "facts" appeared to be the basis of the conflict between the National Gay Task Force and the Family Research Council, the fight went far beyond the data. It was a fight over the nature and validity of social science and over the role of surveys in establishing accurate information about sexual behavior. And it quickly became a political battle over the right to define normal behavior and the nature of the evidence to be used in such definitions.

Sexual behavior is a volatile and sensitive topic, and surveys designed to reveal it have both great power and great limits. By revealing the private behavior of others, they provide a way for people to evaluate their own behavior and even the meaning of information the surveys produce. And they provide experts with information they urgently seek to understand society and develop social policy. Social scientists often view surveys as providing hard facts about behavior, yet results are limited by researchers' often unrecognized preconceptions about what the important questions are and also by respondents' ability and willingness to reveal what they have done. Surveyors frequently assume that the facts are ahistorical realities to be tapped by experts rather than transitory events that are open to interpretation. And the "truths" surveys reveal have enormous implications.

As Voeller understood from the first, 10 percent was large enough to represent an attack on heterosexuality as the accepted norm and indeed on the conventional meaning of gender. It implied that at least one gay person existed in almost every extended family in America. It challenged the underlying principle of family life: the "natural" sexual attraction between men and women. No wonder the leaders of the Family Research Council expended enormous energy in challenging this figure at every possible opportunity. The size of the gay population was critical for determining whether being gay constituted a normal identity. Those who believed the answer to be affirmative knew that a large gay population would strengthen demands for social inclusion, while conservatives seeking exclusion strove to prevent "deviants" from claiming normality.

For most of Western history, religion decreed appropriate standards for sexual and social behavior. By the twentieth century, however, secular social scientists had become the experts. Even conservatives like Knight, who want to espouse the cause of religious fundamentalism, defend their arguments not with theology but with statistical data and other scientific evidence. In deciding what is normal, experts have viewed private behavior, particularly sexual behavior, as an important indicator of personal stability and well-being. They have regarded their assessments as scientific but have based them on assumptions about gender, assumptions promoted by biologists as scientific fact.

Biologists have viewed men's and women's different reproductive systems as inevitable sources of difference in all aspects of their lives, making men and women not only different but complementary, in need of each other to be fulfilled.[5] In this view, fundamental gender distinctions find particular expression in sexual activity between men and women, whose intense natural physical attraction to each other is the centerpiece of their relationship and of the societal ideal of the couple. Individuals may deviate widely from this norm, but such assumptions provide powerful incentives toward conformity. To be normal sexually means to do what is natural, that is, heterosexual. If gay sex is shown to be widespread in the population, it challenges the assumption that men and women are natural sexual partners. Although the presence of a few sexual "deviants" underscores the meaning of normal sexual attraction, the presence of many undermines it.

The French intellectual Michel Foucault argued that with the development of the modern nation-state sexual identity became a central component of Western identity.[6] This emphasis on sexual identity, he explained, arose as a mechanism for monitoring individual behavior in a world where external authority had declined. As feudalism eroded, the bureaucratic state replaced the absolute power of kings. Thus power became decentralized. If social order was to remain in this new world, people must assume responsibility for their own behavior. Furthermore, population increase, the rise of cities, and the consequent growth in impersonal social relations threatened individuals at a time when they could no longer expect the authorities to guarantee social order.

In such a world, Foucault argued, citizens learned to control their own behavior by checking on the normality of their acts. Private behavior became especially vulnerable to personal scrutiny, since its very nature makes it difficult for others to police. As science replaced religion as the source of advice, biology became the basis for determining what constituted normal sexual behavior. Experts deciphered sexual activities, evaluated their normality, and gave advice to potential practitioners. While Foucault wrote little about gender, those influenced by his work have noted that this normal sexual behavior was gendered. As sexologists catalogued sexual types, they described men and women as having fundamentally different sexual desires, responses, and roles to play in their relationships with each other.

Foucault took issue with the twentieth-century view that the nineteenth century was a period when human sexuality was subjected to a repressed silence. The Victorians, he argued, discussed sexuality obsessively, since they viewed out-of-control sexuality as a threat to social order. In doing so, they created new sexual identities through which to catalogue sexual acts: for example, the child who masturbated or the sexual deviate whose behavior could be interpreted only by experts. The most famous of the early experts, Richard von Krafft-Ebing, classified a huge array of sexual types, providing detailed descriptions of the personalities of those who engaged in various behaviors or displayed various tastes.[7] Krafft-Ebing and others educated physicians about the existence of these types and the threat they represented. In this view, sexuality and society were at odds with each other, and social order faced constant threats from an out-of-control sexuality.

Victorians extolled the virtues of an orderly private life as a protection from the modern menaces of the public world, but the existence of the sexual side of this private life suggested the possibility of less easily controlled behavior. Although governments could attempt to legislate morality and police private lives, the cities, in particular, afforded sexual marketplaces with a broad spectrum of flourishing sexual activity. Such an atmosphere occasioned great anxiety about sex and its practice among the general population.[8]

The citizens of villages and towns in earlier times could scrutinize their neighbors' lives more easily. Proximity made shame a potent force for the regulation and repression of illicit sexual activity. Once people could keep aspects of their lives hidden from families and friends, preventing transgressions became a personal rather than a collective responsibility. Guilt, not shame, ensured conformity. Guilt was especially powerful in a country where immigrants from all over the world flaunted different and sometimes frightening behaviors. Concerns about others' most intimate acts exacerbated fears about moral taint and threats to health.

Turn-of-the-century writers still viewed sexuality as in conflict with society rather than as a product of it, but they were more sympathetic to sexual variety. Sigmund Freud was convinced that the normal path to sexual maturity lay in heterosexuality. Yet he assumed that everyone had to repress a variety of other sexual desires in order to achieve this, and he was tolerant of those who took a different path. Freud's contemporary Havelock Ellis went a step further by describing sexual variety itself as part of the natural order of things. Ellis thought scientific sexology would liberate individuals from the constraints of a repressive social system.[9] But even Freud and Ellis helped increase the pervasive sense that the sexual world held dark secrets. The existence of sexology created the possibility of watching for signs of deviant behavior and rooting it out.

During the twentieth century, experts following in the footsteps of Freud and Ellis espoused increasingly liberal views of sexuality and, like Ellis, sought to liberate sexuality from societal repression. Foucault viewed this twentieth-century espousal of sexual liberty as an endless discussion that, rather than creating actual liberation, increased concern about sexual normality while changing the definition of normal. There were other contributors to this discussion as well. Individuals and institutions concerned with the general welfare, including the government, public health officials, the media, and social scientists, continued to worry that private acts threatened public safety.

All those providing sexual advice viewed the family as the bedrock of social stability and the gendered couple as its foundation. For them, women and men occupied separate spheres of control. Men's assertive personalities, symbolized in their role in sexual intercourse, were ideally suited to run public life, while women were keepers of the private sphere who provided sustenance, sexual and otherwise, to those who ran the world. Over the century, despite significant modifications of these assumptions, the gendered nature of private sexual behavior remained central. Likewise, a pervasive sense that sexuality is so inherently unstable and irrational that society must be ever vigilant kept experts busy proffering advice. This fear that private behavior could affect public well-being fed repeated panics about such issues as venereal disease, teenage pregnancy, and indiscriminate sex, while it fostered an interest in expert counsel.

The first sexologists relied on their own insights supplemented by clinical records to document the dangers of sexual excess. In the twentieth century this task fell to social scientists. Since the Progressive era, American social scientists have viewed their disciplines as capable of furthering human progress by alleviating such panic. They approached this task using scientific methods, in particular statistical methods. In each time of sexual crisis they perceived an urgent need for information. Yet they did not collect data with the scientific disinterest they imagined. Instead, their assumption that men and women differed from each other sexually dictated the form of their questions about the nation's social and sexual health. Believing that solutions start with the facts, the experts produced their urgently needed data through a filter of gendered sexuality.

Given the long-standing American belief that numbers provide factual representations of the world, surveys are an obvious source of information.[10] Since sex is an arena in which what others do is unclear, actual information about sexual behavior had two ready-made audiences: experts concerned that private behavior had a negative impact on public order, and individuals anxious to use hard evidence to evaluate and regulate their own behavior. Since 1892, when the biology student Clelia Mosher started asking upper-middle-class married women whether they liked intercourse, how often they had intercourse, and how often they wanted to have intercourse[11]—information she never had the courage to publish—researchers have asked hundreds of thousands of people about their sexual behavior and *have* published their findings for others to read.

This intense scrutiny created a window into the sexual lives of ordinary women and men that exposed private behavior to professional interpretation. Experts relayed this information to the public in reports and press releases. They evaluated the meaning of the data for what men and women should do, what they should like to do, and what they should fear doing. They not only reported what they believed to be the facts but helped create these facts in line with their own ideological positions, particularly their beliefs about gender. These facts, in turn, helped create sexual practices in two ways. First, reports about what others were doing suggested to readers that they should model their behavior on those who appeared to represent them. Second, surveys evaluated the behavior of those in the surveys, and this also provided lessons to readers. Thus even reports that accurately described aspects of the behavior of a particular group at a particular time created behavior by acting as guides or warnings to others. Since the most consistent assumption on which the surveys rested was of a gendered sexuality, albeit a changing one, surveys helped sustain a vision of sexuality as innately contained within masculinity and femininity.

The potential impact of such revelations is the reason those who disagree with results find it necessary to discredit them. Since the meanings attributed to the data have political implications beyond the facts, those who conduct sex surveys feel pressure to meet certain social needs. Investigators do not operate in a cultural vacuum. They approach their research holding beliefs about what is normal and what they expect to find, beliefs shaped by their personal experiences and desires, by their social circumstances, and by the findings of earlier researchers. Furthermore, when survey results become public, readers may change their sexual behavior as a result of finding out what others "like them" do, and researchers find themselves influencing what they had merely hoped to record.

Survey researchers, sensitive to charges of subjectivity, claim that as scientists using modern survey methods they can eliminate the effects of the expectations and biases they bring to their research. They concede that, without the advantage of modern techniques, early researchers were less objective, but they insist that today's methodology can take care of such problems. Asking questions of persons one at a time and aggregating the answers appears to reveal reality. Such scientific surveys seem the perfect way to amass information about a variety of social problems—venereal disease, divorce, teen pregnancy, for example—in order to develop informed public policies aimed at alleviating their ill effects.

Modern survey practice evolved throughout the twentieth century but came into its own after the Second World War.[12] Nowadays, letting prior hypotheses influence outcomes is decried as poor technique and a betrayal of the fundamental principles of science. Researchers view the scientific method as demanding hypotheses, or at least research questions, which they test in ways that do not influence the outcome. Although there has been little acknowledgment that the choice of research topic inevitably represents a point of view, four phases of the survey process have been the subjects of methodological studies intended to achieve this goal of objectivity. These are decisions about whom to interview; methods of data collection, including interviewer training; content and structure of the interview schedule; and the analysis of data.

Early researchers did not understand either the importance of interviewing all segments of the target population or that researchers who chose which respondents to interview might influence the results. They consciously surveyed "the better part of the middle class," or those who were "not pathological mentally or physically," in order to present the best possible case for their arguments.[13] The use of random sampling in surveys, a technique that ensures that each person in the target population has an equal, or a known, probability of being selected, developed in the 1930s. In this method, researchers completely remove themselves from decisions about which persons to interview. By 1940 the U.S. Bureau of the Census had adopted random sampling for its monthly survey of employment and unemployment.[14]

While sampling techniques changed survey research, sex researchers were slow to adopt these superior methods. Alfred Kinsey, who undertook his survey when modern sampling was in its infancy, did not believe random sampling was possible in sex surveys, and many subsequent sex surveyors followed his example. Kinsey believed that people contacted at random would refuse to answer personal questions. Instead, he selected respondents himself. Unlike his predecessors, Kinsey understood that all segments of the population should be included, so he went to great lengths to represent all sexual tastes. Unfortunately, in his determination to be inclusive, he most likely overestimated less common sexual activities such as same-gender sexual behavior.

Since the 1980s this avoidance of random sampling has ended. A number of recent sexual behavior surveys, for example the Battelle survey, have successfully used random sampling techniques to select respondents. While a 100 percent response rate is unlikely in a random sample, and nonrespondents can bias the results, the use of this method of selecting respondents has improved the reliability of the data immeasurably.

The history of interviewing in sex surveys is more complex, and many issues remain unresolved. From the beginning some researchers insisted on using face-to-face interviews on the grounds that this would create the intimacy and trust necessary for respondents to reveal their sexual secrets. But they did not understand the problems involved when researchers personally conducted the interviews. Gilbert Hamilton, who surveyed the sexual adjustment of married couples in New York in the late 1920s, did all the interviewing himself and imposed his own notions of intimacy and trust idiosyncratically. Commenting that his interviewing technique produced frequent "weeping and trips to the toilet," he maintained scientific objectivity by noting all such occurrences and by tying "the subject's chair to the wall in order to forestall the tendency that most persons have to draw closer to the recipient of confidences as these become more intimate."[15] Kinsey also was too early to understand the importance of using professional interviewers, of keeping the hypotheses from interviewers, and of training interviewers to ask sensitive questions.

By 1955, when the sociologist Ronald Freedman conducted the first national survey of married women's contraceptive practices, he and his colleagues used properly trained and monitored interviewers; and techniques have further improved since then.[16] Today investigators make well-informed decisions on whether to have interviewers ask the questions or to ask them in other ways, such as by computer. Interviewers receive extensive training and are held to rigorous standards. Researchers study the impact of interviewer traits like gender and race on different respondents. From the beginning some researchers avoided interviews. Instead, they designed self-administered questionnaires for respondents to fill out and return. This method assures respondents of confidentiality and increases their willingness to disclose sexual secrets. But it produces lower response rates and creates problems for respondents who have difficulty reading.

All surveys, regardless of interview method, require some type of questionnaire. Because the researcher holding the hypothesis selects, words, and orders the questions, questionnaire design is particularly vulnerable to researcher bias. In the early years of sex surveys, surveyors did not understand the problem, and, in order to protect themselves from respondent outrage, wrote reassurances that the sexual acts respondents were being asked to describe were normal. Katharine Davis's 1920 mail-in survey of the sexual experiences of middle-class women included a long prefatory statement to her questions on masturbation communicating the opinion—shared by other progressive thinkers in her day—that, in spite of condemnation, masturbation was not harmful for women. Indeed, some experts, she said, maintained that it was "a normal stage in the development of the sex nature and must be passed through if sexual development is to be complete."[17]

Davis expected to find that many women masturbated, and not surprisingly she found this. In modern questionnaires, such reassurance—which may push a respondent in the direction of a particular response—rarely appears. Before the survey takes place, pretesting helps achieve clear, nondirective questions. Careful wording and ordering of questions produce more accurate responses. It is more difficult to examine the effect of turning abstract concepts into terms that respondents can understand, or to ascertain what a respondent might reasonably remember. Even here, however, research has made progress. For example, one source of variation in estimates of the size of the gay population is the questions asked. Not only does asking the gender of respondents' sexual partners produce different results than asking respondents if they are homosexual, bisexual, or heterosexual, but the specific wording of the question makes a difference. It is hard to compare the findings of the Battelle researchers with those of Kinsey because of the differences in the questions.

During the final phase, data analysis, bias was endemic but often unrecognized in early surveys. Indeed, obtaining impartial data and analyzing them in a manner unfettered by the investigator's agenda was not always the aim. Max Exner, who in 1913 embarked on one of the earliest sex surveys, stated that "we are in urgent need of facts which would enable us to speak with reasonable definiteness" about the need for sex education as a way of curbing young men's excessive sexual desires.[18] Although draped in scientific garb, Exner's questions and analysis reveal that for him the survey was not a tool to discover information. He used it to support his preexisting "knowledge" that learning about sex from the street led to unhygienic sexual practices.

Over time, with increasingly rigorous survey methods, such obviously prejudiced practices ceased. Researchers even began to realize that their unconscious biases could influence the outcome. With more sophisticated data analysis techniques, researchers could be more certain of their conclusions and less able to shape them to satisfy an agenda. Yet they remained largely oblivious of the fact that the questions they ask of the data reveal a point of view. The Battelle researchers insisted that the furor over their reported incidence of male homosexuality was misplaced. This, they said, was not the main target of their research, and they did not have sufficient data for accuracy. But they revealed this result in a carefully orchestrated manner that seemed designed to maximize publicity.

Throughout the century, survey researchers interested in sexual behavior viewed their results as improvements on earlier findings. Indeed, this brief description of survey practice suggests that a history of surveys of sexual behavior should be a history of the growing sophistication of researchers and the increasing certainty of their conclusions. In order for this to be the case, two conditions would have to hold. First, researchers would have to be neutral observers of sexual behavior, an unlikely proposition in a world where no one escapes pressure to monitor personal sexual standards and desires. Second, sexual behavior would have to be independent of history and culture. In such a case, questions such as the proportion of gays in the population would be technical, not political or historically specific questions.

In fact, while survey improvements have produced more accurate reflections of historical moments, surveys do not divulge universal truths, only those relative to their time and place. Furthermore, even with the best intentions, researchers have managed their surveys in such a way as to produce findings reflecting their own beliefs about gender and normality and their concerns about the dangers of sex research. Responsible researchers adopted techniques to neutralize the effect of their biases, but their very choice of research topics assumed a certain view of sexuality. When, in 1992, the research team quoted in the epigraph to this chapter finally received funds for a large national survey of American adults, they used the latest survey techniques. Yet they conducted their research in a climate in which sexual coupling, especially with strangers, was perceived as potentially fatal. Their concern over "promiscuity" colored all aspects of the survey.[19]

In addition to researchers and respondents, two other groups had an impact on what information surveys revealed: those who funded surveys and those who interpreted the results for larger audiences. At first sex surveys were commissioned by private organizations interested in promoting a particular point of view. In later years the federal government took over much of the funding. Those who dispensed federal dollars also had a point of view to promote, although they did so in a less directive manner.

In the early years, researchers not only controlled who respondents were and what their answers meant; they also controlled the dissemination of results to other experts and the general public. As more sources of dissemination appeared, it became difficult to exert such control. Once the media began reporting the results of surveys, their goals differed widely from those of the researchers, who often found their results presented in a distorted manner. The Battelle researchers experienced this. They used the media to promote their survey, but they quickly lost control of the debate. As discussion raged over the percentage of men who were gay, the rest of the results, including those of most interest to the researchers, almost disappeared from view.

Do these limits and problems mean we can learn little from surveys of sexual behavior? On the contrary, such surveys teach us a great deal about sexuality in America, about the beliefs that have shaped sexual behavior, and about the concerns that have driven researchers to ask questions. They show the changes in these concerns and in assumptions about sexuality. Tracing these changes reveals the history of sexuality in the twentieth century. Furthermore, as survey practice improved, the ensuing descriptions of sexual practice not only provided a behavioral control but provided comfort and encouraged people to act on their desires.

We tell this story in the belief that sexuality is not a trait with which individuals are born but a crucial aspect of identity that is socially created. Researchers often assumed that sexuality was innate and that their task was to reveal what already existed. In contrast, we believe that the assumptions driving the research helped create the sexuality the research revealed. Researchers' assumptions were the product of the larger society, of the researchers' positions within that society, and of the findings of their predecessors. While the culture changed over time and researchers did not occupy identical social or professional positions, two factors remained almost constant. First, researchers shared general beliefs in the existence of innate differences between men and women and viewed such differences as the basis of sexual attraction. Second, most researchers were men and viewed the world through the eyes of male privilege. They assumed a straightforward male sexuality while puzzling over "the problem of female sexuality." In this, their major concern was that women should satisfy men's needs. Female sexual pleasure was increasingly viewed as a way to make men happy and families secure. It was not until the 1980s, when women began to undertake sex surveys, that the focus began shifting to female pleasure as a woman's concern.

Researchers believed that women become aroused slowly and through love, while men experience constant arousal. These beliefs influenced surveys and were so powerful that researchers did not always know how to handle contrary findings. For example, the few women surveyors in the early decades described a strong female sex drive, more similar to than different from men's.[20] Yet even as male experts reported these women's results they ignored the voices behind them, choosing instead to reinterpret findings to fit conventional assumptions. Furthermore, these assumptions about gender and sexuality differed according to respondents' race, class, and age. Middle-class adults received the most attention because of beliefs that only they had the time or education to achieve sexual bliss. Only during periods of crisis when sexuality became a symbol for concern about other social changes did groups other than the white middle class become the targets of sex research.

Part of the reason for caution over whom to interview involved researchers' need to justify sex surveys while protecting themselves from charges of prurience. Those undertaking sex surveys found them to be a dangerous enterprise. Sex talk, with its forbidden overtones, was often embarrassing because it was exciting. Doing the research involved invading a private sphere. This affected the nature of the research questions and the explanations given for asking them. Surveyors rarely justified sex surveys on the grounds of interest. Instead, they used the urgent social problems of the day as an explanation for their questions. Their justifications had implications for the collection of data, for the questions asked, and for what constituted knowledge. Discomfort over sex talk, even in scientific guise, made sex surveys more vulnerable to personal pressures at every stage of the survey process.

Researchers in many areas claim their results are definitive, but these claims have a particular cast in sex research because worries about criticism often lead to overstatement of the reliability of conclusions. In reaction to the claims of conservative opponents like Senator Jesse Helms that "most Americans resent even being asked to answer questions about how often they engage in sex, with whom, their preferences for sexual partners, and which sex act they prefer,"[21] researchers tended to downplay the methodological and theoretical challenges of their research. In such a climate they were loath to consider the impact of their research on behavior. They tried to convince skeptical audiences that asking questions about sex was easy and the results were trustworthy. Paradoxically, this need for certainty created resistance to research on the methodology of sex surveys, since such research requires an acknowledgment of uncertainty. It also made researchers hesitant to share their experiences with other researchers, which, in turn, slowed the accumulation of knowledge on which to build. This made researchers vulnerable to attack on methodological grounds even from those whose objections were actually political.

Nevertheless, the history of sexual behavior surveys remains a history of the optimism of researchers and of the enlightenment of readers. Living in a culture in which no topic has been considered too difficult or too private for scientific inquiry, and believing that knowledge would further human progress, surveyors saw themselves as pioneers venturing where others dared not go and doing so without fear of personal consequences. Their goal was to delve into the most secret and shame-laden human behavior, and to reveal it for all to see in the hope that the truth would liberate people from ignorance and stigma. In recent years many writers about sexuality have agreed with Foucault's argument that talk about sex does not liberate sex but is merely another way of controlling it. Researchers had a limited understanding of how they shaped the results of surveys. But they showed courage in following their beliefs that social stability is best served by exposing practice rather than by hiding it. Their work reveals an important thread of cultural and sexual history in the twentieth century.

2

In Urgent Need of the Facts

Increased sterility, marriage late or never, the falling birthrate . . . , unhappy marriages, frequent divorce, increasing promiscuity and sex crimes, . . . an army of unattached women vicariously sacrificing their natural desires of love and maternity for anti-vivisection and female suffrage propagandism or for men's vocations, and last and most alarming of all, the infection, sooner or later, of the majority of men and women with lax ideas of sexual morals and with the two fearfully destructive venereal diseases, gonorrhea and syphilis, are ample apology for serious work on any or all sex questions.

—Walter Robie, 1916

IN 1898 a secretary of the college department of the YMCA, F. S. Brockman, undertook a study of "the moral and religious life" of boys in early adolescence. Rather than interview young boys directly, he mailed questionnaires to men attending colleges, universities, and theological seminaries asking them about their preparatory school years. Echoing an increasing concern of the YMCA, Brockman described adolescence as a time of "moral and religious crisis" for middle-class boys. By collecting the "plain unvarnished facts" about a variety of topics, particularly religion, Brockman hoped to document the existence of a crisis of religious and sexual development. Three questions addressed his fears about sex: "What was your severest temptation?" "Did you yield?" "To what extent?"[1] It is difficult, a century later, to know the exact meaning Brockman's questions had for himself or his respondents. At the time, the 251 young men who returned completed questionnaires understood them, and although Brockman never used the word "sex," they responded to his queries with details of sexual temptations and "yieldings."

The publication of Brockman's results in G. Stanley Hall's *The Pedagogical Seminary* provides further clues about the author's intent. Hall was an important early figure in American psychology and its greatest popularizer.[2] Like other leading social scientists of his day, he viewed the scientific method as the tool with which to build the perfect society. By the turn of the twentieth century the social sciences took shape as independent disciplines, and practitioners began collecting empirical data for a variety of social purposes. The European forefathers of these disciplines believed that only the methods practiced in the natural sciences could produce knowledge. They saw human society as an organic whole that developed according to general rules, which were predictable and could be discovered by a rigorous methodology. Following Newton in the physical sciences, they believed knowledge of the social world could be obtained by direct observation and measurement of phenomena. Such knowledge could demystify social relations and behavior. American social scientists also believed this knowledge could alleviate social ills and improve the human condition.

Hall combined his commitment to empirical science with a strong religious faith derived from his puritanical family. While studying in Germany he became interested in psychology and committed to viewing science as the way to progress. He spent most of his professional life at Clark University, where he was the first president and where he built a strong empirically based psychology department. Hall was taken with the ideas of the nineteenth-century British philosopher Herbert Spencer, who argued that societies underwent evolution in much the same way as species. From this Hall argued that the passage from childhood to adulthood followed all the stages of the development of the Northern European "race" from savagery to civilization. Believing that individually acquired characteristics would become inheritable at the end of maturation, he focused on adolescence as a critical developmental stage for advanced societies. In his view, boys started out as uncivilized savages but, under the right circumstances, grew into wise and mature men. They would pass their wisdom on to their children and advance the race only if they were raised slowly to full maturation. The most crucial problem for adolescent boys, Hall warned, was "precocity" or premature development of adult interests, which quickly led to degeneracy. This was best illustrated by working-class youth, who went straight from childhood to adulthood. Hall concluded that, therefore, the future depended on middle-class boys.

To support his ideas, Hall built a child development program whose participants used questionnaires to collect masses of data on all aspects of childhood. Surveys were an ideal tool for social education and engineering, providing empirical evidence about behavior that could not always be observed.[3] The international secretary of the YMCA, Luther Gulick, was a follower of Hall's. Gulick submitted Brockman's research to Hall's journal, and he used Hall's arguments, bolstered by Brockman's research, to move the YMCA toward a more developmental approach to building moral men. Gulick built a youth program for boys aged twelve to sixteen. The program's healthy activities would occupy their minds and prevent them from focusing on adult pleasures too early.[4]

With its twin emphases on religious conversion and masturbation, Brockman's survey reflects the crisis these men perceived in the lives of middle-class boys. Gulick and Hall both believed boys should not undergo religious conversion until late adolescence. Both worried about youthful masturbation, which they described as the greatest deterrent to proper conversion. While rejecting the most lurid nineteenth-century fears about the effects of masturbation on boys' physical and moral state, Hall warned that it caused a depletion of energy. Masturbation was a threat to the bodies and souls of immature boys. Unused semen should be reabsorbed into the body to provide the great energy necessary for proper religious conversion.

Brockman's data underscored their worst fears. Of the 232 respondents who answered his survey, 132 declared masturbation to be their severest temptation, and all but one had yielded. Fifty-seven young men said their greatest temptation was laziness, which Brockman interpreted to mean "an indisposition to study rather than to physical exercise." Since, like Hall, Brockman believed premature intellectual development to be a major cause of precocity in adolescence, he took comfort in laziness: "In view of the terrible strength and ravages of the sexual temptations, as recalled in these answers, one is led to wonder whether this indisposition to books is not a call to out-door exercise, and whether the failure to obey this demand of nature may not account in some measure for the distressing failure to control the sexual appetite."[5] Furthermore, religion offered little protection. The majority of respondents had already converted by age seventeen, "the day when the young man is most prone to drift out of the church." Among those yielding to masturbation, Brockman was horrified to discover, at least twenty-four had done so after deciding to become ministers. Sixty-six respondents had even more precocious ideas: sexual intercourse was their severest temptation, and seventeen had yielded.

Brockman's was the first published sex survey. While worries about masturbation were not new, he used empirical research to confirm fears about the impact of secret sexual acts on public health. Brockman undertook his survey at a time of great social upheaval.[6] Improved nutrition and public health caused middle-class young men to grow taller and reach puberty earlier. At the same time, their education was extended, delaying their entry into the labor force. In an increasingly secularized society, sexual tensions were rising as young men's church attendance was dropping. The problem appeared to be exacerbated by city living, which allowed young men to associate with undesirable friends away from their parents' eyes. Gulick argued that the city itself caused degeneracy; after two or three generations there, families discovered that their children became morally, intellectually, and physically weaker. A reason for this was certainly the opportunity the city provided for young men to learn about and practice "self-abuse" or masturbation. Such behavior, he and others believed, would lead to successively weaker generations.

While Hall hoped to delay adulthood until the early twenties for both boys and girls, he thought girls were less cause for concern as they were better adapted to sexual sublimation. Unlike boys, adolescent girls experienced little temptation. Hall, expressing a Victorian truism, declared that women were more interested in mothering than in the marital bed. He believed that biological differences in sexual interest between the sexes resulted from evolutionary progress and were getting wider. Thus ideal women were particularly uninterested in sexual activity. They remained tied to their families, attended church regularly, and were not tempted to early sexual excess. Hall warned that intellectual activity for women would cause them to turn away from childbearing and marriage and so would be disastrous for the race. Development for girls meant that their adult life should continue on the path set in their childhood. They did not need the self-discipline necessary for white-collar capitalism.

Boys not only were more easily tempted than girls but had to develop much greater self-control if they were to become men of substance, capable of advancing social progress. If they followed their constant and unending sexual urges, society could not prosper. Experts needed to know the facts about the sex lives of young men because the future of the nation truly depended on such knowledge. The YMCA, which saw religious conversion as less for the service of God than for the preservation of civilization, was the perfect organization to collect such information.

The YMCA's leaders soon discovered, however, that single-sex recreation and religious conversion were insufficient to prevent the sins of the flesh, and so they tried for a more direct approach. Gulick and his followers at the YMCA had been writing pamphlets promoting sexual abstinence since the late nineteenth century, and by 1908 Hall was recommending sex education for both sexes but different for boys than for girls.[7] Girls should learn about menses in order to develop the habits of hygiene necessary for reproduction, but boys needed to learn more than their physiology if they were to develop sufficient sobriety to resist temptation. They needed to learn first and foremost of the evils of masturbation but also of the sacred nature of sexual intercourse.

Middle-class Victorians believed that sex should not be too central in marriage lest passion overwhelm a more spiritual intimacy. For them, sex was not a bond to tie the marital pair together in intimacy and privacy. Couples set themselves apart from others with love of a less carnal sort. Perfect intimacy was based on a spiritual bond between husband and wife. Sex, as a pleasure for its own sake, debased this marital relationship. Ideally, sex should occur solely for purposes of reproduction, between a man and a woman whose souls already had intertwined; it signified the existence of love, but it did not represent love. Undoubtedly many individual Victorian couples did not live up to, or even agree with, these ideals. Some were old-fashioned enough to believe, as the Puritans did, that married couples required sexual happiness, but most nineteenth-century writing on the subject took the more modern Victorian position.[8]

In 1911, believing that education could become more important in promoting the spirituality of sexual acts, the YMCA appointed Max Exner as director of sexual education. Exner, an M.D. who had immigrated to the United States as a child, soon decided that he needed to know more about his subject. He too believed in asking questions to obtain facts. On his travels to universities around the country lecturing on sex education, he started distributing questionnaires on sexual attitudes, learning, and behavior to the college men in his audiences. He obtained almost a thousand completed questionnaires.

Exner's mission was to expose the deplorable state of early sexual learning for young men, to show the disastrous consequences of this, and to prove that sex education would solve the problem. Like those who came before him, Exner was utopian in his assumptions about the power of the right education to teach premarital sexual control. His questions on sexual learning reveal his viewpoint as well as his willingness to lead respondents to make connections between education and behavior:

- At about what age was the subject of sex first brought in a striking way to your consciousness—that is, in such a way as to make a permanent impression?
- Through whom was it thus brought?
- What, in general, was the effect of this information upon you as you look back on it now?
- Indicate in what way this information was good or bad for you.
- Have you received any instruction in matters of sex? If so:
    At what age did you receive it?
    From what source?
- Please give fully your opinion regarding the influence of this instruction on your life. Have you received any definite education relating to your sex life in college?
- If so, what was its nature?
- What impression did it make upon you? What influence has it had in your life?

Exner ventured to ask only three questions about actual sexual behavior, which he characterized as the most "personal questions." Staying away from detail, he asked:

- Have you at any time indulged in any sexual practice?
- What was its nature?
- At what age did you begin?[9]

Given Exner's goals and the way these questions directed respondents' answers, it is no surprise that 90 percent of respondents reported having learned about sex from "unwholesome sources" and, more important, that 79 percent thought the information had had a bad effect on them. Descriptions were replete with confessions to "a premature and unnatural" focus on sexuality and a resulting tendency to degrade women. And degeneracy bred degeneracy. Exner described how information was transmitted from an older, already defiled boy who delighted in passing it to younger, more innocent ones. Almost all had received their "first striking impressions" of sex before age thirteen, that is, before the onset of the critical period of adolescence. This method of learning coupled with a lack of wholesome sex education explained why many yielded to "the habit of self-abuse" before age fifteen, Exner's age of puberty. These findings provided further evidence of the crisis. The precocious sexual interest of boys threatened not only their own futures but those of their younger schoolmates.

In the tradition of Hall, Exner saw precocity as directly linked to "self-abuse." The evidence on self-abuse, he wrote, "is the direct and terrible answer to the questions relating to the sources and the effect of the earliest sex impressions in childhood and youth . . . The conditions here shown in the lives of these college men are for the most part the result of precocious stimulation of sex interest and of the early misdirection of the sex instinct through unfortunate sources of information and appeal."[10] Exner's solution was total sexual continence outside marriage. He believed in the YMCA credo that men could be as sexually pure as women. Masturbation was the ultimate self-indulgence for boys. Its control distinguished the middle classes from those below them and justified their superior station in life.

In Exner's survey science and morality went hand in hand. Sex education of the right sort would convince young men to postpone sexual interest until they were older and had an appropriate, but still limited, outlet in marriage. By the right sort of education Exner meant that which would satisfy existing curiosity but not stimulate an interest in sex. Exner and his compatriots believed that men's overdeveloped interest in sexual intercourse harked back to an earlier evolutionary period when polygamy was widespread and men needed to impregnate numerous wives. In the modern world, sexual intercourse twice a month was sufficient to produce offspring and was in keeping with the more delicate asexual nature of women. Men who developed early self-control would be able to manage their sexual urges without resorting to birth control, something these moral guardians viewed as an encouragement to sexual degeneracy.

These beliefs were rooted in a view of sexuality as an essential and powerful instinct that society must control. This instinct was natural, necessary, and completely honorable if properly managed, but if allowed to develop rampantly it might bring down the entire social order. The correct path was hard work. Exner concluded with a call to arms:

> It is also to be borne in mind that the sex instinct exerts a more profound influence upon human life than any other instinct, and that it is more easily misdirected. The sex instinct furnishes the greatest undercurrents of life, especially during the life-shaping, character-determining period—

adolescence. It gives character and direction to life more than any other human instinct. It is therefore of the utmost importance that the earliest sex impressions shall be of a wholesome nature and proceed from responsible sources.[11]

A great ambivalence about sex, including the sense that any misstep could be disastrous, underscores the seriousness with which early researchers approached their work.

While fears about the evils of masturbation remained influential among psychologists and educators, a new and more pressing menace appeared and, with the First World War, took precedence.[12] In 1904 a New York physician and reformer, Prince Morrow, had shocked the nation with his declaration that gonorrhea, "the most widespread and universal of all diseases in the adult male population," infected at least 75 percent of men in New York City, while syphilis "though not nearly so universal [has been] variously estimated at from 5 to 18 percent."[13] In the second half of the nineteenth century, activists had viewed prostitution as a menace to family life because of the subjection of hapless young women to men's sexual lusts. These views changed with new discoveries about the transmission of venereal disease and its long-term consequences. Hall had added venereal diseases to the list of topics to cover in sex education for boys, but he did not focus on it as he did masturbation. Yet between 1905 and the First World War many cities undertook studies of prostitution and broadcast the frightening news that most middle-class men had risked their health and that of their families with prostitutes.

Morrow's social hygiene movement attracted groups like the YMCA, since it complemented their existing goals. Advocates of sex education organized meetings across the country warning about the dangers of sex with prostitutes, explaining the ease with which venereal disease was transmitted, and describing its terrible consequences. Concern reached new heights during the First World War as young men who left home to join the armed services gained new sexual freedom. Although Exner had not included venereal disease in his survey, he was concerned about it, and he involved the YMCA in an effort to ensure celibacy among the troops by providing information to soldiers in Europe on the dangers of contracting venereal disease from prostitutes.

These early writers promoted sex education as a way to decrease sexual activity. This caught them in a dilemma. They were part of an ever expanding public conversation about sex. Indeed, they were describing the activities of respectable middle-class Americans, whose shocking behavior, they believed, had been shrouded in silence too long. Yet the very act of asking about sexual activity was part of making private behavior public and thus was vulnerable to resistance. Those promoting sex education risked charges of profligacy. Hall, in particular, was widely criticized by other prominent psychologists for his writings on sexuality; sometimes his own proclivities were even subject to innuendo. Surveyors, for their part, justified their interest in sexual acts on the highest moral grounds of public health and well-being. Still, they realized that the sensitive nature of their questions might evoke less than honest answers from their respondents. When young men in New York reported lower rates of sexual activity than those in the West, Exner believed that since he had not been available personally to hand out questionnaires and explain why the survey was so important, he had not been able to obtain the personal trust of the New York respondents, and that this had caused widespread underreporting.

Those who wished to control sexual longings were not the only early sex researchers. In 1916 Walter Robie, a neurologist active in the conservative wing of the birth control movement, published the results of a survey of "the better part of the middle class." Robie shared some of the assumptions of the earlier writers but made some novel departures. Like earlier researchers, he chose to interview only members of the middle class. He explicitly shied away from interviewing either upper- or lower-class people in his determination to portray the sex lives of normal adults. The rich were unsuitable as their idleness allowed temptation full rein. As for the impoverished "submerged tenth," Robie believed that young and old and male and female sleeping in one room meant that sex talk and sex acts would occur in the presence of children, so the sexuality of the lower class would differ widely from the "normal." In other words, normal did not mean that which was common to large numbers of people, but that which was morally acceptable. Random sampling was still in its infancy, and Robie did not understand that selecting only those he deemed normal would bias his results.

Robie also shared the social hygienists' belief in the need for sex education to preserve the health of individuals and of society. He asked his respondents leading questions about "early surroundings and teachings which kept the sexual instinct from coming into consciousness or enabled [them] to control it if it did come into consciousness." He believed educational intervention in sexual matters should begin by adolescence to ensure that young people were warned of the dangers of promiscuous intercourse.

To support his argument, Robie resorted to the data used by the leaders of the social hygiene movement but translated it to serve his message. Stating that 60 percent of young men and 20 percent of young women were infected with venereal disease at the time of marriage, "to say nothing of the loose habits and low conception of public morals which must inevitably have come during the acquiring of these diseases," he called for widespread sex education on this issue. Without an all-out effort, marriage, "the only course which can lead to the greatest personal happiness and the greatest public good," would be a failure for many. For Robie the moral family was the cornerstone of individual happiness and social solidarity.[14]

Yet, in important ways, Robie's viewpoint differed from those of his predecessors. As an advocate of birth control, he supported the many middle-class couples who were reducing their fertility and viewed this as having great implications for their marriages. These were the people he was interested in surveying. He was critical of what he saw as an overemphasis on the sex lives of the aberrant rather than a celebration of the normal. Where earlier writers had emphasized danger and disease and had viewed desire as sinful, Robie initiated a limited celebration of sexual pleasure. While agreeing that the nation suffered from rampant venereal disease, he blamed sexual repression not sexual licence. Reticence and prudery had led to ignorance about sexual matters, which had precipitated this crisis. Though others had also wanted to lift the blanket of silence from sexual behavior, they had sought to rein in desire. Robie, in contrast, saw men's sexual appetites as natural and as one of their greatest sources of happiness. The goal was not to repress these appetites but to direct them properly.

Even more radical was Robie's position that women too experienced strong sexual desire and passion; indeed, "all normal women as well as men have within them the instinctive cravings and physical necessities of physical love, as well as potentialities for undreamed-of heights of idealistic or spiritual love."[15] Consequently he interviewed not only the professionals and businessmen among his acquaintances but also their "wives, sisters, and daughters." This represented, albeit tentatively, a break with earlier male experts who did not view female passion as significant for female health or well-being.[16]

Robie was influenced in these views by the writings of Freud and the British sexologist Havelock Ellis. Freud had first visited America in 1909, invited by Hall, and his ideas were gaining wide distribution among experts in human sexuality and personality. Freud argued that both men and women suffered if sexually repressed, a position that caused Hall to maintain his distance, but that others began to accept. Ellis was even more influential in the short run. Although he did not view men and women as alike sexually, he did celebrate female sexuality. In his view, men and women were made for each other. Women were much slower to reach arousal than men, but male pursuit stimulated the normal woman. Robie shared these ideas and stated that the husband must be "the seeker and gentle aggressor in the preliminaries." All assumed heterosexuality to be the normal expression of male and female passion.

The implications of Freud and Ellis were profound for sex researchers. Where Exner and others in the social hygiene movement despised any unsublimated sexual expression except marital intercourse and believed that masturbation was the precursor to consorting with prostitutes, Robie defended masturbation as an appropriate and even necessary extramarital sexual outlet, an idea promoted by Ellis. Moderate indulgence in auto-erotism, he declared, helped prevent nonmarital intercourse with its possibly disastrous consequences for marriage. He asked his respondents whether they practiced masturbation, how they had learned the practice, and what its physical and emotional consequences had been. He sought to establish a link between a failure to masturbate and "irregular (extra-marital) intercourse" with the following questions:

- If you, for a short time only or never, practiced this habit, please tell what your sexual life has been.

- If you have had irregular (extra-marital) intercourse. If so, how frequent?

- If continent, how frequent emissions did you have, if a male, or were there voluptuous dreams with orgasm at or near the menstrual epoch, if female?[17]

No longer were respondents to confess their yieldings. Now they were being asked to divulge the consequences of *not* masturbating. Robie's questions also communicated to respondents his assumed differences in male and female sexual response. Like Freud and Ellis, Robie tied female sexuality to reproduction, and he believed that while men were always sexually ready, women's desires were cyclical and were strongest around the menstrual period. At the time, biologists believed the menstrual period to be the human counterpart of heat in mammals. Robie expected to find women most sexually receptive around menstruation, and his questions educated his audience as to the appropriate answer.

To bolster his argument that women experienced strong sexual desire,

Robie described a young woman who did not masturbate because she was told that masturbation might cause death. Unable to control her desires, she started having sexual intercourse, became a prostitute, and died of syphilis at age eighteen. Thus female sexual desire could cause unmarried women to become prostitutes. This changed the understanding of who was to blame for seduction. If women did not experience strong desire, they could only be led astray by men, but libidinous women might themselves initiate the sexual conquest of vulnerable young men.

For Robie the worst possible sexual sin was premarital intercourse, both because it posed the danger of venereal disease and because it lacked the spirituality that only marriage could provide. But, as a practical matter, the unmarried did need a sexual outlet. The sex drive was so imperious that it could not be totally suppressed, merely controlled, and Robie concluded that those who occasionally masturbated rarely engaged in extramarital relations. He also argued that early marriage would enable young people to channel their urges properly, a benefit to themselves and to society. Exner had argued that men should defer marriage until age thirty or older when they would be able to support a family, but for Robie delayed marriage could only lead to trouble. Early marriage and a healthy sexual appetite within marriage were solutions to the threats the family faced from unwholesome sexual practices beyond its domain. Robie wished to break with what he saw as a dangerous repression of sexual pleasure: "Psychic love to the exclusion of the physical has been to such an extent the ideal of the home that it is in a way to ruin all health, to rob of all virtue and efface all happiness. In short, it is this exaltation of the psychic or spiritual at the expense of the physical or sensual which has made the brothel possible and allowed the continuance of all the shameless extremes of license and lust in our modern society."[18]

By the end of the First World War Hall's idea of the developmental nature of childhood was firmly entrenched, and psychologists applied it in ways Hall would not have countenanced. Experts began taking the position that young men's masturbation was simply a normal developmental phase which they would outgrow. A survey by the psychologist Paul Strong Achilles shows this developmental view of sexuality in the detailed questions he posed to young men. Achilles wanted to evaluate the effectiveness of a series of sex education pamphlets in changing undesirable behavior, and he included a set of questions measuring the development of interest and activity in a sequential way:

Try to give accurately the age at which you experienced each of the following:

First feeling of curiosity about sexual matters.
First feeling of shame connected with sexual matters.
First feeling of disgust, or repulsion, connected with sexual matters.
First feeling of humor in sex matters, or joking about them.
First feeling of bashfulness connected with sex.
First feeling of strong attraction for members of the other sex.
First feeling of being in love with a girl.
First feeling of definitely sexual desires.
First seminal emission or "wet dream."
First masturbation or self abuse.
First sexual intercourse.[19]

The study of male masturbation culminated with the psychology professor William Sentman Taylor, who took the position that it was essential. In 1919, to show that men who were unable to marry early could not be expected to sublimate all sexual desire into other activities, Taylor interviewed "forty superior single men." He excluded "rakes" and "morons, neurotics, and other abnormal personalities" and included only "moral" men with a "great capacity for physical and mental work," all of whom had "evidence of aesthetic need or outlet."[20] Before asking about their behavior, Taylor told each respondent that he believed sublimation impossible since all his previous superior respondents had reported masturbating. He delayed publication of the results because ten men insisted that they had never masturbated. In 1929 he reinterviewed these, giving them a chance to change their stories, and every one of them did so. Thus he was able to produce the results he wanted.

By the end of the war masturbation was relegated to the role of necessary evil. Venereal disease had become the leading concern of sexual surveyors. From the experiences of soldiers, many experts viewed prostitution as the root cause of venereal disease, and some researchers nervously began to question young men about consorting with prostitutes. The first to include such questions were the psychiatrist M. W. Peck and the psychologist Frederick Lyman Wells, both of Boston Psychopathic Hospital. Their two studies of college graduates from "one of the more favored social groups" emphasized continence, but they also assumed that their respondents were actively trying to control urges that were a normal part of their development, and their questions indicated this assumption:

- What has been the greatest force working for continence in your case? Moral Principle—fear of disease—influence of some one person—dictates of the church—timidity with other sex, etc.

- Do you feel that sexual thoughts and unsatisfied sexual cravings interfere with your work and to what extent?[21]

While masturbation was a phase of normal sexual development, controlling the urge to engage in premarital sexual intercourse was a sign of well-being and socioeconomic success. Robie believed sexual desires were so strong that they *would* find an outlet somehow, but Peck and Wells took the view that developmental maturity enabled men to direct sexual energy elsewhere.

However, not all their respondents were able to do so; 35 percent admitted to having sexual intercourse before marriage. Peck and Wells noted that this was somewhat lower than others had estimated and explained that their respondents had "a greater share of satisfaction in life than the crudely erotic" because of their greater "means of 'sublimating' such urges, owing to more favorable economic status."[22] For these investigators, the major problem their prominent young men faced was the sexual advances of lower-class women. A tenth admitted going to prostitutes. Peck and Wells thought this was a low figure and wondered if their respondents were sufficiently able to identify a prostitute. When only one man reported venereal disease, rather than questioning the accuracy of the incidence reports about venereal disease, they assumed respondents either were "repressing" the truth or did not understand that the term included gonorrhea. They continued to insist that these young men were in danger of contracting venereal disease from women who were not their equals, for this justified their survey.

In a second survey, Peck and Wells's concern that socially prominent young men were being tempted by the wrong women continued. They asked questions that seemed designed to demonstrate this. One item involved the effect on young men's sexual feelings of "mixing socially with the better class of girls at dances, parties, etc." In the first survey respondents could choose only between "Increase" and "Decrease," and over half reported feeling decreased sexual impulses in the presence of nice girls. This concerned the authors, who believed social and psychological health was best maintained through a class-based social order that assumed mutual attraction within each class. Believing the either/or choice to be the problem, they added a third choice, "Indifferent," to the second survey. When this category was chosen by two-thirds of the respondents with the rest evenly distributed between "Increase" and "Decrease," the authors were relieved. The poor showing for nice girls on the first survey, they surmised, occurred because middle-class girls did not try to be sexually alluring. But "if 'nice girls' did not afford erotic stimulation at least equal to that of their more liberal sisters, the whole social function of modesty would be called into grave question." Any other interpretation would "give the devil a controlling interest in eroticism," an unsound view in their opinion.[23] In this way they transferred the responsibility for sexual mixing between social classes from the wayward sexual desires of young men to the sexual allurement of lower-class women, a viewpoint that would have been incomprehensible two decades earlier.

During the first twenty-five years of sex surveys, male experts began moving away from the position that sexual activity was permissible only if undertaken for the higher purpose of reproduction within marriage. As long as this view held, male sexuality was seen to be the problem, and young men were targeted as the group to be questioned about the facts. These facts informed experts that education would help young men deal with the dangers of late marriage and the temptations of "extra-marital sex." A few interviewers in this era, like Robie, challenged the prevalent view by including women in their surveys. They acknowledged that women had sexual urges, although they viewed these as weaker than and even dependent on men's, but if women had sexual problems, researchers saw these from the point of view of men.

It took a female researcher to consider women's sexual behavior with concern for the women themselves. Only two surveys before 1925 focused on women. Both were conducted by women, and both suffered similar fates of silence. The first survey, by Clelia Mosher, did not become part of the knowledge about sex circulating in her day. The second, by Katharine Davis, produced facts that were frequently cited, while her different point of view was ignored. These women's concern with female sexual experience was ahead of its time, and their interest was quite removed from the concerns of the male surveyors.

Clelia Mosher was the first person to ask Americans about their sexual behavior. In 1892, while a student at the University of Wisconsin, she embarked on a project that spanned twenty-eight years, interviewing upper-middle-class married women as opportunity arose. Respondents on many of the forty-five surviving interviews graduated from elite colleges including Stanford, Cornell, Radcliffe, and Vassar.[24] Since Mosher never wrote about her project, it is not clear what prompted the survey, but her medical career, during which she challenged notions about female frailty, provides clues. An advocate of exercise for women, she sought to dispel the widely held belief that female breathing originated from the upper chest and was shallower and weaker than male diaphragmatic breathing. She published papers on such topics as why women did not need bed rest during menstruation.[25] It would seem to follow that she interviewed women about their sexuality in order to argue that, as in other areas, women were men's equals. Yet, despite holding progressive views about their potential for equality, she thought American women were becoming too sex conscious, and that this posed a threat to marital and social stability. By the 1920s she was lecturing young women about their racial obligations to marry and have children. By this she meant that middle-class, non-immigrant white women must reproduce if American ingenuity and superiority were not to be diluted by increasing proportions of the inferior masses.[26]

Mosher began her survey six years earlier than Brockman and, unlike him, asked detailed, probing questions about sex. Her standards of propriety did not deter her from asking whether respondents had orgasms, how often they had intercourse, whether they enjoyed it, and whether they used birth control, all questions no one asked of men. Her questions reveal concern about an ideological shift in college-educated women's views toward sex. Some educated women were practicing birth control and having fewer children than their mothers. These women were already struggling to define a new form of marriage in which two equal partners would find love, companionship, and even erotic pleasure independent of reproduction. Among her questions, Mosher inquired:

What do you believe to be the true purpose of intercourse?
  (a) Necessity to man? To woman?
  (b) Pleasure?
  (c) Reproduction?
What, to you, would be an ideal habit?[27]

While these questions may seem strange today, Mosher's respondents understood them and produced detailed answers. A minority claimed that the only justification for sexual intercourse was procreation. A few went to the opposite extreme and said that sex was important in its own right. The majority located themselves between these extremes. They wanted to experience sexual pleasure but were wary of carnal feelings and often disappointed by sex in practice. Their comments reflected the transition between the Victorian ideal of controlled sexuality and the twentieth-century view of sex as central to marriage. Many respondents approved of nonprocreative sexual intercourse but for spiritual reasons having little to do with physical passion.

Mosher never revealed her own beliefs about the nature of the female sex drive. Her respondents clearly believed it did not equal men's, and a majority said they would have preferred to have sex less often. This conviction that women's sexual urges were weaker than men's was to persist for most of the twentieth century. In consequence, as men's sexual desires became normal, to be celebrated rather than controlled, women's supposedly lesser drives gave them responsibility for sexual control. Florence Fitch, the dean of women students at Oberlin College, put it this way when summarizing a 1915 survey of experts' views: "Even if we come to the full recognition of absolute equality between man and woman in their rights and responsibilities, we cannot do away with the fact that woman is physically the weaker, that there is an unalterable difference of duty, and that she must inevitably bear the greater burden in case of wrongdoing however equally society may distribute its condemnation."[28]

In 1920, however, Katharine Bement Davis took a different position in her study of the sex lives of 2,200 upper-middle-class married and single women.[29] Davis was not a traditional woman. She never married. She described herself as not "the sort with whom men are always falling in love."[30] She was active in the suffrage movement, and her friends were professional women whose interests she shared. The early male researchers were psychologists and psychiatrists who wished to understand sex in order to explain human development, but Davis had a Ph.D. in political economy from the University of Chicago, where she studied under the famous empirical sociologist W. I. Thomas. She knew most of the male sex researchers: Exner helped her obtain funding for her survey, and she cited many male colleagues in her report. She worried about some of the same issues, but her solutions differed.

Appointed as superintendent of the Bedford Hills Reformatory for Women, whose inmates included many prostitutes and others convicted of moral offenses, Davis argued against the prevailing view that most felons were mentally defective. From her own research Davis believed that environment and education were prostitution's main causes and that psychological testing could separate the redeemable from the truly defective. John D. Rockefeller Jr., who was concerned about prostitution and venereal disease, had created the Bureau of Social Hygiene to bring scientific skills to the study of these problems. He learned of Davis's work and in 1917 appointed her as the Bureau's secretary. Davis agreed with male experts that sex education would prevent sexual ills, but she departed from their argument that men particularly needed this education. She considered it more important for women because much of women's pathology concerned their sexual behavior.

Believing that facts would enable experts to design an effective program of education, Davis began her survey. She formed a cooperating committee of professional women to help with her survey design. Consistent with her training and the committee's serious interest, her survey was the largest and her analysis the most comprehensive to date, replete with tables analyzing cause and effect.[31] Davis's committee helped her take several risks. They justified her decision to include unmarried as well as married women and, even more outrageously, to include questions on same-sex relations. Yet she reflected her times in insisting on "normal" women who were capable of adjusting to their social group and were not "pathological mentally or physically." Like other researchers, she believed the sexual development and adjustment of the educated middle classes was of key importance for the future of the race. She had demonstrated that poor women could learn to live useful and productive lives, but she agreed that the middle class had superior intelligence and thus greater social importance. In fact she confined the survey of single women to college graduates because these more "intelligent" women had responded more conscientiously than others in the study of married women. She took the additional precaution of expanding the single women's questionnaire by defining terms like "autoeroticism" and repeating assurances of confidentiality.

Davis was pulled in two directions. Trained and professionally active in a male-dominated world, she was complicit in many aspects of men's view of sexuality. But women's roles were beginning to change. The First World War had had emancipatory effects, and talk of the "new woman" abounded.[32] Davis worked for these changes. She broke with other surveyors in acknowledging women's capacity for, and right to, sexual pleasure. Even more radical was her understanding of the nature of this capacity. Not for her the argument that it took ardent but loving husbands to evoke sexual feelings in women. For Davis sexuality was a biological necessity felt by both sexes, which could find satisfaction in marriage but also existed and needed satisfaction among those who did not marry.

Davis revealed her belief in women's capacity for sexual pleasure through her liberal views on masturbation. She alone discussed it in great detail, including why women began masturbating and if and why they stopped. She argued that pleasure in handling one's sex organs was not masturbation unless it led to orgasm. Thus she made explicit the right to sexual pleasure as physical rather than psychic or emotional. Among her unmarried respondents, 60 percent had masturbated, something Davis assured them was normal. These single women did not deny themselves sexual pleasure, nor did Davis think they should. Furthermore, she reported no difference in marital sexual satisfaction between the almost 30 percent of married women who had masturbated before marriage and those who had not. For Davis normalcy meant statistical normalcy: if enough people did something without ill effects, then it was normal. This was a significant break with earlier definitions of normalcy, which carried both moral and medical judgments.

Davis was interested in all aspects of women's sexual pleasure. Many of her questions, particularly to married women, revealed conservative normative assumptions, such as whether "knowledge of contraceptive measures prior to marriage contribute[s] to the incidence of illicit sexual relations." Yet, unlike those who came before or after, Davis offered no negative judgments of those who indulged in illicit sex. She reported that a mere 7 percent of the married said they had had sex relations before marriage. Of these, a higher than average proportion had received sex education. Among the unmarried, 10.5 percent had had sexual relations. Davis concluded her chapter on marital happiness this way: "We are able to show that for the group under consideration preparation for the sex side of married life is a factor making for married happiness; that there is a correlation between preparation and attractiveness of the married relationship itself as it comes into experience; that when these first experiences are attractive there is a greater chance for subsequent happiness." This conclusion that good first sexual experiences were beneficial, regardless of when they occurred, was a far cry from the panic about illicit sex implied in the surveys of men.[33]

Even so, Davis believed in gendered sexuality. Like Robie, she inquired as to whether women experienced heightened desire before, during, and after menstruation, an idea popularized by Havelock Ellis.[34] Of the 808 unmarried women who said they experienced sexual feelings, 272 reported that sexual desire was periodic and highest around the menstrual period. Where Davis differed was in not implying that women necessarily depended on men for pleasure. She asked respondents about their sexual experiences with women.

The only survey before Davis to include questions about same-gender sexual activity had assumed a norm of heterosexual desire. The Seattle psychiatrist Lilburn Merrill interviewed one hundred boys, aged seven to seventeen, who appeared in juvenile court charged with misconduct. These were not normal middle-class boys, and Merrill believed that he was not depicting normal sexuality; in fact he wanted to document the perils, for individuals and for society, of inappropriately channeled sex instincts. He defined the topic of his study, "sexualism," as "an habitual, pathological functioning of the sexual mechanism." Of the boys interviewed, 71 percent, the "sex group," presented "symptomatology of an erotic nature and an addiction of interest and practice"; that is, they had no control over their sexual impulses. All were habitually autoerotic, with a frequency of orgasms ranging from three times a week to five times a day. Thirty-one of his respondents had engaged in fellatio with other boys during prepubescence, a finding Merrill interpreted as indicative of a serious problem. He was somewhat relieved that most of the boys engaging in these homosexual acts nevertheless displayed "normal amative desires and probably were limited in their heterosexual relations only by their environment." While he believed such behaviors would end with appropriate education, he viewed homosexual acts as delinquent.[35]

Davis took a different position, and her questions responded to a different concern: fears about lesbianism among educated middle-class women. Although communities of male "fairies" had existed in most large American cities since the turn of the century, lesbians continued to be invisible. Lesbians represented a distinct threat; their existence meant that women could live without men.[36] For experts who were just beginning to imagine that women might have sex drives, it was hard to understand the existence of women who not only experienced desire but initiated sex with other women. But lesbianism did not evoke much concern until coupled with growing fears that women's increasing economic and social independence might encourage middle-class women not to marry and reproduce the race. The end of the First World War had brought many changes for women. They appeared in public in short dresses, wearing makeup, with short hair, and with a new ability to do whatever they wanted and go wherever they wished. Much of the concern centered on women's colleges. A decade earlier college authorities had looked benignly at young women's "smashes" on one another as infatuations that were passionate, romantic, but not carnal. By the 1920s they frowned upon what they now called lesbianism. These colleges had to protect themselves against charges that their unnatural environments turned young women's passions away from marriage and children and toward the unnatural.

Davis's questions about homosexual behavior responded to these concerns but did not play into them. Though she wrote nothing about why she included the questions, she reviewed theories of homosexuality and commented that her own experience showed homosexual behavior to be more common than most were willing to admit. The survey of single women concentrated on the existence and timing of "intense emotional relations" between women but also included three questions on the sexual component of relationships. The survey addressed a serious question of the day: whether women's relationships were merely noncarnal passionate friendships or involved sex:

- Was the experience associated with sex in your own mind at the time? Later?
- Was the experience without physical expressions other than kissing or ordinary endearments of close friendship?
- Did the experience include such physical expression as bodily exposure, mutual handling of organs, mutual masturbation, or other intimate contacts?

Protesting that she would not attempt interpretation, Davis, with a vision unmatched in her time, calmly defended homosexuals as no different from heterosexuals in their sexual adjustment or overall normality. In addition to her survey results, Davis drew on her work in single-sex institutions, particularly prison, to strip away some of the myths. Homosexuality among women, she stated, was not "morphological," that is, not part of women's physical makeup. Such practices had "always been observed as common where groups of men are isolated from women for considerable periods of time," and were "also common in boarding-schools and colleges exclusively for girls and women and in penal institutions of all types."[37]

Half of Davis's single respondents and one-third of the married ones reported erotic feelings for other women. Of these, half were merely romantic crushes and half were sexual. Davis reported few differences between these two groups or between women who had such feelings and those who did not. She found no difference, for example, in levels of happiness between women who had been emotionally or sexually involved with other women and those who had not. Few unmarried women cited homosexual experiences as a reason for not marrying, and among the married those with homosexual experience adjusted to marital sex just as well as those without. Of unmarried women who ended a homosexual relationship, one-third reported that such relationships were "abnormal, wrong or disgusting," and Davis dismissed this as merely reflecting public opinion since almost half of the remainder reported their homosexual relationship to have been "helpful" or "stimulating." By positing homosexuality not as an exclusive identity but as something that any woman might harmlessly experiment with, she allayed fears that lesbianism threatened the family.

Whereas the male researchers had retained control over the meaning of their results, Davis was not able to. The men had used their expertise to underscore other experts' views about appropriate behavior, and the audiences for their ideas were physicians, social workers, educators, and others who dealt with the young and who shared their viewpoint. Davis's data on premarital intercourse and on marital sex were cited for decades, but selectively. Her evidence that women could and did enjoy sex without men, through either masturbation or sex with other women, was largely ignored. Assertions that women might have sexual appetites equal to men's, and might even satisfy them without the aid of men, created more profound fears among male researchers than did out-of-control male sexuality. In response, researchers soon turned their attention away from threats to the family from without—that is, from venereal disease and other types of male extramarital sexual risk-taking as well as from women who did not need men—and focused instead on strengthening the family from within. Male surveyors whose agenda was to save marriage and maintain a patriarchal social order turned their attention away from un-married men as subjects and toward the spousal couple.

3

Sex in the Service of the Conjugal Bond

An increasing number of persons would like to bring an educated intelligence into consideration of such matters as sexual adjustments in marriage, the sexual guidance of children, [and] the pre-marital sexual adjustments of youth . . . Before it is possible to think scientifically on any of these matters, more needs to be known about the actual behavior of people.

—Alfred C. Kinsey, Wardell B. Pomeroy, and Clyde Martin, 1948

DIVORCE had caused consternation since the turn of the century, but in the 1920s this consternation exploded. The detonator was a Census Bureau report showing a 31 percent increase in divorce between 1916 and 1922.[1] Experts on the family agreed that the trend had serious implications not only for the future of the family but for American society. Reports that the birth rate had fallen to an all-time low exacerbated the apprehension. The sociology professor Ernest Groves pointed out what was most dangerous about the low birth rate: "its sinister meaning appears in its concentration on the middle class."[2] The middle class, to most social scientists, represented the best of the race, and thus the nation's future was severely jeopardized.

In accounting for these trends, writers listed a number of forces. For example, economic ties no longer kept families intact. Before industrialization, men, women, and children had worked together in the home for their collective benefit. Now men and women could support themselves independently in the labor market, and the self-denial fostered by the earlier system was becoming a thing of the past. Children, once a source of labor, were now a costly burden. Now individuals came together for happiness and pleasure, and if families could not supply these they would look elsewhere.

In this climate sexual pleasure ceased to appear dangerous to marital intimacy. Instead experts began to develop the position that sex formed the basis of the marital relationship. While Groves worried that this emphasis on pleasure put a tremendous burden on the family, he nonetheless hailed the trend as positive. And it was not only academics who thought this. The new ideology of sexual pleasure was celebrated in magazines, newspapers, and movies. Advertisers used sexual desire to sell products, and "Sexual freedom . . . itself became a commodity."[3] Men began to feel they had a right to sexual happiness rather than a duty to suppress desire.

This emphasis on sexual pleasure made the marital bond central to family life. But this bond appeared threatened by the emergence of female autonomy and the decline in male dominance within the family, trends that writers also saw as related to the increase in divorce. This problem was most apparent among young, educated men and women, the very group on whom the future of the middle-class family depended. As Groves explained it, young men and women had ideals belonging to separate generations. Men looked backward, wishing to marry women as subservient as their mothers, while women looked forward to a new equality.

The growing acceptance of more explicit expressions of sexual feelings led to new anxieties. If women became sexually demanding, how were men to respond? Walter Robie and Katharine Davis had both "discovered" that middle-class women possessed a sex drive as natural as men's. In contrast to Robie's descriptions of a female sexuality that depended on men for arousal, Davis had suggested a disquieting level of female autonomy. With her descriptions of female masturbation and lesbian sex among unmarried women, Davis had tapped into an emerging fear. If women had autonomous sexual urges, they might even initiate sexual activities without men. With unmarried women of all socioeconomic classes able to work before marriage, worries that those with college educations might not marry played into the eugenic concern that the educated classes were not reproducing themselves. The nature of the female sex drive was much discussed by the psychiatrists and psychologists who dominated sex research. And experts claimed it was as puzzling to girls themselves. Along with "physiological changes, sexual feelings become part of the girl's life," declared one pair of writers. Yet, they added, these feelings and the dreams they arouse are likely to be "unacceptable to her waking consciousness. Thus she may feel she is abnormally constituted and different from other girls."[4]

One solution to anxieties about female sexual autonomy was to define the normal female sex drive as geared toward men and as central to women's happiness. If this view was accurate, the liberation of women's sex drive might solve the dilemmas of rising divorce and female autonomy. In the 1920s many writers began to take the position that Victorian prudery was a cause of unhappy marriages and to hail the positive evaluation of the erotic as beneficial. They began to propose a new type of marriage, "companionate marriage," based on equality of, but differences between, the sexes. In one of the best-known books of the decade, *The Revolt of Modern Youth*, Judge Ben Lindsey and Wainwright Evans argued that a recognition of equality, strong bonds of love and affection, and sexual pleasure all cemented the marital union.[5]

Such marriages would be based on the idea of complementary male and female sexuality. In this argument, male sexuality was natural, urgent, and relatively undiscriminating in its object, but female sexuality, which was central to women's happiness, was aroused by falling in love. Women needed to marry. The problem women faced in satisfying their sex drives was the repressive Victorian upbringing to which many had been exposed. If divorce was rising, it was because many women could not overcome this training and abandon themselves to their husbands. Lindsey and Evans urged sex education not so men would control their rapacious desires, but for the marital preparation of middle-class girls. In their view properly responsive wives would enhance family security, since husbands would no longer resort to prostitutes.

Lindsey and Evans assured young women that marriage, rather than a career, was what would make them happy. Those who pursued careers would suffer sexual frustration. Thus fears about the dangers of careers and of female sexual autonomy were averted by descriptions of a female sexuality that was dependent on men and marriage for its fulfillment and could not exist independent of them. This heterosexual imperative became the basis of the middle-class family, something surveys could document.

The first survey of the sexual life of married men and women was undertaken in 1929 by Gilbert Hamilton, a physician with training in psychology. Since Freud's work was now widely accepted among psychologists, Hamilton believed that women could and should experience orgasms, albeit the "vaginal" kind. He asserted that inadequate sexual training caused severe problems in many marriages. Indeed, "a great many spouses who go on living together find in marriage a hateful bondage, a dreary, long-drawn-out harassment, and a stultifying relationship." Hamilton interviewed two hundred "highly cultured," normal, married women and men from New York City for an average of eight hours to measure the relationship between the quality of their sexual relationships and the success of their marriages.

To see how common good marriages were, Hamilton rated those of his middle-class respondents using thirteen questions:

- What is there in your marriage that is especially unsatisfactory to you?
- Have you any habits to which your spouse objects?
- Has your spouse any habits to which you object?
- Are you and your husband (or wife) socially and intellectually well-mated, or otherwise?
- What is the principal source of trouble between you and your husband (or wife)?
- How long after you were married did you begin to be seriously dissatisfied with any serious lack or shortcoming of your spouse?
- Do you wish to go on living with your spouse . . . because you love him (or her)?
- If, by some miracle, you could press a button and find that you had never been married to your husband (or wife), would you press that button?
- Knowing what you now know, would you wish to marry if you were unmarried?
- Describe your husband's (or wife's) disposition as well as you can.
- What things in your married life annoy and dissatisfy you the most?
- If your marriage is an unsuccessful one, what do you believe to be the chief cause of its failure? [This question was worth two points.]
- What changes would you make in any of the following mental qualities of your husband (or wife): Temper? Talkativeness? Thriftiness? Carefulness of dress? Selfishness? Tendency to scold? Intelligence? Social standing? Religious life? Truthfulness? Tendency to flirt? Capacity for showing affection? Strength of sex desire? Vanity? Serious-mindedness?[6]

To receive a positive score for an answer, respondents had to describe absolutely no problems, even though most questions suggested problems existed, and respondents had to score ten out of a possible fourteen to be rated happy. It is not surprising that only one-quarter achieved this. Hamilton recommended that unhappily married people should divorce and find out if they were "matrimonial incompetents," a category in which he included impotents, homosexuals, lesbians, and the frigid.

Faced with his finding of so many unhappy marriages, one might be tempted to see Hamilton as a man who did not support the institution. Yet he thought it central to personal happiness, and he explained his dismal findings as mainly caused by one factor: "orgasm inadequacy." He explained this as the result not only of repressive upbringing but also of evolution: "Since in the case of women, the orgasm is not essential to fertility or even to intense enjoyment of the sex act, it might be regarded as a relatively unimportant aspect of the sexual phenomenon if it were not for the nervous tension and sense of dissatisfaction that are so often associated with its absence."[7] Women with this problem included not only forty-one wives who never experienced orgasms but also five who had multiple orgasms. Evidence of overwhelming female desire was apparently threatening. One-fifth of the wives (including four of those with multiple orgasms) were "serious psychoneurotic cases," who could not engage in normal sexual intercourse. The "orgasm inadequacy" of the rest Hamilton viewed as having mixed physiological and behavioristic causes, particularly childhood and adolescent conditioning that created negative reactions to heterosexuality. Poor sexual functioning on the part of women was partly inherent and partly a result of Victorian repression.

Hamilton's understanding of female orgasm was based on Freud's argument that fully mature women would have vaginal orgasms in contrast to the immature and unsatisfactory clitoral orgasms of childhood. Hamilton took this one step further by arguing that a woman who masturbated as a complement to copulation could expect to have a "complete normal orgasm during the sex act," but that masturbation as a substitute for copulation would operate "against the chance of having the normal orgasm."[8] The five respondents who had multiple orgasm, he reported, had not given up masturbation in favor of the more mature pleasures of penetration.

In spite of these emphases on biology and childhood conditioning, Hamilton maintained that couples could improve wives' sexual functioning. In particular, they could use birth control. Except for those who wished to become pregnant or who believed they were sterile, all his female respondents used contraception. Hamilton's opinions on birth control were consistent with his view that sex had importance in marriage beyond its procreative role.

Two years after Hamilton's study appeared, long-awaited reports by the physician Robert Latou Dickinson and the professional writer Lura Beam helped refine his findings. Dickinson was a gynecologist who collected patients' detailed medical histories, including sexual histories, from the end of the nineteenth century on. He became a central figure in the effort to collect information on sexual behavior during the 1930s. Beam analyzed Dickinson's voluminous data and wrote *A Thousand Marriages* using 900 married women's sex histories and *The Single Woman* with 350 sex histories.[9] Although these are usually referred to as Dickinson's work, Beam's consciousness as a modern woman was evident throughout. She complied with male scientists' understanding of gender differences in sexual response but challenged Hamilton's explanation for this sorry state of affairs.

Beam's main focus was marital adjustment. She reported that the majority of brides had difficulties adjusting to marital sex. Dickinson had diagnosed 120 of the married women as frigid, and 175 more reported pain during intercourse, which Beam determined to be a form of frigidity. But where Hamilton blamed innate tendencies and repressive upbringing, Beam thought husbands at least partly responsible: "It takes two persons to make one frigid woman . . . the husband's function is in question as well as the wife's, and the male component to the female frigidity must be ascertained."[10] Sadly, she added, husbands' techniques were often inadequate. Still, Beam agreed with male writers that women and men differed sexually. Both had the same lifelong capacity for sexual desire, but this was inconsistent and fluctuating in women. Yet female sexual pleasure, while difficult to achieve and maintain, was essential to marital happiness. This made it important for husbands to practice and perfect their technique.

These ideas, that marriage was central to the future of the middle class and that women's lack of sexual response was the most important problem within marriage, pushed away fears about female sexual autonomy and turned attention to marital sexual behavior. In the next decades few questioned women's capacity to enjoy sex or that this capacity depended in part, but only in part, on men's skill in arousing them. Sex became the cement for middle-class marriages, and wives' sexual inadequacy appeared as the new crisis. Those undertaking sex surveys turned their attention to curing women's orgasmic inadequacy.

By this time social scientists were ready for this new crisis of private life. The social science professions were well established in universities, and a new university-based generation of male researchers took charge. They shared the optimism of their predecessors that they could cure as well as diagnose problems, and they greatly enhanced survey practice. Sex surveys in the service of marital happiness were conducted in this period at a number of major universities, including Chicago, Stanford, Michigan, and Indiana.

For the first time sex surveyors began to allow respondents to answer in ways that the surveyors did not completely control. And they developed new audiences for their work. Unlike the earlier generation of surveyors who had written mainly for other experts, the academic researchers wanted to take their results directly to those who most needed them:

middle-class individuals, especially women who were preparing for marriage or struggling to make existing marriages work. The venues for the dissemination of this expertise were marital-advice books, the developing field of marriage counseling, and, most important, college-level courses in family life designed to help middle-class youth make informed choices about whom to marry and how to succeed in marriage. These interpreters of the results inserted their own views of reality into the findings and were often more cautious and conservative in their presentations than the surveyors themselves.

Whereas the earlier experts had been psychologists, the family life movement was dominated by liberal sociologists.[11] With their emphasis on social influences on behavior, they argued that marriages could be changed to meet what they saw as new challenges. One of the movement's founders, Ernest Groves, promoted marriage counseling, wrote popular marital-advice books, taught the first college-level course on family life education, and, with William Ogburn, wrote the first college textbook on marriage and the family. In his textbook Groves said that the cultural upheavals of the twentieth century had created a "movement of family change [that] has already reached a momentum that draws the attention of all thinking people."[12] And education was central to the solution. In the textbook's introduction its editor, Howard Odum, bemoaned the lack of instruction in marriage and family relationships and envisioned a time when students would be required to take such a course to graduate.

While these sociologists emphasized the social basis of values and beliefs, they did not examine their own. They assumed that their own views of the world as educated men had no bearing on their neutrality as scientists. Odum's conviction that college students needed such a course showed the continuing focus on the middle-class family. Surveys by those in the family life movement involved college-educated middle-class couples almost exclusively, since researchers assumed them to be the only group capable of creating companionate marriages. So pervasive was this view that the Columbia University sociologist Willard Waller, who in 1938 published the most influential and widely quoted textbook, *The Family,* described it as "a study of the family life of middle-class persons in the United States of America . . . intended for use as a textbook in college courses on the family."[13] That is, "the family" of the title was the middle-class American family.

Family courses proliferated in the 1930s, and by 1949 almost half the nation's colleges had a course designed to prepare students for marriage.[14] These courses created a demand for marital adjustment surveys to provide scientific evidence about marital problems and their solutions. In their wish to help people select the best possible mates, researchers measured the causes of unhappy marriages and the reasons for successful ones. They used their results to develop tests that students could take to see if they and their potential mates were compatible. Since no mate could be perfect, this careful scientific selection was followed by advice on marital adjustment.

Whereas those surveying sexual behavior had earlier been reticent about relaying their results to the general public, they now used these courses to disseminate their results directly to those who most needed the information. In doing so they provided young middle-class audiences with a vision of the importance and achievability of sexual bliss in marriage. Typical of sociologists who thought science could create happy marriages was Ernest Burgess, a professor at the University of Chicago, who during the 1930s conducted two marital adjustment surveys. Burgess asked: "Is it feasible to bring love and marriage within the purview of science, of prediction, and control?" He answered this with the title of the report on his first survey (written with Leonard Cottrell): *Predicting Success or Failure in Marriage.* This survey involved interviews with recently married couples. To test the power of his prediction scale, Burgess undertook a second study. This time he and Paul Wallin made predictions on the basis of interviews with engaged couples and checked them with reinterviews one year after marriage. Another prominent researcher, Lewis Terman, a psychology professor from Stanford University, used a different method of verifying his scale, comparing the scores of 1,133 married couples with those of 109 divorced couples.[15]

Since these researchers considered sexual adjustment central to marital adjustment, they included questions in their surveys about sexual problems in marriage. And in doing so they made assumptions about gender. Terman was trained by G. Stanley Hall, and like Hall he thought gender differences were innate. Terman had developed a widely used scale to measure "masculinity" and "femininity." He decried "the once widely prevalent belief" that women were not as intelligent as men, but asserted that "the sexes differ fundamentally in their instinctive and emotional equipment and in the sentiments, interests, attitudes, and modes of behavior which are the derivatives of such equipment." Furthermore, he argued for "the existence of individual variants from type: the effeminate man and the masculine woman."[16] Every person had a mixture of masculine and feminine traits, with normal men and women located at the gender-appropriate end of the scale and variants closer to the "wrong" end. This allowed for tender men and aggressive women without challenging the basic assumption that men and women were opposites.

Although Burgess and Wallin asked men and women the same questions, they too showed gendered expectations. For example, they asked a series of questions designed to measure sexual fulfillment and satisfaction with the partner's demands:

- Amount of relief from sexual desire usually obtained from intercourse?
- Wife's frequency of orgasm?
- Fear of pregnancy makes intercourse less enjoyable?
- Spouse overmodest or prudish in attitude toward sex?
- Spouse not sufficiently modest?
- Would individual like spouse to take more initiative in requesting intercourse?
- Does spouse demand too much foreplay?
- Can husband prolong duration of intercourse?
- Is spouse too forward, frequently suggesting intercourse when individual does not desire it?[17]

These questions implied innate sexual urges, the fulfillment of which made for personal well-being and happiness for both men and women. At the same time, the questions clearly communicated a second message: that wives had difficulty with orgasm while husbands might have difficulty holding back until their wives became sufficiently aroused.

Terman too asked detailed questions about sexual adjustment, and he conveyed more explicit messages about gender than did Burgess and Wallin. His questions covered a wide arena: frequency of intercourse, preferred frequency, whether the spouse was more or less sexually passionate than the respondent, length of intercourse, and frequency of orgasm. Terman asked about a variety of potential problems involving the spouse, such as, "penis too large or too small," "too animal like," and "vagina not moist enough." He asked wives whether they would like husbands to take the lead and be more dominating, whether they experienced periodicity of sexual excitement, and whether fear of pregnancy made sex less enjoyable. He asked husbands if their wives were overly prudish or modest or demanded too much foreplay. His questions communicated to his subjects his expectations about what he would find.

The questions asked by marital adjustment researchers informed respondents that the problem lay with wives who were unable to achieve the abandon required for sexual pleasure. But these men not only wanted to document the existence of problems, they wanted to fix them. And the solution also lay with wives. Burgess and Cottrell, for example, reported that wives often suffered from lack of sexual desire, which led to a "considerable avoidance of or actual resistance to sexual activity, with consequent frustration and resentment on the part of the sexually unsatisfied mate."[18] This problem had its origins in the childhood and adolescence of middle-class girls. But there was hope for young women who had been raised under such repressive conditions. Burgess and Wallin wrote that, unlike men's more natural sexual drive, women's was overlaid with the cultural value that love was more important than sex. If women could peel away the layers of cultural conditioning, they could hope to unleash innate sexual urges in the service of erotic marriage.

Similarly, Terman concluded that two sex factors seriously contributed to marital happiness: wives' "orgasm adequacy" and husband-wife differences in the strength of the sex drive. Terman asked, "Why is it that one woman out of three rarely or never succeeds on reaching the normal climax of sexual intercourse?"[19] As a psychologist, he was less sure than the sociologists that these problems were cultural. Asserting that women who did not have orgasms were lacking in vigor of all kinds, Terman wondered if their inability had biological causes.

When it came to solving marital problems, these university professors saw themselves as having a key role in educating their young charges. Most sexual problems, they stated, were caused either by lack of sexual knowledge and skill or by the wrong attitude. Among Burgess and Cottrell's 49 couples, 35 had problems that sex education could solve, either by providing needed information or because discussing sex openly would overcome repressive upbringing and liberate sexual impulses. Burgess and Cottrell believed in sexual variety in marriage, and taught this to their students and those who would teach other students: "There is no normal sexual act in the sense of a mechanically standardized routine of actions or experiences. There is wide variation in the sexual act from couple to couple and from time to time in the activity of the same couple. There is variation in the intensity of desire, . . . the nature and extent of preliminary sexual inter-stimulation before coitus, . . . the height of feeling in the orgasm, the time taken in the sexual activity, and the intervals between coitus."[20]

These statements show the great change in views about sex and marital happiness in the few decades since the beginnings of sex research. Terman, however, was more cautious. While he agreed that many had a deplorable lack of education in sexual matters, he found no relationship between sex education and high scores on his marital-happiness scale. In his most famous work, the seven-volume *Genetic Studies of Genius,* a longitudinal study of people with very high measured IQs, he concluded that these highly educated geniuses were no different from others with regard to sexual problems.[21] Yet, like his contemporaries, Terman argued in favor of marital preparation in college.

Some writers struggled with a second, more dangerous solution. If wives came to marriage sexually ill-prepared, should they obtain a little sexual practice with their husbands-to-be before tying the knot? Those surveyors who cautiously collected information on premarital sexual activity were extremely tentative in their conclusions. Even Burgess, who was more liberal than other researchers of his day, was cautious. About half the respondents in his survey with Wallin admitted to having had sexual intercourse before marriage, but in examining the consequences of this finding the two men straddled the fence. Engaged couples with no premarital sexual experience scored higher in predicted marital success than those with experience. Yet wives who had engaged in premarital intercourse reported more frequent orgasms during marital intercourse, especially if their earlier experience was with men other than their husbands. Furthermore, couples who reported having sexual intercourse while engaged believed it had strengthened their relationship.

Burgess and Wallin interpreted their confusing findings by postulating the existence of three groups. A minority of couples were vehemently opposed to premarital sex. Another minority indulged without guilt. The majority were in the middle: tempted but overwhelmed with guilt and fearful of pregnancy. Rather than link this to societal attitudes, Burgess and Wallin took no stand either for or against the desirability of premarital sex. Instead they took the safer position that their job as scientists simply involved presenting and, where possible, interpreting the data. In the 1930s college professors dared not undermine the institution of marriage by advising students to engage in premarital sex.

Terman concluded that women who married as virgins had happier marriages than those who did not. Still, he noted: "Premarital sexual experience on the part of the woman, even when known, no longer makes her an outcast or bars her from an advantageous marriage. The data we have to present seem to indicate that premarital chastity has lost most of its significance so far as relation to marital happiness is concerned."[22] Terman reported higher rates of premarital intercourse than did others of his era, with 60 percent of husbands and 30 percent of wives saying that they and their spouse had had sexual intercourse before marriage. And among those born after 1910 the rate increased to 86 percent for husbands and 68 percent for wives.

These and other survey findings proved invaluable in marriage classes. These courses appealed particularly to women, and surveys informed them that they most needed help. Thousands of young women across America answered the question of why someone who was only going to marry should have a university education by enrolling in these courses. They learned that sexual happiness was central to marital happiness, but that many women like themselves, through some combination of femininity and upbringing, failed to become the kinds of sexual partners their husbands wanted and needed. From the 1930s through the 1950s, the textbooks these young women read took a stand against premarital sexual experience, selectively citing authors, especially Terman, Burgess, and Katharine Davis, as showing that those with no sexual experience before marriage had happier marriages.[23] In addition to learning how difficult it was for wives to overcome orgasmic inadequacy, young women learned that it was risky to try to solve this problem before marriage. A woman who practiced would incur societal disapproval and might find herself abandoned.

If all else failed, there was one other solution. Burgess and Wallin advised a woman who loved her husband to find happiness in his pleasure if she experienced none of her own. Terman was more explicit. Although it was harder to have a happy marriage if the wife suffered from orgasm inadequacy, "our data do not support the frequently expressed opinion that it is the one major cause of unhappiness in marriage. In our group, there are numerous marriages in which both spouses have very high happiness scores despite the fact that orgasm is never experienced by the wife."[24]

No one but Hamilton questioned the institution of marriage. Companionate marriages depended on mutual sexual satisfaction, and researchers told their audiences that this was attainable. Their analytic framework led them to emphasize the individual traits each partner brought to a relationship rather than negotiations by couples. They told their largely female, college-student audiences that women were to blame for any sexual incompatibility. And, Terman's caveat notwithstanding, they reinforced this message by using surveys to demonstrate that orgasmically inadequate wives caused unhappiness to themselves and their husbands. The young women in these classes anticipated first intercourse differently from, but as nervously as, any nineteenth-century maiden. For them, marital happiness depended on their ability to produce regular orgasms.

In contrast, male sexuality was relatively straightforward and uncomplicated. While classes were open to men, fewer took them. Those who did learned that men needed regular sexual intercourse ending in orgasm and would be content in marriages providing this. They learned that sexual pleasure meant orgasm and that sexual play was to prepare women for penetration. Surveyors applied a male model to female sexual response and, on finding that many women did not have orgasms, or at least not regularly, did not enquire if women enjoyed other aspects of sexual relations. Instead, they blamed "Victorian" attitudes for what they assumed was a problem.

Although social scientists were convinced that they could help young women achieve their goals for marriage, or at least could diagnose their problems, they found it difficult to obtain research funds. In 1922 the National Research Council (NRC) had formed the Committee for Research in Problems of Sex. The NRC had been founded by Congress as part of the National Academy of Sciences, but its funding for sex research came mostly from John D. Rockefeller or his foundation.[25] The NRC's natural scientists resisted paying for social science research and used the money for biological research instead. When Hamilton applied for funds, the NRC opposed his study so the committee turned him down. He received some support from the Rockefeller-funded Bureau of Social Hygiene,[26] as did Burgess. Terman was the first social scientist to receive funding from the Committee on the Problems of Sex, and in supporting him the committee gave sex research a new legitimacy. The NRC influenced government policy and frequently wrote reports on topics of concern to the federal government, so the committee played an important role in getting sex research onto the federal agenda.

After Terman, the Committee for Research in Problems of Sex funded the most prominent sex researcher of the century, Alfred Kinsey. As a biologist, a hard scientist as opposed to a social scientist, he secured the confidence of the NRC. This is ironic because he openly proselytized for permissive sexual standards as no previous researcher had dared. Kinsey asked respondents about a range of topics, but his main interest was marital adjustment. He did his first interviewing while teaching a marriage course at Indiana University. More than any other researcher, he viewed sexual adjustment as the basis of marital happiness, and he focused on inadequate female sexual response as one of the major barriers to achieving this.

Like his predecessors, Kinsey believed there was a terrible shortage of facts about sexual behavior. These facts were needed to provide guidance to students and others, and in collecting them, he did not favor half-measures. From 1938, when he started interviewing, until his death in 1956, he, along with Wardell Pomeroy, Paul Gebhard, and others, collected 20,000 sex histories, about 40 percent of which Kinsey obtained personally. Using about 18,000 of these interviews, he published two books, *Sexual Behavior in the Human Male* and *Sexual Behavior in the Human Female.* Kinsey considered science to be the only appropriate basis for the study of sex, and he argued that scientific practitioners had an obligation to remain neutral on issues of morality. He criticized most of the earlier work as narrowly moralistic and unscientific because the researchers had been prudish about sex and too influenced by society's values to say what they really thought.

Yet Kinsey's own values intruded. Some of these were similar to those of his predecessors, while others diverged markedly. Like earlier researchers, Kinsey was pro-marriage, but while he defended marriage in both books and viewed rising divorce rates with alarm, his defense was pragmatic. He used a functionalist model, common in marriage courses in his day, that marriage and the maintenance of the home were universally important to social stability. Without the family, he argued, children would receive no care, individuals would not have their sexual needs met, and social disarray would result. Families provided a "regular sexual outlet for adults" and controlled "promiscuous sexual activity." Kinsey considered sexual problems a major cause of divorce. Any group interested in maintaining the family, he stated, had to be concerned with "the sexual factor." Other factors besides sex were important to marriage, but no scientist could fail to appreciate the significance of coitus to marital stability.

Kinsey agreed with Terman and Burgess that the greatest obstacle to sexual satisfaction was poor sexual adjustment among wives. But he differed in his explanation of this. Although poor sexual performance was produced by repressive upbringing, this was not only a problem for women: "Specifically, the sexual factors which most often cause difficulty in the upper level marriages are (1) the failure of the male to show skill in sexual approach and technique, and (2) the failure of the female to participate with the abandon which is necessary for the successful consummation of any sexual relation. Both of these difficulties stem from the same source, namely, the restraints which are developed in premarital years, and the impossibility of freely releasing these restraints after marriage."[27]

Despite this pro-marriage ideology, Kinsey was a sexual libertarian. He proselytized in favor of tolerating all kinds of sexual tastes, a stance seemingly at odds with his insistence on scientific objectivity. Where earlier standards of sexual normality were based on either religious or medical prescription, Kinsey based his on the statistical distribution of sexual acts. Whatever existed in nature must be normal, so Kinsey was open to all that he observed and heard. While others were anxious not to offend, Kinsey presented himself as a scientific pioneer venturing where others could or would not go. In his introduction to *Sexual Behavior in the Human Male* he stated: "The present study, then, represents an attempt to accumulate an objectively determined body of fact about sex which strictly avoids social or moral interpretations of the fact. Each person who reads this report will want to make interpretations in accordance with his understanding of moral values and social significances; but that is not part of the scientific method and, indeed, scientists have no special capacities for making such evaluations."[28]

Kinsey's approach resulted from his background as a taxonomist. Since the eighteenth century, when Carolus Linnaeus created his typology of species, biologists had constantly modified and refined it. Taxonomists were less interested in estimating the relative frequencies of population characteristics than in discovering all variations. As a taxonomist, Kinsey viewed the range of human sexual behavior as more important than the relative frequency with which any particular behavior occurred. This led him to argue that normality included anything found in the normal distribution. He stated this clearly: "the fact of individual variation is one of the fundamentals of biological reasoning."

Kinsey argued that the amount of variation in species was greater than had been realized, and that, although scientists assumed a dichotomous variation, much of it was continuous: "Biologically I can see only two bases for the recognition of abnormality. If a particular type of variation is rare in a given population, it, perhaps, may be called abnormal. The rarity of adults who measure under three feet or over eight in total height is, perhaps, some reason for calling such extremes abnormal. I should prefer to call them 'rare.' The second biologic test of abnormality is the physiologic malfunction which it may produce. In that sense cancers and tumors may be called abnormal." Finally: "Scholarly thinking as well as the laymen's evaluation still needs to be tempered with the realization that individual variations shape into a continuous curve on which there are no sharp differences between normal and abnormal, between right and wrong."[29] To Kinsey, being a scientist meant being nonjudgmental, and this meant embracing sexual variety. But he never fully realized that these ideas challenged assumptions about gender opposition.

If normality was a function of frequency, scientists must collect enough cases to include all variations, and Kinsey tried to collect data on every type of sexual behavior. However, he did not realize that his decisions as to which characteristics were important were influenced by his own social position as an educated upper-middle-class man.[30] Kinsey was the first to interview all social classes rather than just the upper-middle or middle class. He romanticized what he called "the lower level," that is, lower socioeconomic classes, as more spontaneous, less inhibited, and less conforming to conventional morality. Earlier writers had seen the more permissive sexuality of lower-class women as a threat to middle-class marriages. Kinsey approved of what he perceived as their more spontaneous sexuality. He did not recognize the patronizing aspects of this view, or that his message was directed toward the middle class for whom the lower strata provided an object lesson.

He had difficulty obtaining interviews with "the lower level," and his data came largely from prisoners. As Paul Gebhard noted, he did not see this as a problem: "Kinsey was having trouble getting people with less than a high-school education, and he discovered that the prisons were full of them. His feeling was that they were pretty representative of that social group anyway, because he really believed that, for grammar school educated people, part of their culture was going to jail."[31] This assumption almost certainly excluded the many working-class persons living law-abiding lives with sexual proclivities carefully shaped by institutions such as religion. Kinsey also refrained from publishing data on the sexual behavior of blacks in his two books, because he did not have enough middle-class black respondents and he did not want to confound class and race. After the volume on men drew extensive criticism for his working-class sample, his associates stepped up the pressure, and Kinsey dropped the prison population from the women's volume.

Just as his class blinded him to diversity in other social strata, Kinsey's gender figured in his choice of orgasm as the sole measure of a sexual event.[32] And in spite of his tolerance for diversity, in his volume on women, published in 1953, he agonized over women's frequent failure to achieve orgasms easily. Kinsey saw women's sexual inhibitions as products both of their upbringing and of physiological variations that caused a natural range of sexual response much greater than in men. He also insisted that women were naturally monogamous, unlike men. Men married to secure regular sexual relations, while women married to establish a home, develop a deep affectionate bond, and have children. He interpreted his findings through the cultural lens of his day. Furthermore, he argued that the great range of women's sexual responses inevitably led to problems among them:

> Because there is such wide variation in the sexual responsiveness and frequencies of overt activity among females, many females are incapable of understanding other females . . . To the third or more of the females who have rarely been aroused by psychologic stimuli, it may seem fantastic to believe that there are females who come to orgasm as the result of sexual

fantasy, without any physical stimulation of their genitalia or of any other part of their body. Sensing something of this variation in capacity and experience, many females—although not all—hesitate to discuss their sexual histories with other females, and may prefer to carry their sexual problems to male clinicians.[33]

The idea that women would find it easier to talk to men than to other women about their sexual problems illustrates Kinsey's lack of understanding of women and his blind assumption that men could explain women to themselves.

Yet, while Kinsey thought women and their sexual incapacity were the major cause of marital unhappiness, he was optimistic about prospects for change. He did not accept the widely held view that penetration was the most likely way for women to reach orgasm, and he stated boldly that the clitoris, not the vagina, was the site of female pleasure. For this reason, he argued, masturbation was not only acceptable but increased women's ability to achieve orgasm in heterosexual intercourse. When 14 percent of his female respondents reported multiple orgasms, Kinsey, unlike Hamilton and Terman, saw this as good news, although he was not sure all women had the capacity. Unlike his predecessors, he unambivalently concluded that premarital coitus helped women achieve orgasm during marital coitus. Women who denied their sexual urges in their early years, he said, had difficulty becoming sufficiently abandoned to achieve orgasm.

This contradiction between his defense of marriage and his acknowledgment that women did not really need men for sexual pleasure shows two aspects of Kinsey. He truly believed science was a neutral endeavor, and this made him less likely to evaluate behavior negatively in the manner of other experts. He did not confine his interest to orgasms achieved during heterosexual intercourse (Kinsey preferred the word "outlet" to "orgasm"), and he collected data on the frequency of different types of outlet. Yet he wrote about the importance of preserving marriage and family, and he himself had a traditional, even patriarchal, marriage in which his work and his desires took center stage. His conservative tastes ran to gardening and classical music, and he was formal in dress and manner. Pomeroy described him as a man who "got along with his neighbors," adding that "except for his interest in sex, he was the same as everybody else."[34] Since he saw himself as a scientist, Kinsey could not acknowledge the personal prejudices he held about gender.

Since Kinsey's ideas about female sexual autonomy were overshadowed by his more vigorous defense of marriage, his data on female sexuality were not his biggest challenge to the sexual knowledge of his day. He was most controversial in his opinions that one sexual outlet was as good as another and that homosexuality was not only an acceptable outlet but represented only behavior and not a type of person. This idea flew directly in the face of accepted convictions that sexuality and gender were intimately intertwined and that homosexuals had confused genders as well as deviant desires.

The shocking nature of Kinsey's position can be seen by contrast with the only other survey of homosexuality undertaken in the 1930s: George Henry's study of "sex variants." Henry was sympathetic, but he portrayed homosexuals as abnormal people with gender confusion:

> The sex variant is not an uncommon person and he is found in all classes of society. Moreover there is little scientific basis for precise classification of humans as male or female. Masculinity and femininity are quantitative and qualitative variations. These variations are registered in structural, physiological, and psychological attributes which are peculiar to each individual. Regardless of the sex, a person gives expression to masculine or feminine traits in accordance with his innate tendencies to maleness or femaleness and in proportion to the opportunities for expression of these tendencies.[35]

Following Terman, Henry argued that some unfortunate persons had a greater proportion of traits associated with the opposite sex. This produced women with the sexual desires of men and men with those of women.

Henry's research grew out of the interest of several prominent sex researchers in homosexuality and the threat it represented to marriage. In 1935 Dickinson formed the Committee for the Study of Sex Variants. Dickinson had collected limited data on lesbians as part of his study of single women, and while he found no evidence of "organic differentiation," he assumed homosexuality was a developmental problem involving a confused gender identity. That is, some people had childhood experiences that caused them to adopt the gender of the opposite sex. Henry, a professor at Cornell University Medical Center and a past president of the New York Psychiatric Society, was one of several psychiatrists on the committee, which also included Terman.

The committee sponsored Henry to do a study with a lesbian, pseudonymously called Jan Gay, as his research assistant. In addition to giving their histories, Henry's respondents submitted to a variety of procedures including measurement of the cranium and examination of the pelvis. Presenting the "facts without personal bias," Henry concluded that, in addition to constitutional factors:

The sex variant is a person who has failed to achieve and maintain adult heterosexual modes of sexual expression and who has resorted to other modes of sexual expression. The sex variant seems to be in part a by-product of civilization. In our present civilization he is an expression of his inability to meet the responsibility of establishing and maintaining a home which involves the rearing of children. The manifold demands made upon parents as a result of our high standards of living often discourage heterosexual adjustment and foster substitutive sexual activity.[36]

Henry's views matched those of most sex researchers of his day. He considered homosexuality a sickness, resulting from faulty development, which should be kindly treated but nonetheless should be treated. For Henry, heterosexuality was synonymous with normality, and gendered opposition, the natural attraction of men and women for each other, was the basis of marriage.

The Sex Variants Committee did not confine their interest to "inverts." Members worried about threats to the family from those who could not adjust normally. They no longer argued that these behaviors were always congenital but saw maladjustment largely or solely as a result of faulty social development. This position increased anxiety that families could unknowingly produce children whose adjustment to married life would be problematic. That is, the family was the unwitting source of problems that threatened its future. Concerns during the 1930s reflected the Depression, which created genuine threats to family stability, and isolationism, which made Americans even more fearful of family variety than before. During this decade many people could not afford to marry. They lived on the edges of society, traveling from place to place in search of jobs, and increasing the sense of threat felt by the more fortunate, who saw the economically disadvantaged as pathological.[37]

Persons with potentially problematic sexual development included not only homosexuals but women whose inability to enjoy sexual activity was so severe that they could not function as wives. The Columbia University professor and Sex Variants Committee treasurer Carney Landis received funds from the Rockefeller Foundation and the Committee for Research in the Problems of Sex for two studies in the late 1930s, one comparing the sexual responses of "normal" women and female psychiatric patients and the other of physically handicapped women.[38] He justified these studies as important for understanding normal female sexual development. Normal development was so hard to define that the truly abnormal were needed for contrast.

Henry's study was published in 1941 and reprinted in 1948, the year Kinsey's volume on men appeared. In marked contrast to Henry, Kinsey challenged the idea that gender and sexuality were fundamentally intertwined:

> In studies of human behavior, the term inversion is applied to sexual situations in which males play female roles and females play male roles in sex relations . . . A more elaborate presentation of our data would show that there are a great many males who remain as masculine, and a great many females who remain as feminine, in their attitudes and approaches in homosexual relations, as the males or females who have nothing but heterosexual relations. Inversion and homosexuality are two distinct and not always correlated types of behavior.[39]

As part of this challenge, Kinsey denied the existence of "the homosexual" as a type of person, and insisted that he was simply describing behavior. He did not like the term "lesbian" because it erroneously implied "that there are fundamental differences between the homosexual responses and activities of females and of males."[40]

Kinsey argued that all sexual "outlets" were equal as long as no one was harmed. Yet he still treated the gender of partners as having special importance by developing a scale to measure relative amounts of heterosexual and homosexual experience. He did not think one's position on the scale was fixed; it might change over time as one developed new sexual practices and discarded old ones. He also provided several estimates of homosexual experience depending on the time frame and the exclusivity of practice. For men these percentages ranged from 37 percent with at least one homosexual outlet after puberty to 4 percent whose outlets were exclusively homosexual throughout their lives.

Kinsey defended homosexual activity while maintaining his argument that marriage between men and women, whose mutual sexual attraction kept them together, was important in preventing the disarray that would result from total sexual freedom. For Kinsey homosexual sex was simply one type of extramarital sex, and he argued for tolerance about such lapses, none of which need threaten the family. While some men and women had exclusively homosexual histories, just as some had exclusively heterosexual, a considerable proportion of the population experienced a mixture of homosexual and heterosexual activity. Such persons were found in every social group, married or single. For some professional women it was a matter of convenience, because they found pursuit of a career difficult to combine with marriage; and for some men, married or single, "homosexual relations" were "sometimes a substitute for less readily available heterosexual contacts" and sometimes simply "a different type of sexual outlet."

Because he believed that homosexuals, rapists, and pedophiles often engaged in perfectly normal behavior, Kinsey was critical of the practice of placing sex offenders in jail. He was particularly incensed by state laws passed during the 1930s in response to panics about "sexual psychopaths." The work of experts like Terman and Henry, added to fears about the homeless unemployed, had led some states to "modernize" their laws and treat sexual outcasts as psychopaths by committing them to mental hospitals for indefinite stays. Other states gave courts the discretion to sentence convicted sex criminals to either an indeterminate sentence in a psychiatric institution or a fixed prison sentence. To most Americans homosexuals were perverts whose existence threatened the American way of life. It was more palatable for liberal researchers to view homosexuals as a unique category in need of civil liberties than to make Kinsey's more radical argument that any person might have such experiences.

While his training led him to accept sexual variety, Kinsey's colleagues acknowledged that his proselytizing tendency went beyond this. Gebhard attributed it to his upbringing: "He was brought up by a very puritanical family. They wouldn't even let him play the piano on Sunday. During his adolescence, he was sure he was going to burn in hell-fire because he masturbated. There was no one to talk to about it, but he knew it was evil and dreaded he would go to the insane asylum. Later, as a scientist, he could see what an unfortunate situation this was. He once said to me, 'I decided I didn't want any young people going through the nonsense I went through.' "[41]

Kinsey's position was dangerous since it questioned the very basis of the family. To imply that the family was not a biologically necessitated human institution but simply an effective way of maintaining social stability made people nervous. Kinsey was aware that this was controversial, and, to maintain respectability, he controlled every aspect of the research. He even created a myth that he had not been especially interested in doing sex research but had been forced into it when asked to coordinate a marriage course for which Indiana students had lobbied. In his version he sought answers for the hordes of students who came to him for sexual guidance, so he started collecting their sex histories to use as data. When this caused contention, he had to choose between his new research agenda and the course. He claimed to have reluctantly chosen the former. Thus he described himself as coerced into sex research by young people's need for sex education.

In fact, by 1938 when the marriage course started, Kinsey's interest in sex research was already of long standing.[42] He had written a sexually explicit high school biology text in 1926. At the university he encouraged graduate students to talk to him about sexual problems, gave a number of lectures on the topic, and worked with students to lobby for the marriage course. In 1941 Kinsey wrote that his interest in sex research had been sparked by reading Dickinson's work a decade earlier. Furthermore, his elaborate interview schedule was complete well before 1938. Kinsey deliberately obfuscated the origins of the research, probably out of fear that his interest would seem prurient and imply a lack of scholarly impartiality.

In the end, problems with his methodology were probably as important as the radical implications of his conclusions in causing his reputation to diminish and his funding to be cut. At the time, it was standard practice for researchers to do the interviewing themselves using a written interview schedule. To achieve confidentiality, Kinsey dispensed with the schedule, and he and the few others he trained memorized five hundred possible topics. Questions changed according to interviewers' judgments, and responses were recorded using a secret code. Instead of asking neutral questions, Kinsey put the burden of denial on respondents; for example, he asked "When did you first masturbate?" instead of "Have you ever masturbated?" Pomeroy described the procedure:

> It's important that, as interviewers, we not be evaluative. Of all the interviewing skills you need, that is the key. You do this by talking to yourself. Do not think about why someone is a rapist. That is for him and his conscience. You just have to say that it's not your business. Sometimes this was difficult. Kinsey was made furious by—the term is "dirt"—someone who would beat up a homosexual after having sex with the person. But he realized that "dirt" had a story to tell. I had trouble with anything that involved violence, but I had to train myself to minimize this feeling. You can minimize bias if you work at it. For example, occasionally, when interviewing, people would come on to you. You had to teach yourself not to lean forwards as if you were interested, nor to lean backwards.[43]

Sometimes it did not work out this way, as in the following account from Gebhard: "We would make encouraging noises. In fact we got in the habit of saying 'Good. Good.' Pomeroy got caught by that once. Some guy told him about his extra-marital intercourse and Pomeroy said 'Good. Good.' The guy stops and says 'What's good about it?' "[44] As this story shows, being nonjudgmental led to a position in favor of diversity and communicated to respondents a tolerance for, and perhaps an expectation of, all sexual acts.

As a result of Kinsey's nonjudgmental, even encouraging approach, he reported higher levels of most sexual activities than other researchers did. But this method undoubtedly gave people permission to reveal their deepest secrets, which other researchers may have underestimated.

A more certain cause of overestimation is the way Kinsey obtained subjects. In 1938, probability sampling, in which everyone in the population being studied has an equal or known probability of selection and survey directors exercise no choice over whom to select, was gaining acceptance. Kinsey's staff had limited statistical expertise, and they did not use this method. His respondents consisted of people who crossed his path, plus what he called 100 percent samples, that is, interviews with all the members of a group.[45] In selecting groups Kinsey sought the greatest diversity possible. He interviewed many men in prison, often for minor sexual offenses. He went to great lengths to interview homosexuals, pedophiles, and others whose sexual tastes were against the law. This is the opposite of probability sampling, in which those with less common behaviors are not overrepresented.

Kinsey dismissed all criticism of his work as prudish, even though most academic reviews were positive except for criticism of his sample. However, given the controversy surrounding his volume on men, these methodological critiques and Kinsey's dismissal of them worried his funders. By 1948 Kinsey was receiving almost all of the money available to the Committee for Research in Problems of Sex. Its parent organization, the National Research Council, asked the American Statistical Association to review his research techniques. The unpaid review team consisted of three world-renowned statisticians, William Cochran, Frederick Mosteller, and John Tukey, who found much to praise.[46] The study improved on previous sex surveys, with better coverage of material, a broader sample, a greater variety of methodological checks, and more sophisticated statistical analysis. They were interested in the interviewing techniques, which they compared favorably to standard methods. They had only one major criticism: the absence of random sampling made results impossible to generalize. Describing the ways in which small probability samples might verify his results, the team strongly recommended that Kinsey try one.

Unhappy during the team's visit, Kinsey reacted with public caution but private fury, particularly at Tukey, who had told him "I would trade all your 18,000 case histories for 400 in a probability sample."[47] Kinsey ignored their advice and in fact never understood it. He liked to quote his friend Raymond Pearl, a population biologist who had himself surveyed sexual behavior. According to Pearl, with so many cases Kinsey did not need to worry, since "statistical theory is largely a substitute for adequate data."[48]

Because Kinsey did not differentiate supportive criticism from that of conservative ideologues, he did not see a more serious attack on the horizon. The University of Pennsylvania sociologist A. H. Hobbs and his colleague Richard Lambert wrote a blistering attack on Kinsey's views about homosexuality and premarital intercourse.[49] Kinsey, they stated, ignored the serious consequences of breaking down social mores. If some people fell short of society's sexual standards, this should not lead to the abandonment of those standards. Hobbs and other conservatives wrote to their congressmen about Kinsey's access to foundation support. In 1954 they reached the Tennessee Congressman B. Carroll Reece. Some liberal foundations had funded an inquiry into the House Un-American Activities Committee, so in retaliation Reece formed the House Committee to Investigate Tax Free Foundations. The first and only topic this committee raised was Rockefeller Foundation funding of Kinsey, and it called only witnesses hostile to Kinsey, including Hobbs.

The new head of the Rockefeller Foundation, Dean Rusk, refuted the committee's final report but also cut Kinsey's funding. In addition to feeling intimidated, the foundation was irritated by Kinsey's refusal to respond to criticism. Most large foundations do not support projects indefinitely, and the congressional investigation was a propitious moment for a break. Kinsey never recovered from this loss and spent his last few years in a fruitless search for financial support. Those close to him witnessed his grief at being "at the height of your fame and going around with everybody being superficially cordial but actually treating you like you were a pariah."[50]

While Kinsey's work did not have the impact he envisioned, it permanently changed the public's attitude toward sex surveys. From a late-twentieth-century vantage point it is hard to envisage the tentative nature of the pre-Kinsey public discussion of sex. The *New York Times,* for example, refused to accept advance advertising for Kinsey's first volume. By carefully managing the press, Kinsey created a new audience for sex surveys, and, after the first volume was published, the *Times,* like the rest of the print media, published reviews as well as the reactions of religious leaders, psychiatrists, and other authorities. Surveys, which previously had served as tools for experts or as resources for educating college students, were increasingly directed straight to the public by way of the media.

Once the media became involved, Kinsey lost control of the results of his study as they lived on after him. He had managed the voices of his respondents, and he had been able to create media interest and to control the presentation of data to journalists. But the media summarized his findings into sound bites small enough to digest and not too controversial for family newspapers. And it was these media versions, not Kinsey's, that lived on as "fact." Although both volumes were bestsellers, Pomeroy described them as the least-read bestsellers ever, written in a style that made them "scientific" and therefore inaccessible. The media reported selectively. In doing so they ignored many of the most radical arguments, including those on female orgasm and on homosexuality.

These press summaries, especially the finding that premarital intercourse was more common among women than previously supposed, filtered into the general consciousness and helped form public knowledge about what Americans did sexually and what it was permissible to do.[51] From then on, many of Kinsey's findings became accepted truths even among those who never heard of Kinsey. Textbooks on marriage and marital-advice books readily incorporated Kinsey's findings about heterosexual intercourse. They interpreted his results as evidence that a satisfactory sex life was the most important basis for marriage. They reinforced the widely held belief that sex was more interesting to husbands than wives. Kinsey's agreement with his predecessors that female orgasm was a special problem perpetuated the idea that men and women were innately different and had difficulty in reaching sexual accord.

Kinsey had opened the private world of sexual activity to public scrutiny, and in doing so had created a demand for more information. Between 1900 and 1950 just over fifty surveys of sexual behavior were conducted in the United States. By 1970 the number increased to well over one hundred per decade. But while questions about sexual behavior appeared in more and more surveys, research on marital adjustment floundered. Although a few surveys on sexual satisfaction and marital adjustment continued to appear until the early 1960s, these tended to look backward by citing the earlier studies as guides. Researchers confirmed the role of the wife's sexual adjustment in marital happiness, emphasized the importance of simultaneous climax, and measured sexual fulfillment by the level of satisfaction with genital intercourse.[52]

The men in charge of these studies continued to argue that wives who could not learn to enjoy sex were largely doomed to marital unhappiness and even failure. Some elaborated on Kinsey's reports of the effects of premarital sexual experience on women's marital adjustment, but they generally concluded that such experience had a negative effect on women's sexual response within marriage.[53] Young people should certainly get to know one another through some petting before marriage, but should save coitus for after. To go against societal codes, these writers opined, would be so difficult that women who did so would suffer. Using societal norms as their moral standards, these researchers ignored the premarital sexual experience of men. The main purpose of marital adjustment studies continued to be to provide information for textbooks used in courses on marriage and the family.

In addition, new areas of inquiry began to attract researchers, including studies of contraception and fertility. Kinsey had asked about contraception and abortion but had asked relatively few questions about fertility. While fertility studies had their origins in demographic research rather than in sex research, Kinsey's reports made intimate questions easier for demographers to ask. Furthermore, the birth control movement and the world of sexology overlapped. Even so, for a long time demographers asked few questions about sex. They were uncomfortable with such questions, and in focusing on births and contraception among the married, they were able to assume the existence of sexual activity. In fact, the widespread availability of contraception was probably more important than any study of orgasmic adequacy in promoting the importance of sex in marriage.

By the late 1930s demographers were worried about declines in American fertility, in particular middle-class fertility. Since the middle classes were assumed to produce superior children, their low fertility created fears about the nation's economic and genetic future. Demographers had long worried about the breeding habits of the poor, as had those in the birth control movement. In 1942 the Birth Control Federation of America changed its name to the Planned Parenthood Federation of America, symbolizing the movement's switch from an almost exclusive focus on birth control for the unfit poor to one encouraging all families to plan for the number of children they could afford. This implicitly encouraged fertility among the better off. Around this time the demographers John Riley and Matilda White fielded a study of nearly 3,500 upper-middle-class married women to see if their contraceptive practices were linked to the falling birth rate.[54] The study was funded by the Market Research Corporation of America, which was interested in the growth of this segment of the population. The authors found that almost all nonsterile women used one or more birth control methods. Their assumption that women alone were responsible for fertility and contraception decisions was to persist for decades.

In 1941, one year after this study appeared, a team of demographers led by Clyde Kiser and Pascal Whelpton interviewed more than 1,000 white Protestant couples in Indianapolis.[55] Their explicit goal was to advise the government on how to encourage larger families. The study was funded by the Milbank Memorial Fund and the Carnegie Corporation, foundations with a history of supporting the eugenics movement and with fears about population trends. Kiser and Whelpton concluded that couples used birth control to limit family size and to space their children. Their finding of a negative correlation between socioeconomic status and effective contraceptive use concerned them greatly. It seemed that the wrong women were having the most children.

This problem righted itself as fertility rose in the wake of the Second World War, and by the 1950s overpopulation replaced low fertility as the problem. Demographers responsible for the Census Bureau's population projections, including Whelpton, had incorrectly assumed that high postwar birth rates were the temporary result of delayed childbearing. By extrapolating the fertility rates of prewar cohorts, they projected a slow growth, or even a decline, in the postwar population. Instead, fertility rates stayed high during the prosperous 1950s as middle-class couples, aided by federal housing legislation, moved to the suburbs. Open spaces, economic opportunity, and a family-centered ideology turned women's attention toward husbands and children. After their failure to predict the postwar baby boom, Whelpton and his colleagues realized that they lacked information for population forecasts. Survey research proved the ideal tool. This was an era when husbands were often the sole financial support of their families and women took on the job of family management. Ronald Freedman, a University of Michigan sociologist who had worked on the Indianapolis study, suggested to Whelpton that demographers should ask women about their fertility intentions.[56] Freedman, along with Whelpton and Arthur Campbell, conducted the first Growth of American Families study (GAF-I).

Prying into the private lives of citizens was a serious business, especially for men who were demographers not sex researchers, and it required weighty rationales. With the Cold War under way, the nation's well-being became the study's justification: "many long range plans depend on population forecasts."[57] The lofty goal of the GAF-I demographers was to help define the role American families should play in securing the country's future. The title of the study implied that all families in America would be included. Although it was no longer confined to the middle class, only white, married women, aged 18–39 and living with their husbands were interviewed. Young single women were asked about future plans under the assumption that they would not be sexually active until marriage.

The surveyors used the latest scientific methods, which they explained in detail. These included a probability sample, trained interviewers who did not know the study hypotheses and thus could not unwittingly influence the results, and extensive pretests of the questionnaire to ensure the questions measured what they were intended to measure. The entire process was staged to avoid causing scandal. With reassurances that they were not sensationalists like Kinsey, Freedman and his colleagues obtained funding from the Rockefeller Foundation. All research at Michigan required approval by the university's Board of Regents. The Regents questioned Freedman about his proposed research and decided that his questionnaire must be approved by the Detroit Archdiocese. To further insure against any appearance of impropriety, the researchers assembled two distinguished advisory committees, one of physicians and one of lay people. These cautionary measures did not completely alleviate the team's nervousness about interviewing a random sample of strangers about intimate aspects of their lives. To their delight, the survey produced the highest response rate (91 percent) for a noncaptive audience in the history of the University of Michigan's Survey Research Center.

Freedman and his colleagues found widespread use of contraception among all groups they interviewed. As a result, family size was becoming homogeneous, around two to four children. Catholics wanted and expected larger families, but few wanted more than four. Many families had more children than they wanted, but this was a result of lower education and a consequent inability to practice contraception effectively. The middle class appeared to have expanded. Almost all white families shared the norms of moderation and a gendered division of labor.

Freedman's success placed surveys firmly at the center of social science research. It promised methodologically rigorous solutions to sticky problems, and it had a profound impact on both fertility and sex research, topics that had seemed too dangerous for probability samples. The survey, which was repeated in 1960, led to many other fertility surveys and set the stage for government funding of demographic research.[58] By 1965, when the National Institute of Child Health and Human Development (NICHD) funded the National Fertility Studies (NFS), the researchers even included questions on sexual behavior. The demographers Norman Ryder and Charles Westoff asked only three such questions, none of which used the word "sex":

- In the past four weeks, how many times have you had intercourse?
- (Since your last pregnancy) How many months, if any, have there been when you stopped having intercourse for any reason—such as sickness, husband away from home, or so that you wouldn't have a baby too soon?

- (Since your last pregnancy) Have you douched regularly within half an hour after intercourse?[59]

Ryder and Westoff used policy-oriented justifications for the questions, such as needing to know if frequency of intercourse was related to contraceptive failure.

In the 1970 and 1975 rounds of the NFS, each set of respondents reported greater frequency of marital intercourse than in the previous survey.[60] Ryder and Westoff credited this to the greater openness and permissiveness of the sexual revolution of the 1960s.[61] They also acknowledged the importance of the pill and of legalized abortion. Previously, women's apparent lack of interest in sex had been blamed on either upbringing or constitution. No one had anticipated that when women ceased to fear reproduction their sexual activity would increase. This finding of a possible connection between sexual desire and reproduction acknowledged, for the first time, the relevance of sex research to an understanding of fertility.

By the 1960s fertility started to fall. This time anxiety about world population growth led demographers to see this as a positive trend. Rather than raising fertility among the advantaged, they wanted to lower that of the disadvantaged. This meant examining black fertility, and the 1965 NFS included a black sample large enough for separate analysis. With the civil rights movement in full swing and the war on poverty commencing, the relationship of black fertility to poverty was beginning to receive attention. In 1970 the black sample was even larger.

As government funding for policy-oriented social science research increased, twin ideas about the causes of poverty competed for attention. Many agreed that the poor, particularly the black poor, were ill-prepared to compete in a postindustrial society with rising unemployment for the untrained. But the old belief also resurfaced, that victims of poverty caused their own misery by their uncontrolled fertility. Where, for the middle classes, sex was the glue that held good marriages together, for the poor, it was their undoing.[62] Ryder and Westoff noted that the gap between desired number of children and expected number of children was larger for black women than for white women.

Once race was introduced, another problem appeared. The practice of interviewing only currently married women seemed inappropriate when more than one-third of black fertility involved women who were not married at the time of the pregnancy. This led to the inclusion of the unmarried in fertility surveys, which necessitated more questions about sexual behavior. With married respondents researchers assumed that sexual intercourse occurred regularly, but they could make no such assumption for the unmarried. From this point forward sexual activity, at least of the potentially reproductive kind, became an integral feature of fertility surveys. And the focus on the disadvantaged meant that researchers stressed the negative consequences of sexual activity. In 1960 the sociologist Lee Rainwater had published a book that served as a catalyst for these concerns.[63] Rainwater portrayed sex as one of the poor's few pleasures and children as a burdensome by-product. In fertility surveys of middle-class couples, husbands' desires received little mention, but Rainwater described poor husbands as pursuing their own pleasures while disregarding their wives' often negative feelings.

J. Richard Udry at the University of North Carolina took a similar position, insisting that in order to understand reproduction it was essential to ask even married people about sex, and that men should be interviewed as well as women. Udry differed from other demographers in his sociobiological explanations for sexual activity.

Starting in the late 1960s, Udry published a number of surveys over the next decades.[64] The largest, funded by NICHD, involved the evaluation of family planning programs for the poor. He, Naomi Morris, and Carl Bauman described a series of studies conducted from the late 1960s through the 1970s with black and white women aged 15–44.[65] In these evaluation studies Udry made the argument that IQ and fertility were related. Furthermore: "Following this argument to its logical implications for program application, we can infer that low-IQ women are in need of permanent methods of fertility prevention when they have reached their desired family size if they are to be able to control their fertility as well as high-IQ women. It should be emphasized that, according to our data, education is not necessarily the answer, since the differential in unwanted births for women at risk by education net of IQ is not significant."[66] In these surveys of poor women, the surveyors' interpretation of the meaning of sexual activity for the marital relationship had changed drastically from its beneficial role in middle-class marriages.

By 1975, with widespread use of the pill and sterilization, variations in fertility by race and religion were too small to be of interest to demographers. The NFS was replaced by the National Surveys of Family Growth, which began in 1973. The National Institute of Health Statistics has fielded this survey every five years since then for the use of researchers. But since those who will analyze the data do not collect it, it is difficult for individual researchers to get their voices heard. For example, although the National Surveys of Family Growth expanded the definition of the family to include ever-married women plus never-married women who had given birth, it was not until the 1982–83 round that all women aged 15–44 were included.

For a long time demographers, like marital adjustment researchers, confined their interest in sexual behavior to the safety of sex within marriage. But the audience for much of their work was college students, who learned in their marriage courses not only about the importance of satisfactory sexual adjustment but also about family planning. It is not surprising that, having learned how difficult and important their own tasks would be in this arena, and having learned, too, about methods of birth control, the female members of the audience began to wonder if a little premarital practice might not improve their chances of making their marriages work. While demographers were writing about birth control within the family, young women began experimenting sexually, and sex researchers turned their attention away from marriage to this more dangerous topic.

4

Sex before Marriage

Two basic criticisms of research on premarital sex were that it lacked data on the all-important areas of attitudes toward sex in addition to the actual behavior and that the research utilized poor samples. I sought to meet these criticisms in my own work on premarital sex.

—Ira Reiss, 1972

I N 1960 the family sociologist Lester Kirkendall proposed a solution to an issue troubling teachers of family courses: what to tell students who came for advice about whether to have sexual intercourse before marriage. Addressing his colleagues in the journal *Marriage and Family Living*, Kirkendall recommended that, in deciding what to do, couples should consider the consequences for their particular relationship. This meant examining their moral values and the strength of their feelings for each other. Lest his audience conclude that he was abandoning his own moral standards, he added that if the young followed his advice it would eliminate most premarital intercourse, since "the great bulk of it appears to be exploitive and advantage-taking."[1]

By this time "functional" family courses, that is, courses preparing students for marriage and family life, were a mainstay of sociology departments everywhere. One year earlier a report in the same journal had said that 82 percent of colleges and universities offered such courses, in which about 100,000 students enrolled annually.[2] The majority of students in the courses were women. Most students came to the courses to learn how to have a good marriage, and many wanted to know what their professors recommended about the troubling issue of premarital sex.

The journal published a symposium of reactions to Kirkendall's recommendations, and these reveal the turmoil professors felt about the issue.[3] If professors told students to wait for marriage, they risked seeming outmoded and irrelevant, but if they told students premarital sex was acceptable, they could be accused of encouraging the young to flout social rules. How could they retain the paternal authority so necessary to gain students' respect, yet not offend parents, state legislators, and others? Some of the symposium writers noted that if professors followed Kirkendall's recommendations students would realize their teachers were avoiding the issue and would lose faith. Others took the position that schools must uphold societal mores and forbid sex before marriage. Yet others answered that premarital sex was part of a changing society that professors should encourage, for it would help students achieve sexually satisfying marriages. This professorial debate occurred against a background of growing parental fears that children lived in an "adolescent society" whose values were at odds with those of the adult world.[4]

It seemed clear to all the professors that before they could recommend any behavior to students they needed to know what kinds of sexual activities their young charges were engaging in. In the late 1930s, when data from the marital adjustment surveys indicated increases in premarital sex, researchers had slowly begun interviewing the unmarried. By 1960 they had already completed about twenty such surveys. But in the permissive 1960s this mushroomed, and by 1975 over eighty surveys of the sexual behavior of unmarried young people appeared, almost all focusing on college students. The use of students was partly a matter of convenience but also resulted from a continued concern about the middle class.

Most of those writing before 1960 took it for granted that students should avoid premarital sex. Yet many were sympathetic to the strain this caused college students, whose lives away from home were filled with temptation and opportunity. And, while they believed both men and women would experience strain, researchers assumed that these would affect the genders differently. Men's desires were strong and innate, and arguments that they could withstand their hormonal urges had all but disappeared by World War II. College "girls," in contrast, experienced temptation after they fell in love and, even then, they were rightfully cautious about "going all the way."

The first survey of college students' sexual behavior was undertaken not by male professors but by two female journalists. In 1938 Dorothy Dunbar

Bromley and Florence Haxton Britten promised readers the unvarnished truth in their report on interviews with students at a variety of colleges. For Bromley and Britten most of the consequences of sex before marriage were personal, not social. They considered college a serious place where young people should devote themselves to getting an education. Particularly anxious that young women not be distracted, they gave practical advice. Sex was problematic because "an intense love relationship tends to be more disturbing than tranquilizing" and "may interfere seriously with class work." Even so, it was not always to be discouraged, since "the chances for ultimate happiness seem to be about as good for deeply committed couples who adjust themselves to a complete physical relationship as for those who endure great strain, grow irritable and perhaps against their preferences turn to other mates whom their tricked and disappointed bodies have chosen instinctively as more likely sexual prospects."[5] Giving in to desire was wrong only in the pragmatic sense that love and work might not be compatible. This was particularly true for women, since for them premarital sex carried a heavy burden of secrecy.

While Bromley and Britten were unusual in depicting strong female sexual desire, they accepted contemporary beliefs about differences in male and female arousal. They took it for granted that women were aroused by love, while noting that, given the availability of attractive men in college, love was hard to resist. In these tempting surroundings, they reported, only 12 percent of their female respondents easily contained their desires. These had been raised in "the Victorian mode" by parents whose emphasis on chastity delayed arousal of their daughters' sex instincts. In contrast, most young women who remained virgins were "fully aware that the tempting fruit hangs heavy, heavy over their heads."[6] Bromley and Britten saw different pressures facing college men. Most lived in a state of great arousal and had happily given in to temptation. The few who had not had unusually low sex drives. These young men felt social pressure to test and prove their virility and even apologized for their lack of experience.

Other authors shared Bromley and Britten's beliefs about gender differences in sex drive, but not their ideas about the importance of women's careers. A decade later Winston Ehrmann interviewed almost 12,000 students at the University of Florida and, in a much-cited report on his survey, justified a double standard of sexual behavior.[7] Ehrmann posited that women's sexual interest resulted not only from love but also from a man's emotional commitment, and in the postwar world of the 1950s his message was unmistakable. Bromley and Britten had argued that early marriage was a poor solution to sexual urges because it interrupted women's education. Now marriage was the main goal of college women and that idea seemed an outdated vestige of early-twentieth-century feminism. Furthermore, if successful marriages rested on a strong erotic component, then for women love, not education, was the goal.

By now writers took a benign view of young men's uncontrollable urges. Where surveyors had once described young men's sexual incontinence as a threat to the family, they now reported that young unmarried men would inevitably acquire sexual experience. In 1950 Kirkendall undertook his first survey of young men. He found high rates of premarital intercourse and concluded that men who could not marry until well into their twenties could not remain virgins until marriage.[8] This assumption that young men "needed" sexual intercourse led Irving Tebor at Oregon State to examine the "problem" of male virgins, who, he stated, experienced teasing and a lack of support from family and friends.[9]

Ehrmann described sexual desire as one of the most important defining characteristics of manhood. This desire began to develop in early adolescence or even before. Since middle-class young women did not respond sexually until they fell in love and, ideally, married, this posed a problem for their male counterparts. Ehrmann described his male respondents as solving this by having "sexual relations" with lower-class women and "social relations," which might include sex, with women of their own social strata. His college men reported much higher rates of heterosexual intercourse than his female respondents, and Ehrmann explained this as due to a few sexually active young women who were not college students. Thus Ehrmann assumed a double standard of behavior among middle-class youth. Men would have extensive sexual experience with women other than their future spouses, but women would save sexual intercourse for the men they married. This was normal.

A rare study of young men from more varied social backgrounds provided a contrasting picture of these sexually active women and suggested that working-class Americans were less committed to the double standard. During World War II the physicians Leslie Hohman and Bertram Schaffner interviewed 4,600 army inductees. They asked these men to describe both their own sexual behavior and that of the women they knew. Eighty percent of the white inductees had engaged in sexual intercourse, and 71 percent evaluated their partners as "nice girls." In addition, "practically all Negroes have had sexual relations by the time they are twenty one years old, and in practically all cases they regarded the girls as nice, that is as girls they would have married." In the eyes of these young men, sexually active young working-class women were not "sexual outlets" to be discarded after taking care of a man's sexual needs.[10]

Ehrmann's idea, that the sexual needs of college men were satisfied by lower-class women, received a blow from a study showing that college men did not, in fact, practice restraint with women from their own social backgrounds. In two studies Eugene Kanin, a sociologist at Purdue University, found rampant sexual aggression against college women by their dates.[11] Approximately 60 percent of women described an offensive episode during the previous year, and in about 30 percent of cases this involved attempted intercourse. Far from protecting women they wished to marry, men were more likely to attempt intercourse with women if they were a "regular date," "pinned," or "engaged." Perhaps this was why the most offensive episodes were the very ones young women had discussed the least.

Not only did Ehrmann argue that college men satisfied themselves sexually with the type of women they would not marry; his work and other work like it unintentionally encouraged young men to think of themselves as sexually "needy." Perhaps a shortage of exploitable young working-class women was one reason men turned to those of their own class. Ironically, women kept the myth of male protection alive through their silence, which partly explained Ehrmann's finding of lower rates of sexual intercourse among college women than among college men.

Besides defining the double standard, Ehrmann made another lasting "discovery." On the basis of his interviews, he described normal sex as following a predictable progression of behaviors that built excitement and defined the experience: "Heterosexual behavior falls into highly compartmentalized *stages* of increasing degrees of intensity, as judged by the young people of our society, both with respect to physical intimacy and to moral judgement. These stages range from no physical contact, at the one extreme, on through holding hands, kissing, general body embrace, and the fondling of various portions of the body, to sexual intercourse at the other."[12] In 1954 Lawrence Podell and John Perkins arranged these behaviors into a fifteen-item ordered scale of sexual experience. From then on, surveys of college students assumed the existence of such a progression, and young people knew that this was the way a proper seduction proceeded.[13] Neither the researchers nor the young understood the social creation of this progression. Like young men's urgent need for sexual outlets, it was simply "natural."

By 1960 the exploitative nature of the double standard began to bother researchers. Since they could see no way to contain young men's sexual needs, they tried to redirect them. If premarital sex could be confined to serious love relationships, young men would gain their sexual experience with women they respected, not those they denigrated. This would have positive consequences for the way middle-class men treated women and therefore for marriage. Professors who took this position could use moral justifications for their arguments and avoid the dangers inherent in advocating premarital sex. This would also endear them to their largely female classes. Two works in particular promoted this view, and these aroused great interest and debate: Kirkendall's second study, some time before 1961, of 200 male students, and Ira Reiss's series of surveys of students' premarital sexual attitudes, which he undertook between 1959 and 1963.[14]

Both men remained cautious about surveying youthful sexual behavior. The turn of the decade was still a time of conservatism and quiet on American college campuses. Researchers who asked what students were doing sexually could be accused of promoting promiscuity. Kirkendall confined his survey to those respondents least likely to take offense, men reporting coital experience, and he used only volunteers, many from his classes. Reiss was more daring. Early in his career he challenged the assumption that premarital sexual intercourse was wrong for women but excusable for men. He noted that this created a predatory attitude among young men, making them eager to classify women as "bad" or potentially so. This caused problems for marriage, since "double standard premarital sexual intercourse leads to many maladjustments: there is male selfishness and female inhibitions; there is past association of thrills and sex, and restraints due to 'bad' associations. Finally we may add that a double standard male may carry over this standard to extra-marital sex relations and thereby risk an increase in over-all marital maladjustment by engaging in extra-marital sex conduct."[15] Even so, Reiss cautiously added that, as a scientist, he was not taking a moral position on the double standard.

Reiss was among the first sex researchers to use random samples, which meant that he could not select whom to interview or use only those who volunteered. This took courage, but he was careful to confine his questions to relatively safe topics such as sexual attitudes. He asked questions about behavior only of a volunteer sample of University of Iowa students, and even then his language was cautious. He asked a series of questions about "kissing," "petting," and "full sexual relations." For example:

- During the time that you have accepted your present standard [of sexual behavior], have you engaged in *full sexual relations?*
- In regard to full sexual relations, would you say you have done less than your standard would allow you to do?

as much as your standard would allow you to do?
or would you say your behavior with regard to full sexual relations
has exceeded your standard?[16]

He went on to ask how frequently standards had been violated, why this had happened, the level of guilt, and which partner was more to blame for the violation. The framing of these questions told students that decisions about sexual activity were serious, and allowed Reiss to conclude that students were increasingly permissive, but not approving of "promiscuity." This protected Reiss and was in line with his goal of abolishing the double standard.

Both Reiss and Kirkendall maintained that when serious young people satisfied their normal sexual desires in emotionally committed relationships, these relationships developed in an atmosphere of mutual trust and would create lasting marriages. Young men whose sexual needs were met in this way would be less likely to exploit women they had no intention of marrying. Still, Reiss warned that, given differences in male and female roles, such behavior would continue.

In spite of his precautions, Kirkendall felt it necessary to assure readers of his opposition to frivolous unmarried sex by labeling most premarital sex reported in his survey as "highly exploitative," since it involved sexual intercourse without serious commitment. His 200 respondents described 668 different sexual liaisons, only 18 of which were with fiancées. If sex was permissible only under Kirkendall's restrictive criteria, students might not listen. Reiss was more realistic about college professors' ability to manage the behavior of the young, so he had more influence on other researchers. Still, he was careful to coat his sexual liberalism with science, because, as he noted thirty years later, "I was taking a straight mainstream science stance, so I could say 'Look, don't kill the messenger. I'm just telling you what's happening.' I think it was clear that I liked what was happening, since I was constantly describing all these trends without a word of warning. But I didn't make that crystal clear. I did not think of it as 'protect yourself by playing the scientific role,' but had I come out and said, 'I love what is happening, isn't this great?' I would have got a lot of criticism."[17]

Reiss asserted that the double standard was being replaced by "permissiveness with affection." He reached this conclusion on the basis of his widely used sexual attitude scale, which consisted of a series of sexual scenarios. For example: "John and Mary have no particular affection for each other. They engage in full sexual relations, since they both feel that having full sexual relations does not require any particular affection between the couple." Respondents evaluated John's and Mary's behavior and answered a series of questions on their own values about kissing, petting, and "full sexual relations" under a variety of circumstances.[18]

These options allowed student respondents to take a position in favor of premarital sexual intercourse. At the same time, most indicated that they approved only when emotional bonds were strong. Reiss was able to stay on high moral ground by concluding that while women were becoming more permissive, young men's promiscuity was declining. Furthermore, permissive young women were still "good." They felt guilty about past sexual practices and had only accepted this behavior when in strong relationships: three-fifths of engaged women thought sexual intercourse appropriate for themselves, compared with only one-quarter of those not emotionally involved. Reiss justified his caution in asking students about their sexual standards, rather than about what they were actually doing, by contending that no evidence existed of a sexual revolution. He doubted that students were more sexually active than in earlier years. Instead, their values were increasingly consistent with their behavior. This positive interpretation of the sexual realities family sociologists heard daily in their classes further allowed them to present themselves as not promoting sex.

One way of showing that sexually active college women were "good girls" was to demonstrate their continued sexual difficulties. In the late 1950s and early 1960s some researchers began claiming that, in addition to having repressive childhoods, young women were apprehensive about becoming too responsive to erotic overtures.[19] They had well-grounded fears of bad-girl reputations, so they crushed their spontaneous sexual desires when engaging in premarital petting. Such habits, once acquired, were difficult to break. Reiss noted that women supported the double standard more strongly than men. He warned that "years of developing inhibitions in accord with the double standard view of women cannot be discarded at will," and that such women needed "understanding and time to chip away the veneer of culturally imposed inhibition." His caution paid off when Reiss obtained three of the first government grants awarded for sexual surveys. In applying to the National Institute of Mental Health (NIMH), he was warned not to put sex in the title, so he called his proposal "A Study of Attitudes." His funders assured him, "No-one's going to pick this out because it doesn't have the word 'sex' in it."[20]

These early surveys of college students created a new vocabulary to describe sexual problems between women and men. In the lectures on female sexual response, the double-standard woman whose inability to become a fully orgasmic partner arose from a discrepancy between her values and her behavior replaced the sexually unresponsive one. Where before all sex outside of marriage was "extramarital sex," students now learned of the still-forbidden "extramarital sex" plus the ambivalently regarded "premarital sex," terms rapidly picked up by the media. "Premarital" assumed that marriage would follow, so such experience might prove functional for middle-class marriages rather than exploitative. Just as the marital adjustment researchers had seen the middle class as the standardbearers for sexual intimacy in marriage, so the premarital-sex researchers thought educated middle-class students would negotiate a new courtship standard based on mutual trust and respect. In 1960 Reiss predicted that, led by college students, permissiveness with affection would become the dominant societal ethic for premarital behavior.

In the years that followed Reiss's reports, most surveyors of college students' sexual behavior cautiously promoted permissive standards. Rather than risk random sampling, professors kept control of their respondents by conducting surveys in their own classes. This allowed them to show students their own sexual standards and to define these as appropriate. It had the effect of encouraging behavior the surveys purported merely to document while safeguarding the professors against the potentially negative consequences of undertaking sex surveys.

Even if they were more directive than they acknowledged, researchers did not completely control their findings. Their research involved listening to students, not just telling them what to do. In contrast, textbooks intended for marriage courses in the early 1960s often selected their findings carefully to produce more conservative messages. For example, in a widely distributed 1963 text Judson T. Landis and Mary G. Landis asserted that young couples should concentrate on learning how compatible they were but should avoid sexual intimacy: "Normally well-adjusted young people will suffer no ill effects from following a plan which includes self-control and emphasizes avoidance of excessive sex interest until they can marry. The advantages are all on the side of this course of action. Here, as in many other phases of marital and post-marital experience, the long-time view point is of fundamental importance. What is most desirable for life as a whole? Permanent satisfaction in marriage must outweigh other considerations."[21]

But this advice was increasingly falling on deaf ears. In the first five years of the 1960s, surveyors found a growing indifference to their elders' opinions among college students, especially young women. In addition, while students were learning sexual values in college, these were not coming from the classroom. Harrop Freeman and Ruth Freeman's study of 1,100 women plus a few men at a variety of colleges between 1962 and 1965 was typical.[22]

Parents, they contended, rarely knew about their daughters' sexual activity and would be horrified if they did. College replaced parental influence with the peer group's standards, and, since two-thirds of respondents viewed their campuses as sexually liberal, it was not surprising that young women's own attitudes had become more liberal too. The Freemans also noted that the double standard continued: half their female respondents agreed with it, and many who did not gave men more permission than women to have premarital relations. In spite of more liberal attitudes, the Freemans assured readers that young women were not irresponsible. Away from home, and pressured by the men they loved, they simply learned that their mothers' sexual standards no longer applied.

By the early 1960s research on this sexual revolution began in earnest. Vance Packard, in his bestselling *The Sexual Wilderness,* concluded that a revolution was occurring because women now allowed sexual intercourse outside of marriage as long as they were in a committed relationship.[23] And, he continued, many women had had sex in a relationship that had since ended. It seemed that young women moved from one commitment to another because "commitment" justified sex. Horrified by this, Packard proposed a voluntary code of conduct for unmarried youth. They should agree to abstain from sexual intercourse unless they first finished a year of college and were "known to hope" to marry their partner. This was not quite the same reassuring picture as that of Reiss, but it was a picture portrayed in many surveys in the first years of the 1960s.

During this time college students themselves began to change, at least in the eyes of others. The first sign occurred with the civil rights movement. In the summer of 1963 many student activists went south with the Student Non-Violent Coordinating Committee. At first most of this political activity took place off campus, and those who became involved appeared in the media as heroes risking their lives for democracy. But the media soon began to describe another change. A *Newsweek* story in the spring of 1964 entitled "The Morals Revolution on Campus" was typical.[24] Announcing that students now believed that a couple who had a "meaningful relationship" had a "moral right to sleep together," *Newsweek* provided a defense of the Reiss position. Men, the magazine claimed, no longer expected to marry virgins. But since "Sex with anyone except 'Mr Right' is largely frowned upon, as is out-and-out promiscuity," the magazine gave a warning to young women enjoying their new freedom: "The question is, how many 'Mr Rights' make a wrong?"

Even though young men continued to report more heterosexual partners than young women, only one survey, published in 1966, questioned whether students were telling the truth about their sexual behavior. In a questionnaire distributed to male students in an undergraduate sociology course at the University of Illinois, John Clark and Larry Tifft asked about a variety of socially disapproved behaviors, including nonmarital sexual intercourse, pregnancy, sex with prostitutes, masturbation, rape or attempted rape, and same-sex relations.[25] They then offered students eight dollars to do a second interview, at which they announced that the students would have to take a polygraph test. Before this, they could review their questionnaires (which were anonymous and identified with a number known only to the student) and make any corrections they wished. Faced with the likelihood of being caught lying, students changed many of their responses. The two sexual items most often changed were masturbation, which more students acknowledged, and premarital sex, which students were as likely to decrease as increase. This small study was evidence that respondents did not always tell the truth and that men might exaggerate their sexual experience. Its implications for what researchers could learn by asking questions were largely ignored. It was easier to assume that survey respondents told the truth.

By 1965 student activism had come home to college campuses. Over the next few years the media ran stories on the Berkeley Free Speech Movement, sit-ins on staid campuses like Columbia and Harvard, and antiwar activism everywhere. Now students held strikes and, instead of going to class, challenged both their professors' values and their research at campus teach-ins. Sexual freedom was part of this new scene, along with political activism, declines in conservative politics, and independence from parents. The sheer size of the college student population, 5.2 million in 1965 compared to 2.7 million a decade earlier, intensified the sense of crisis.[26]

With this as the framework, the number of sex surveys rose dramatically as researchers documented rapidly changing behavior. Some who had conducted earlier surveys wished to see the extent of change. Others measured change by collecting data at two close but distinct times and analyzing them in one study. Still others compared their data to those collected by earlier researchers. Permissiveness with affection remained researchers' desired mode, but permissiveness in itself was the more and more frequent finding. Researchers stopped assuming that couples having "premarital" sex would marry each other, but continued to assume that they would eventually marry.

Robert Walsh, Mary Ferrell, and William Tolone interviewed unmarried freshmen at Illinois State University in 1967 and 1971 and repeated the interviews when the students were seniors in 1971 and 1974.[27] The relationship between the sexual revolution and other revolutions was not lost on these authors, who interpreted their findings as evidence of troubling social change. They used questions similar to those of other surveys, including Reiss's sexual attitude scale. They asked whether parents or peers most determined students' levels of sexual permissiveness. Besides asking about sexual intercourse before marriage, they asked about its frequency, a question Reiss would never have dared ask. They noted that, between freshman and senior year, students engaged in more sexual activity and became more permissive as a result of lessening parental influence and an increase in that of peers. This change was greatest for women. But this was not because of serious decisions to deepen their relationships with future life-time companions. These daughters of conservative Midwesterners considered sexual experience to be an important part of going to college. Furthermore, students were learning these lessons faster; the younger cohort had higher levels of sexual intercourse than the older.

Even though probability sampling was by now widely accepted as essential, if researchers were to generalize their interviews beyond those they surveyed, sexual behavior researchers did not use it, both because they accepted Kinsey's dictum that this would not be possible and because their research was largely unfunded. As a result, at college after college, undergraduates taking introductory sociology or psychology courses answered questions about their sexual behavior and attitudes and provided evidence of rising rates of premarital intercourse among students, especially female students.

Researchers' explanations for these trends varied, as did their evaluations of them. Some were positive about the trends and argued both that women continued to confine their sexual acts to men with whom they were emotionally involved and that the changes resulted from the death of the double standard. Others contended that impersonal sex was becoming the norm for college students; an engagement ring was no longer a precondition of coeds' decisions to have sexual intercourse. Some saw this as positive and even saw "playing around" as a measure of women's success, contending, for example, that the level of female students' sexual experience was a function of their attractiveness. Those who disapproved often blamed parents. As the researcher Robert Lewis put it, "where parents were the major source of sex education, their maturing children were less apt to be promiscuous and had significantly less often engaged in premarital sexual intercourse." If parents left sex education up to the schools, this might not encourage premarital sexual behavior but it would not discourage it as parents could. And the church was losing its influence over these young adventurers. With parents and churches abrogating their authority, the peer group promoted sexual permissiveness.[28]

In addition to controlling whom to interview, surveyors during the 1960s typically did not pretest their questionnaires. They distributed them to students without worrying about the effect this might have on the accuracy of responses. Questions on sex also appeared in a few funded studies of college student life, but although the samples here were larger and usually random, the relevant questions were few.[29] A notable exception to these mostly unreliable survey results involved a 1967 study of students at twelve universities and colleges. The brainchild of the sociologists John Gagnon and William Simon, it addressed many of the themes of the sexual revolution.

Simon and Gagnon had both been hired by the Institute for Sex Research after Kinsey's death. Arriving in 1959, Gagnon "learned to do the Kinsey interview and may end up being the last surviving person in the world with that archaic skill." Simon followed in late 1964, and funding was so tight that Hugh Hefner paid his salary. Fearing that Hefner's support, if known, would cause the research to be questioned, Simon agreed not to discuss it, and no acknowledgment of it appeared on any of his work.[30] In the summer of 1965, Gagnon and Simon obtained federal funding for three surveys, including a study of college students that was the first sex survey to be funded by the National Institute of Child Health and Human Development (NICHD). Gagnon and Simon also collaborated on a set of essays that became a highly influential sociological statement on sexuality.[31]

NICHD's fears that the survey would not prove viable and would embarrass the government led to protracted negotiations over the number of colleges to be included. Meanwhile Gagnon and Simon wrote and pretested their questionnaire with further funding from Hugh Hefner. In 1967 the two researchers fell out with the director of the Kinsey Institute, Paul Gebhard, and quit. They left two of their surveys at the Kinsey Institute but took the college student study with them, and finished it while several thousand miles apart.

The survey was unusual. The quality of data collection was higher than in similar surveys, and the researchers based the questions on their theoretical argument that sexuality is learned rather than innate. This was the first survey of sexual behavior to use a probability sample and also the first sex survey for which the National Opinion Research Center (NORC) undertook the collection of data. It did this for the Kinsey Institute, which had no data-collection facilities of its own. Much of the expertise in survey research resided in university-based survey research centers, but these had not previously conducted sex surveys. NORC interviewed at twelve schools, selecting 100 students from each, and the overall response rate was a low but satisfactory 72 percent. Unlike those of many other sex surveys, the questionnaire was nonjudgmental in tone. Simon and Gagnon assumed sexual behavior was an integral part of culture and that, although complex, it was amenable to study. Their questionnaire covered an unprecedented variety of sexual activities: topics included childhood sexual conduct, pornography, masturbation, sexual arousal, dating, petting, oral-genital sex, sexual intercourse, orgasm, perceptions of peer group behavior, same-sex sexual experience, sex education, and attitudes toward various sexual practices. Students were asked what they did, if they enjoyed it, how often they did it, how their behavior had changed, if they felt guilty, and what influenced their desire for an act.

In their most explicit statement of the surveys' goals, Gagnon, Simon, and their coauthor Alan Berger discussed sexual adjustment in adolescence and asserted that in American society the physical signs of puberty provided the cue for learning adult sexual "scripts." For boys this learning was less ambivalent than for girls, since the rewards of sexual experimentation were more clearly positive. In contrast, girls had been socialized to be passive and reactive, so they took longer to develop "a sexual sense of self."[32] Sexual experimentation in high school led to success for boys but to a sense of loss for girls. By college the cost of sexual activity for women lessened. Unlike authors such as Walsh, Ferrell, and Tolone, for whom the late 1960s were "days of student unrest," Gagnon and Simon were veterans of the civil rights movement. For them the problem with adolescent sexual experimentation was not its association with political activism but a society that sexualized adolescents yet was intolerant of their sexual expressions.

As a result, Simon and Gagnon took issue with those who believed in the sexual revolution, especially those who tied it to the student activism of the 1960s. Comparing their results with Kinsey's, they claimed that rates of early and premarital coitus had remained relatively stable over time and were still largely a function of courtship. In their view, "the emergence of the middle-class companionate form of premarital sex as preparation for marriage" had, over a period of almost fifty years, become "the dominant form of mate selection in the United States."[33] To call this a sexual revolution was "out of touch with reality" and could cause "anxiety among young people" who did not experience a lot of sexual choice.[34] Although sympathetic to social change, they unwittingly defended the status quo by declaring that things were not as others believed. Sex was no longer to be saved for marriage or even for future spouses. Yet it was a precursor to marriage, and marriage was still the goal. This conveyed a message of permissiveness, but not of the abolition of societal norms. The authors' more radical position that sexual behavior not only was pleasurable to the young but was produced by society, not from the rejection of society, was not made explicit.

Unfortunately, Simon and Gagnon's study had only a limited impact on the field of sexual behavior research. They never produced a monograph, and the various writers of articles about their survey imposed their own perspectives on the data. Later surveyors did not adopt Simon and Gagnon's expensive research design but continued to use college student volunteers and to ask questions that would let them manage the answers. Nor did the study end debate about the existence of the sexual revolution. The idea of revolution had a headline-grabbing quality to which researchers were attracted, and it also made student sexual behavior seem like a break with society rather than a product of it. The media and the researchers informed each other's thinking in this. Researchers used media portrayals of student activism to stir up fears about student sex, even though most of the students with whom they came into contact could hardly be described as radical. However, Simon and Gagnon's study did have some effect. Several important subsequent surveys used their model of adolescence as the crucial time for sexual development, and their precedent made it easier for researchers to take a tolerant position on student sex.

For the first half of the 1970s interest in college students' sexual behavior remained high. Between 1970 and 1975 almost fifty surveys focused on the sexual behavior of young people, and almost all involved students. By this time the interest in political activism seemed to be on the decline, and from 1970 on articles appeared describing a new campus mood. As the chair of the *Harvard Crimson* put it when explaining the attraction of Charles Reich, the bestselling author of *The Greening of America*: "Students are still concerned about the war, racism and poverty; some are very active with ecology groups. But most are just waiting, with their pot and their Dylan records, for the grass to grow through the concrete. Last year they would have laughed Reich right off the campus."[35]

Such students had largely lost interest in marriage classes. Instead, courses on human sexuality appeared. Worry that these might be blamed for promiscuous behavior prompted surveys designed to demonstrate that the courses did not increase sexual experimentation. Researchers at the University of Rochester found no differences in behavior between students who had taken a human sexuality course and those who had not, and surveyors elsewhere noted similar findings.[36]

In this new climate, researchers began to take sexual intercourse among young people for granted and to look for new topics. Surveys of young women's sexual responsiveness began to appear. Some researchers reported that guilt about sex interfered with young women's pleasure. Guilt had replaced orgasmic inadequacy as a barrier to female sexual pleasure. Even in the enlightened 1970s surveyors found that modest young women felt guilty about sex, a finding that was in part a function of the questions. When asked if they felt guilty about having sexual intercourse, many young women felt obliged to answer yes.

The most prolific student of guilt was Donald Mosher, a professor of psychology at the University of Connecticut. Confining himself at first to the safer questions about attitudes, Mosher developed a scale to measure "sex guilt," but over time he included questions about behavior. He originally justified these as necessary to verify that his scale measured what it was intended to. But Mosher wanted to demonstrate that young women could experience higher levels of sexual arousal if they could overcome their guilt. Becoming more adventurous, he designed a series of experiments to measure arousal in response to various sexual stimuli. For example, he showed sexually explicit films to about five hundred male and female undergraduates and asked them detailed questions about their arousal. Women were less aroused than men, especially if they scored high on sex guilt. Since the more sexually experienced, less guilty women described the films as producing arousal, Mosher recommended a massive sex education program and the ending of legal sanctions against pornography as cures for guilt.[37]

Many of those who surveyed college students' behavior were ambivalent about what they saw as the rapidly developing emphasis on hedonism. For them lifestyle replaced politics as the focus of anxiety, and students' sexual behavior became part of a larger set of problems. Young women were gaining a measure of equality by doing their share of misbehaving. As Karl King and his coauthors, who had studied sexual behavior among students in 1960, 1965 and 1970, put it, "college youth of the 1970s are less noted for proclaiming the social and political utopian ideals of the youth movement than they are for having inherited the practice of wearing blue jeans and long hair, smoking pot, listening to rock music, and engaging in premarital sexual behavior. These activities, for the most part, may be engaged in by both sexes indiscriminately."[38] Sexual intercourse among students was now the norm. This caused apprehension not because it meant a radical revolution but because students appeared to be rejecting their parents' lifestyles altogether and to be unconcerned about their futures.

Thus sexual license became a marker for other worrisome behaviors. On the basis of a survey of participants in a computer dating service, James Curran and his associates concluded that the student with extensive sexual experience was "more likely to favor alcohol consumption, be nonactive in religion, be a proponent of a liberal morality, and hold liberal political views." Lee Bukstel and others at the University of South Carolina even concluded that students with high levels of premarital experience expected to engage in extramarital sex after they married.[39] Having a variety of partners appeared to be part of the "declining moral standards" of the hedonistic 1970s.

But college students were not the main target of these concerns. They had already gotten into college and would presumably graduate. The period between 1970 and 1975 was transitional not only because researchers switched from documenting the existence of premarital sexual intercourse to documenting its variety but also for the rise of surveys about high school students' sexual behavior. If college sex continued to cause discomfort, high school sex caused more. Surveys linked it to deviant behavior among the young, particularly to rising crime rates. What actually increased was not crime *rates* among the young but the *number* of young people as baby-boom children entered adolescence. Political activism, media stories about the tune-in, turn-on, drop-out generation, and changes in behavior, particularly among young women, all intensified fears.

Consternation about these problems was so high that William Simon received funding in the early 1970s for two studies, one of working-class youth in Chicago and the other of adolescents throughout Illinois. Also, the National Institute on Alcohol and Alcohol Abuse funded the psychology professor Richard Jessor for a longitudinal survey of "problem behavior." Jessor's survey involved a small random sample of both high school and college students in the Rocky Mountain area from 1969 to 1981. In Jessor's description of the survey's rationale, sex was just another behavioral problem: "Initiated toward the end of the 1960s in the midst of the turmoil that marked that period of American history, the research focused on problem behavior in youth—on drug use, sexual activity, drinking, and the problem use of alcohol, activism and protest, and deviant behavior generally."[40]

Like Simon, Jessor and colleagues had a largely benign opinion of young people's behavior, and they presented adolescence as an important period for personality development. Sexual learning was part of this more general adolescent learning. In spite of rising permissiveness, "becoming a nonvirgin" remained an important transition for young people, and the timing of this was crucial. Premature "nonvirginity" occurred among students who had low achievement in school, were independent and critical of society, had low religiosity, and were tolerant of deviance. In other words, a high school student who would not listen to her parents and who focused on the youth culture rather than school was a problem. But if she waited to go through the sexual transition until college, she would not be much more rebellious than those who remained virgins until marriage.

Jessor and his colleagues reinterviewed their overwhelmingly middle-class respondents in later years and contended that problem-behavior adolescents continued their "deviant" ways as young adults, but that this did not spill over into other areas of their lives. Problem youths claimed as much success in status attainment, work, and general life satisfaction as did their less problematic peers. Had Jessor interviewed less socially advantaged young people, he might have found that socially disapproved behavior had more long-term impact on life chances. He also had a problem with selection bias. His study was plagued by low response rates from the start, and these became more serious with each reinterview. Those who stayed in the study were probably more successful than those who dropped out.

Those who studied problem behavior did not celebrate sexual activity. Middle-class college students from caring families could cope with sex, but it created problems for others, including younger adolescents and youth from less affluent, often minority families. Their parents, researchers believed, were not equipped to guide their children in sexual matters without government intervention—an idea that survived in a modified form in studies of adolescent fertility.

One study in the early 1970s summarized many of the themes of sex surveys of the time and demonstrated the great changes since Reiss's cautious data collection at the end of the 1950s. In 1973 John DeLamater and Patricia MacCorquodale, sociologists at the University of Wisconsin–Madison, obtained funding from NICHD for a survey of premarital sexual behavior among both students and nonstudents. Although the study was relatively small (985 students and 663 nonstudents) and suffered from a low response rate (63 percent among nonstudents), its probability sample and other methodological contributions improved the quality of sex research. DeLamater, who had been trained in survey research at the University of Michigan, understood the methodological shortcomings of sex research and wanted to learn which factors might affect data quality, so he interviewed 238 undergraduates in a large pretest. He tested the impact of changes in wording, order of questions, and the interviewer's gender. He discovered a number of interesting problems; for example, women were less likely to say they had liberal sexual values if asked first about the values of their five best friends; and they tended to underreport their current sexual behavior when interviewed by a man.[41]

In the actual survey, DeLamater and MacCorquodale's conclusions summed up the discoveries of the previous decade. Their one important new finding was that students and nonstudents differed little in sexual attitudes and behavior. Where Reiss had assumed that college students were in the vanguard of change, DeLamater and MacCorquodale showed that almost all young adults engaged in nonmarital sexual intercourse. Like Simon and Gagnon and the Jessors, DeLamater and MacCorquodale considered sexual experimentation a normal part of adolescent development, and they described great increases in permissiveness since Gagnon and Simon's survey of six years earlier. Parents had conservative standards for premarital sexual behavior, so young people's sexual behavior depended on the extent to which peer influence replaced parental influence. Young men and women might take as long as five years to move from first kissing to first intercourse. In deciding if this meant there had been a sexual revolution, the authors noted that women had become more like men, a change that might or might not be seen as revolutionary. For their part, DeLamater and MacCorquodale applauded it. Still, the emotional quality of the relationship remained the most important determinant of sexual intercourse. Women, in particular, continued to hesitate to have sex without emotional involvement.

.   .   .

In the late 1950s most young women could only justify premarital sexual behavior as a form of preparation for marriage. During the 1960s many began experimenting with owning and expressing sexual desire, and by 1973 sexual intercourse outside of marriage was just a normal part of becoming an adult. While it is difficult to say which came first, the pro-sex attitudes of many researchers undoubtedly contributed to these changes. When young unmarried women began to acknowledge that they were having sex, male researchers justified it as premarital sex, that is, sex leading to marriage. When more and more young women reported sexual intercourse with men they had no intention of marrying, the meaning of "premarital" expanded. Surveyors insisted on interpreting young women's sexual experimentation as part of their preparation for marriage, because when sex research on young women contained a pro-family orientation it was a less dangerous pursuit.

Apparently middle-class college women were learning to manage their own sexual careers by handling their sexual feelings more like men, and researchers were coming to terms with this. But adolescent women, often not old enough or middle class enough for college, were also engaging in sexual intercourse. Few studies of college students even mentioned contraceptive use, presumably because pregnancies among college students were likely to cause couples to marry. When sex research moved beyond its middle-class boundaries, concerns about the consequences of sexual activity took on a new meaning.

5

Adolescent Fertility

Most childbearing occurs among older and married women and, in the United States, knowledge about the causes of fertility relates almost exclusively to their rather well regulated fertility. The fertility of young, unmarried women, by contrast, is unplanned, largely unwanted, and until recently, was not seen as amenable to scientific scrutiny.

—Melvin Zelnik, John F. Kantner, and Kathleen Ford, 1981

B Y 1970 the nation began to accept sexual intercourse for adults who were not yet married. Given the high divorce rate, many thought it a good idea not to marry too young. One should first test one's sexual compatibility with a potential spouse, as long as this represented a serious step in developing a relationship and was done discreetly. This increased tolerance did not prepare Americans for the shock of learning that a 1971 federally funded survey had found that many girls were not waiting until they were of marriageable age.[1] Unmarried teenage girls of all races and social classes were engaging in sexual intercourse, and doing so at earlier ages and with more partners than had their older sisters. And discretion was a thing of the past. Many were not even marrying if they became pregnant. Girls seemed to be throwing away their chances for marriage and challenging the rule that marriage should precede childbirth. This was a far different sort of sexual activity from the sort adults had learned to condone or at least tolerate. The study that produced the evidence had a lasting impact on public consciousness as well as on survey practice and federal support for sex research.

Surveys of college students' "premarital sexuality" had helped increase the acceptability of premarital sex but also had raised alarm over the sexual behavior of youth. Such fears increased as a result of student activism against the Vietnam war, which seemed to flout adult standards. Since sex researchers of the 1960s had viewed premarital sex as part of the process of selecting a mate, they had paid little attention to students' use of contraceptives. Any coed who accidentally became pregnant would merely marry a little earlier than planned, so college women who had sex premaritally were not disturbing the centrality of marriage as a social institution. But sexually active unmarried teenage girls constituted a different story, not only because of their youth but because, unlike college students, many were not from the middle class. If less affluent girls became pregnant without being married, and without prospects of marrying, the consequences might be borne by the whole society.

Declining fertility among married women also helped shift attention to teens.[2] By the late 1960s fertility was falling in all social groups in America. Demographers stopped arguing that family size was the cause of poverty and instead pointed to the negative consequences of early childbearing. First promoted by Ronald Freedman and his associates on a fertility survey in Detroit, this view emerged in the government when Freedman's former colleague Arthur Campbell became chief of the Natality Statistics Branch of the National Center for Health Statistics. Taking the position that "it may be more important to delay the first child than to prevent the seventh," Campbell portrayed a stark picture: "The girl who has an illegitimate child at the age of 16 suddenly has 90 percent of her life's script written for her. She will probably drop out of school; even if someone else in her family helps to take care of the baby, she will probably not be able to find a steady job that pays enough to provide for herself and her child; she may feel impelled to marry someone she might not otherwise have chosen. Her life choices are few, and most of them are bad."[3]

In 1970 Congress passed the Population Research Act as part of the war on poverty. This established the Office of Population Affairs at the National Institute of Child Health and Development (NICHD). Campbell moved to NICHD, where he worked to increase fertility research, and at the same time, President Nixon empaneled the Commission on Population Growth and the American Future to examine trends and develop policy.

Among the demographers who applied for survey funding were the Johns Hopkins University professors Melvin Zelnik and John Kantner. Kantner had been Ronald Freedman's graduate student at the University of Michigan, where he had analyzed data from the Indianapolis fertility survey, and Zelnik had studied at the Office of Population Research at Princeton. Kantner and Zelnik proposed surveying two groups about which little empirical research had been done: black women and teenagers. Since NICHD planned to add a large black sample to the 1970 National Fertility Study, Campbell pushed NICHD to fund Zelnik and Kantner for a teen survey, the National Survey of Young Women.

Kantner and Zelnik had experience with surveys but not with sex research, and they believed previous fertility surveys had focused too strongly on psychological explanations of fertility. As Kantner described it, they "thought the essential variables were sexual behavior, the initiation of sex, the frequency, the precautions taken, and the number of partners involved."[4] These interests necessitated more questions about sexual behavior than previous fertility surveys had contained, including age at first intercourse, number of partners, use of contraception and abortion, and both knowledge of and attitudes about sex, reproduction, and contraception. Still, unlike sex researchers, they asked only about aspects of sexuality that related directly to reproduction and asked nothing about satisfaction or interest. They used a national probability sample that included an oversample of black teenagers to be sure there were enough to analyze separately, and the resulting data on sex were more reliable than any that came before. But their reports were still the product of the authors' questions and interpretations. They interviewed young women only, and their questions included no mention of the word "sex." For example:

- Have you ever had intercourse?
- Since you first had intercourse, how many different partners have you had intercourse with?

These questions implied that sex just happened, with little or no decision-making or negotiation.

From the vantage point of the 1990s, when sexual activity among teens seems ubiquitous, it is hard to recall the public impact of Zelnik and Kantner's results. They reported that over half of unmarried teenage women would engage in sexual intercourse before age 20, a rate startlingly higher than previous estimates. Furthermore, this rate appeared to be increasing. Other findings were more predictable but not more reassuring. Black teens had rates of sexual activity more than twice as high as those of white teens, and although teenagers had intercourse relatively infrequently and with few partners, they used contraception sporadically.

Aware of the explosive nature of these findings and the great interest they would arouse, Zelnik and Kantner disseminated their results quickly and widely. They gave press conferences and confined their first article to the data on sexual experience. The article appeared in the October 1972 issue of *Family Planning Perspectives* (FPP). FPP was published by the Alan Guttmacher Institute (AGI), which at the time was the research arm of the Planned Parenthood Federation of America. AGI used public relations techniques to draw media attention to findings representing its point of view. Zelnik and Kantner published nearly all their findings in FPP, not only from the 1971 survey but from their two follow-up surveys in 1976 and 1979.[5]

These surveys and the well-orchestrated media response to them almost singlehandedly created the social problem of adolescent sexuality and teen pregnancy. In the three years before the first survey there had been several studies of contraceptive use among the unmarried, but these had had little public impact. Most had not restricted their study populations to teenagers, and all but two had involved only the middle class. By treating teenage girls as an at-risk group cutting across social class and race, Kantner and Zelnik alerted both researchers and the public to a problem hitherto barely noticed.

Before 1971 the media had showed little interest in fertility research other than the National Fertility Study.[6] But when Zelnik and Kantner opened their first article with a shocking finding, the existence of nearly 2.4 million sexually experienced unmarried teenage girls, the media paid attention. Headlines gave notice that teenage girls who might be the readers' daughters had lost their innocence: "Sex: 46% of Teen Girls Do It." "Outmoded Virginity." "Sex and the Teen-Age Girl." Instead of emphasizing the higher levels of sexual activity among black teenagers, the media focused on the high levels among all teens. *Time* magazine, for example, followed its report on the survey with a cover story on teenage sex that cited Kantner and Zelnik to demonstrate that young people were having more out-of-wedlock sex than ever before.[7] The cover photograph showed a young, long-haired, sweet-faced, white couple of whom any middle-class parent might be proud. Similar couples in somewhat more suggestive poses appeared inside. The article covered several topics terrifying to parents; venereal disease, illegitimate pregnancy, homosexuality, teenage girls' abandonment of sexual guilt. Kantner and Zelnik were among the first to include all social classes in their survey, but the media homogenized the variety of experiences into one middle-class picture and made teenage sexuality a middle-class problem.

This posture was encouraged by AGI, which feared that presenting racial data would increase bigotry. Zelnik and Kantner downplayed the racial differences by arguing that although black adolescents were more likely to have sexual experience than whites and to have started earlier, there were few racial differences in frequency of intercourse and number of sexual partners. To reassure parents that their daughters were not promiscuous, they noted that few had had more than one partner in the previous month and most did not have sex very often. This was consistent with AGI's position of presenting young women as vulnerable to unwanted pregnancy but as worthy of and responsive to help.

It was not until a decade later that Kantner and Zelnik articulated a societal explanation for their findings, influenced by the results of their 1976 survey and the by-then active debate over teenage pregnancy. In 1981 they explained that they had published quick results in FPP because of urgent demands for data from those whose task it was to help young women. With the benefit of hindsight, they ascribed their findings to teenage hedonism produced by "the turbulent and tumultuous sixties" when Americans "became more permissive toward youthful dalliance."[8]

In 1971 Zelnik and Kantner did not blame teens. This would have been inconsistent with AGI's agenda. As a result of their framing of the survey and of the media response, teenage girls became objects of concern. A mixture of motives made discussion about teenagers' sexual behavior disjointed. These included anger at young girls who were sexually active and seemed indifferent to the possible consequences; worry about the daughters of the middle class and their families; fear of the unchecked fertility of the poor; and the impact of the civil rights movement, which made it difficult to acknowledge racial differences in any socially disapproved behavior. Even naming the problem was complicated. Was teenage sexual behavior at issue, or was it teen pregnancy? Whatever the definition of the problem, the largest group of unwed mothers, women in their twenties, received little attention, and adolescent boys and young men were conspicuously absent from any discussion. Surveys continued to focus on adolescent girls.

Kantner and Zelnik's results and the publicity they received led to a change in the content of FPP. Articles on teenage girls' sexual activity rapidly replaced ones on poor women worn down by childbearing. And FPP's message was that contraception was the solution to the possible negative consequences of this behavior, and that "access to effective medically supervised contraception and legal abortion is no more likely to encourage teenage promiscuity than denial of access has been to discourage adolescent sexual activity."[9] The journal implicitly endorsed the view that, while sexual activity among teens might be increasing somewhat, there had been no sexual revolution; teenagers had always been sexually active.

While AGI did not endorse teenage sex, it implied that sex was not the problem. Teenage fertility was. Most researchers preferred the AGI position, but the media were more interested in documenting sexual activity than in arguing that the only problem was a lack of contraception. After 1972 abortion was available in most states. Since that time, teens had been the group most likely to take advantage of this option, terminating an estimated 40 percent of their pregnancies. For those researchers who believed teen fertility was the problem, a high abortion rate, while not ideal, was better than the alternative. But for the minority who saw teen sex as the problem, the high abortion rate was evidence of the crisis. Almost all agreed that the increasing tendency for pregnant young women to stay single could only have bad consequences. This behavior turned previously hidden "unorthodox sexuality" into a public display, and the display was exacerbated by the 1972 passage of Title IX, which forbade schools to expel pregnant students. Furthermore, the increasingly hedonistic youth culture of the 1970s would produce pregnancies among girls too immature for motherhood and too young to be involved with suitable marriage partners. This was no longer premarital sex, and neither liberals nor conservatives were comfortable.[10]

The publicity surrounding Zelnik and Kantner's results dictated their use by those shaping public policy. For example, the Commission on Population Growth and the American Future was about to publish its recommendations just as the first survey became front-page news.[11] It hurriedly included data from Kantner and Zelnik, and so unmarried teenagers became a legislative concern. Although President Nixon rejected the recommendation that the government make birth control available to teens, the Supreme Court declared that unmarried persons should have access to contraception. In addition, Congress amended the Social Security Act and required state welfare departments to offer family planning services to sexually active minors. Over the next few years the federal government became actively involved in the issue of teen pregnancy, expanding the availability of family planning services for the young.

Numerous other studies of the fertility of unmarried teens were undertaken between Zelnik and Kantner's 1971 and 1976 surveys. Several themes appeared. The first was that sexual activity was increasing among teens, and while not necessarily reporting this with outrage, researchers could not imply that this trend was acceptable. Second, since black teens were most likely to be sexually active, all surveys including racially mixed samples had to deal with race. The third and easiest theme for researchers was that the negative consequences of sexual activity, particularly pregnancy, could be prevented most effectively by education.

The presentation of these themes differed by whether or not findings were published in FPP. In the FPP surveys sexual activity appeared inevitable among the young regardless of class or racial background, and the problem was the negative consequences of sexual activity, not the activity itself.[12] In this version, most young people became sexually active before attending family planning clinics, which meant lack of information was the main barrier to the proper use of contraception. Most of the surveys involved probability samples and pretested questionnaires, so authors were not controlling their results in an obvious way. Yet authors were often careful to present findings in a way that fit FPP's expectations. Race, for example, caused the journal a problem. Its surveys typically included black teenagers, since researchers could not seem indifferent to them, but FPP's accompanying photographs depicted a clean-cut, middle-class, almost exclusively white world. And FPP authors usually implied that all teens were similar. Many did not even mention racial differences. When authors discussed race they often did so to demonstrate a lack of racial difference in behavior.

FPP was nervous about discussing racial difference because of the way conservatives used such findings. Discussions of difference could play into arguments that blacks were morally degenerate, so FPP's strategy was to imply that all teenage girls, regardless of class and race, were equally at risk of sex and pregnancy. Their policy of presenting young girls as victims rather than as blameworthy negated any discussion of decisions unmarried teenage girls were making about sexual activity. Since the 1930s the family planning community had promoted sexual enjoyment without fear of pregnancy, but to suggest that teenage girls enjoyed sex was to risk the wrath of the public. To conservatives adolescent sexual activity was bad and preventable; to liberals it was bad but inevitable. No discussion emerged of the circumstances under which teens negotiated sex.

Surveys published in academic journals instead of in FPP were freer to discuss race. At one extreme, Julian Roebuck and Marsha McGee, who studied poor black high school girls in Mississippi, declared that blacks had more permissive sexual mores. This was particularly true of girls living in "matriarchies," since "the black woman has frequently been exploited sexually, but she has also experienced widespread sexual freedom." More typical was George Cvetkovich and Marsha McGee's assertion that young black women's higher rates of unwed pregnancy resulted from their victim status. They had a greater likelihood of a pregnancy being recorded as illegitimate, a greater biological risk of pregnancy, and more partners who rejected contraception. Roebuck and McGee implied that black girls had sex because they had lower standards. In contrast, liberals were uncomfortable defending adolescent sex as a reasonable choice, so they described those who became sexually active as victims.[13]

By the early 1970s sex education resurfaced as a solution to the problem of unmarried sex. Promoting sex education was dangerous, as it had been for those in the social hygiene movement decades earlier. Researchers had to demonstrate that talking explicitly about sex would encourage teens to act responsibly: that it would increase teens' contraceptive use but not their sexual activity. A number of surveys evaluated sex education programs, with generally inconclusive findings. The researchers concluded that sex education increased students' knowledge, not their sexual activity, but that many programs provided too little information and too little intervention to increase contraceptive use.[14]

Kantner and Zelnik's second survey in 1976 confirmed the widespread belief that girls were having sex even earlier and with more partners than in 1971. Yet teen pregnancy rates had not increased.[15] Thanks to access to contraception and liberalized abortion laws, the birth rate among teenage girls was lower than at any other time since World War II. The trend from 1971 to 1976 was toward less marriage, more abortion, and less adoption. While this was partly due to economic factors that made early marriage more difficult, much of the change resulted from teenage girls' own decisions. They were choosing to be sexually active and were not furtive about it. Their overt sexuality evoked powerful emotions in many Americans. More funding was allocated to research on adolescent pregnancy. NICHD had initiated a full research program on the prevention of pregnancies among unmarried teens even before Kantner and Zelnik issued their 1976 results.[16]

About this time themes of racial and class differences began to appear in discussions of the problem. These themes conflated poverty and race: so one image involved poor black girls and the other middle-class white ones. Although Zelnik and Kantner continued to consider all teens at risk, they stated that black teenagers experienced greater risks. Black teenage girls were sexually active at earlier ages than white girls, were more likely to become pregnant, and were more likely to give birth. Old fears revived about the sexual licence of lower-class women and about too many poor children causing a decline in the nation's intellectual ability and work habits. There was also anxiety over the cost of poor babies to the taxpayer. Since these fears could not be voiced outright in the post–civil rights climate of the mid-1970s, they were replaced by declarations that poor teenage girls could not escape poverty if they had children before finishing their education and becoming independent. This assumed that delaying child-bearing increased chances for upward mobility, a position not supported by evidence.[17]

Besides presenting data on black teenagers, Kantner and Zelnik brought the problem home to researchers, legislators, and policymakers by describing white teenage girls as rapidly emulating their behavior. Thus the behavior of poor black girls directly threatened the stability of the white middle class. This new set of fears raised the specter of autonomously sexual daughters who might become too committed to teenage romance and sex. Such girls might further insist on keeping their children if they got pregnant, bringing shame to themselves and their families and compromising their futures. They might also suffer psychological damage from emotions they were too young to handle. Worry about sex and its consequences was evident in almost every discussion of teenage sex or adolescent pregnancy in the late 1970s. The idea of saving oneself for marriage was almost dead, but girls should delay sexual experience as long as possible.

These disparate concerns about poor and middle-class girls led to an explosion in surveys of adolescent sexuality. More than fifty appeared in the decade and a half after 1976, many of which focused on early adolescence. And an outpouring of related research "demonstrated" that teenage girls faced adverse consequences from pregnancies, childbearing, and motherhood to a greater extent than older women.[18] These supposed consequences included, besides economic ones, pregnancy complications, maternal and infant mortality, and low-birth-weight babies. None of these issues had been raised in the 1950s when most teenage mothers were married. And the evidence about these negative consequences applied only to very young mothers. When government policy experts sounded the alarm about teenage pregnancy and childbearing, they implied that a large proportion of it occurred among those younger than 18. At NICHD, the demographer Wendy Baldwin noted, "we could see a huge and growing number of kids exposed to pregnancy and childbearing."[19] In fact, the majority of teenage mothers were 18 or 19 and not really "kids" at all.

Policy experts did not develop this picture alone. The family planning community helped define the problem by interpreting survey findings, especially those of Kantner and Zelnik, for public consumption. In 1976 AGI published *11 Million Teenagers: What Can Be Done about the Epidemic of Adolescent Pregnancy in the United States*. This slick booklet compiled scholarly information into terse, simple statements accompanied by accessible bar graphs and tables and photographs of vulnerable-looking young teens. The presentation was so captivating and straightforward that it created the vocabulary used both by researchers and in subsequent political debates.

Five years earlier the family planning community had promoted contraception for teens with arguments that their sexual activity was inevitable and nothing new. By the mid-1970s AGI adopted the position that teenage pregnancy was an epidemic that necessitated increased federal support for family planning and related services and for research. AGI reduced the problem to its most rudimentary terms using big, round, easily remembered numbers. These included the "facts" that each year 11 million teenagers had sexual intercourse, one million became pregnant, and 600,000 gave birth. Such numbers masked the complexity necessary for a more nuanced picture of teenagers' sexual and reproductive lives. The booklet did not mention Kantner and Zelnik's finding that teenagers had sex infrequently and with few partners. It manipulated age categories to present the data in the worst possible light, and when the numbers were too small to startle it turned to percentages.

Even though the researchers themselves were, by now, noting differences by race and class in the likelihood of childbearing, the report explicitly emphasized convergence: "adolescent sexual activity has been traditionally portrayed as principally affecting minorities and the poor; but recent evidence suggests that teenagers from higher income and non-minority groups are now beginning sexual intercourse at earlier ages."[20] Framing the issue as without racial or class boundaries effectively marketed the problem of teenage pregnancy to white, upper-middle-class lawmakers. By highlighting these pregnancies as unintended and characterizing teenage girls as victims, *11 Million Teenagers* encouraged intervention in the private behavior of all teenage girls. It prompted the Secretary of Health, Education, and Welfare, Joseph Califano, to form an interagency task force to develop policy.[21] This task force led to new legislation, the Adolescent Health Services and Pregnancy Prevention and Care Act of 1978, targeting girls aged 17 and under. The continued focus on very young teens, most of whom were not sexually active and did not get pregnant, suggested that anxiety over girls' sexual behavior was a motivation for the legislation. Americans' ambivalent fascination with pubescent girls, eroticizing them while treating them as children in need of protection, can be seen in the phrase "children bearing children," which appeared as a slogan about this time.

Most legislators described the issue as it was presented in *11 Million Teenagers*. Even though teenage birth rates were at a twenty-year low, no lawmaker raised the possibility that teen pregnancy was not as serious a problem as AGI claimed. For AGI the metaphor of an epidemic was an effective lobbying tool. The emphasis on teenage sexuality, illegitimacy, and the consequences of teenage pregnancy, along with the continued de-emphasis of racial difference, played on legislators' fears that rampant sexuality among middle-class girls posed a threat to families like their own. And teen pregnancy was treated as an exclusively female event. In line with the century-old concept of adolescent male sexuality as all-consuming and uncontrollable, researchers left teenage boys out of their surveys. By ignoring boys, surveys suggested that their sexual urges were unchanged and unchangeable, so it was useless for policymakers to consider them in searching for a solution. Supporters of the legislation even avoided mentioning the financial responsibilities of adolescent fathers so as not to jeopardize increased funding for pregnant girls.

Even when both sexes were mentioned, the responsibility for decisions about sex and contraception was placed with girls, who were thought to be less at the mercy of raging hormones. While "eleven million adolescent boys are sexually active," reported the interagency task force, "more than four million girls (age 15 to 19) have had sexual intercourse—[and] only two million use contraceptives." Few wondered who these boys' partners were or noted that most of these "boys" and "girls" were 18 and 19 years of age and not even targeted in the legislation. As chair of the Senate Committee on Human Resources, Senator Ted Kennedy introduced the bill. He used the theme of teenage girls as children, repeating the AGI mantra of a million young pregnant girls and over 600,000 births.[22]

In committee hearings, Kennedy added that this caused "some of the most tragic human experiences that come upon young teenage girls, with all the impact it has on their future lives." During the hearings, only conservative politicians like Senator S. I. Hayakawa of California felt free to articulate a connection between sexual behavior and teenage pregnancy: "Many of us, when we went through high school, worked after school at odd jobs as delivery boys and all kinds of chores, and that reduced the amount of time available for flirtation and the consequences of flirtation. But today, poverty simply means welfare and food stamps and idleness and therefore sex, and we have created the conditions of ample idleness in which these things can happen." Hayakawa did not see teenage girls as victims. Their pregnancies were consequences of their decisions, decisions encouraged by wrong-headed policies. Americans had passed legislation to provide unmarried pregnant girls with counseling, prenatal care, nutritional guidance, postnatal care, and high school daycare, giving them so much attention that "they are the envy of all the nonpregnant girls." Furthermore, he added, "if we increase the rewards, the attractiveness of teenage pregnancy, well, we simply increase teenage pregnancy."[23]

In the late 1970s, however, most legislators were more sympathetic to pregnant girls, and most of the funding in the new legislation went for the provision of services to them and their babies. In testimony on the legislation, NICHD echoed AGI's arguments in favor of prevention of pregnancy. But legislators rejected AGI's solution to the problem even while accepting its definition. The change in emphasis to the already pregnant reflected prudishness on the part of Califano and President Carter and allowed liberal legislators to circumvent the issue of teenage sexuality. AGI's agenda of preventing unwanted pregnancies was funded, but only as a secondary goal. This funding established a new unit, the Office of Adolescent Pregnancy Programs (OAPP), which reported directly to the Assistant Secretary of Health. Over the next decade this office began to fund surveys of adolescent sexual behavior. This funding in the legislation resulted from a compromise with those who preferred to support services. NICHD's Baldwin described its promotion:

> The issue of adolescent pregnancy had broad appeal—that children were having children. When Congress became interested in this issue, NICHD was able to provide data and describe research in hearings. NICHD did not give advice on policy and programs but rather the information base for them. Sexual behavior figured prominently in this issue. Congressional interest was clearly growing as the research agenda was taking shape in this area. When the Office of Adolescent Pregnancy Programs began, it was clearly supportive of research, although it always had a chastity emphasis.[24]

In the years following the passage of this legislation, surveys of adolescent sexual behavior reflected legislative priorities about adolescent sexuality as interpreted by policymakers and researchers. A typical example is a survey by the Child Welfare League of America. In keeping with the new priority of focusing on the youngest childbearing teens, the interviews involved girls who had given birth before age 16. Although most respondents were black, Shelby Miller, in the report on the survey, defined the problem in terms that transcended race, arguing that the rates for unmarried white teenagers had also continued to rise. Yet, by noting the race of respondents, the survey was part of the increased emphasis on race apparent from the last half of the 1970s. Some researchers, especially those with demographic training like Dennis Hogan and Evelyn Kitagawa, even began to take issue with the oft-repeated statement that unmarried teenage childbearing was pervasive among all social classes, emphasizing instead that the chance of becoming pregnant was greatest for black teenagers from high-risk social environments. Surveys began to include more questions on sexual behavior, but these were always justified as essential to understanding the negative consequences of such behavior. Few asked young women how they became sexually involved or whether they wanted to, and none asked if they enjoyed it. Such questions might have suggested that girls lacked innocence.[25]

These trends of differentiating by race and class and including more explicit questions about sexual behavior were exemplified in two NICHD-funded surveys of adolescents by Richard Udry and others at the University of North Carolina. These provide an extreme example because Udry's explicitly sociobiological perspective makes many of the findings appear more racialized, gendered, and class-specific than those of other researchers. Udry helped change the interpretation of racial differences in sexual activity. Where others saw these as a consequence of differences in the lives of black and white adolescents, Udry's findings implied that race and class differences caused the social problem of teenage sexual activity. His position suited the increasingly conservative mood.

Udry's first survey started in 1978 and involved two rounds of interviews with junior high school students in Raleigh, North Carolina. Unlike other researchers, Udry did not focus on teen pregnancy but on "who is likely to have sex and why." He also insisted on interviewing boys as well as girls because he wished to demonstrate that hormonal differences affected sexual interests. Hypothesizing that age at puberty affected levels of sexual interest and activity among adolescents, Udry assessed this by asking each respondent to compare his or her sexual organs to a set of pictures ranging, for boys, from "a prepubertal penis and no pubic hair" to "a fully developed penis and pubic hair." Additional questions involved shaving, weight, voice, and situations that turned respondents on sexually. Equally detailed questions about sexual experience, contraception, the sexual behavior of friends, and parents' attitudes provided a wealth of information. Udry and associates then weighed the comparative influences of friends, parents, and hormonal development on sexual activity.

Udry was unusual in undertaking data collection for a large, funded survey without using a survey organization, and he apparently had problems with some questions. For example, in 1978 the questions about sexual intercourse (shown here for boys) contained no definition of the term and simply started with:

Please put an ⊠ in the box below that best describes you.
   I have never had sexual intercourse with a girl ☐

I have had sexual intercourse with a girl once or twice in my life ☐
I have done this more than once or twice in my life ☐

By the second round of the questionnaire, in 1980, Udry changed and defined his terms:

> To *have sex* (sexual intercourse) is to put the male penis into the female vagina. This is sometimes called "screwing" or "getting laid." Please mark in the box below that best tells about you.
> ☐ I have never had sex with a girl.
> ☐ I have had sex with a girl 1 or 2 times in my life.
> ☐ I have had sex with a girl more than 2 times in my life.

Without describing this wording change, Udry and his coauthors claimed increases in the frequency of intercourse between the two waves of interviews, as well as inconsistencies in the responses. While there probably was an increase, the changes in wording may account for part of the trend. The effects of variation in question wording had long been documented in survey literature.[26] But these were not the only researchers guilty of this oversight. Many authors claimed increases in sexual activities between their survey and some earlier survey from different researchers without discussing question wording.

Udry and his colleagues portrayed teenage sexuality as heavily dependent on natural sexual development. They separated girls' biological coming of age as sex objects from the "natural" growth in their desire: "Estrogen effects (i.e. breast and hip development) are readily observed aspects of physical maturity and are a part of a girl's sexual attractiveness. Androgen effects, measured by pubic hair development in this study, are not usually observed by others, but instead are hypothesized as responsible for the biological component of sexual motivation which we call libido."[27] In this view, pubescent girls had sex not only because their hormones were on fire but because they sexually aroused boys. When girls grew breasts, they excited those boys whose hormones were ready, and boys naturally went after them.

Udry conducted his second longitudinal study of adolescent sexuality in Tallahassee, Florida, as a result of political flak in North Carolina both from Senator Helms and from the Chapel Hill PTA.[28] This time the researchers set out to test their model explaining coitus in early adolescence. This involved three factors: motivation, which they saw as a function of both physical development and social evaluation; attractiveness, which they believed explained opportunity; and social controls, which they saw as the only area in which others could influence the behavior of the young. They reiterated their position that girls were more subject to social influence and boys to hormones and thus reinforced long-standing ideas about boys' intense sexual desire and girls' greater ability to stop sexual activity. However, they saw some girls as exceptions:

> The mother's sexual experience as an adolescent has an influence on her adolescent child's sexual behavior. Not much of this influence is transmitted via the differential attitudes, communication patterns, or behavioral control attempts of mothers with different adolescent experiences themselves . . . there is reason to suspect that the relationship between mother's and daughter's sexual behavior works at least in part through their biological relationship to one another.

In this argument, girls who were interested in sex had mothers just like them. Black girls were another exception to the rule that girls could control their sexual impulses. Their early sexual experiences, Udry and his associates argued, resulted solely from pubertal development. That is, black girls were like boys.[29]

In 1979, before Udry's second survey, Zelnik and Kantner undertook a third round of the National Survey of Young Women. It was accompanied by the first National Survey of Young Men, but this was barely analyzed for almost a decade. In fertility-related research on sexual behavior, women's sexual activity remained the major concern, so reports on the 1979 survey mainly involved comparisons between the young women and those in the earlier two surveys. Kantner and Zelnik found a convergence between the rates of premarital sexual activity of white and black teenage girls, because the white rate was increasing while the black rate had remained stable since 1976. Where Udry highlighted black and lower-class girls, Kantner and Zelnik continued to raise the specter of sex among middle-class (white) girls. But instead of reiterating their earlier position that this was inevitable, Zelnik responded to the changing times by describing teen sexual activity as a symptom of family decline. He noted that first intercourse usually occurred in the home of one of the participants:

> The degree to which sex begins at home may be surprising to some, but it is certainly consistent with the changes that have occurred with respect to working wives, declining neighborhoods, and the general lessening of parental surveillance and control. Homes unoccupied by parents are far more attractive as places for sexual dalliance than cars or the great outdoors; and presumably something other than studying together (or listening to music together) is going on behind closed doors while parents sit

downstairs congratulating themselves for treating their children as responsible and mature individuals entitled to privacy.

In this view, middle-class wives were abandoning children as their priority and becoming part of the problem, and husbands were acquiescing.[30]

By this time sexual activity among the young was frequently taken for granted in surveys, and its consequence was assumed to be pregnancy.[31] Although natality data showed stable rates of teenage pregnancy, authors often misrepresented these and instead helped create a truism that the number of unwanted pregnancies was growing rapidly. Surveys still followed the AGI's line that teen pregnancy was an epidemic, inaccurately stating that "pregnancy rates have continued to climb" even though "teenagers are trying harder than ever to avoid premarital pregnancy, with more teens using contraceptives and using them more consistently."[32] Yet, in spite of this persistent claim that the problem was solvable with sex education and contraceptive advice, by 1981 the more conservative viewpoint promulgated by Udry and Zelnik began to have an impact. Congress revisited the issue of adolescent pregnancy and passed the Adolescent Family Life Act (AFLA) in an attempt to legislate morality. While retaining the provisions for pregnant teenagers and teenage mothers from the earlier legislation, the new act expressed more explicit outrage about sex among the young.

The Act's sponsor, Senator Jeremiah Denton of Alabama, had told the *Washington Post* in December 1980 that teenage sexuality was his issue, and had added: "No nation can survive long unless it can encourage its young to withhold indulgence in their sexual appetites until marriage! There are just two requirements for civilization—the family and agriculture. There wasn't civilization until some kind of moral code inhibited people sufficiently to stay together as husband and wife and exercise self-discipline to raise children." The co-sponsor, Senator Orrin Hatch of Utah, similarly located the problem by stating that adolescent involvement in sexual activity struck "at the heart of family life."[33] Such sentiments, reminiscent of writers like Max Exner in 1913, showed the continuing power of adolescent sexuality to raise discomfort levels. Researchers had various goals, but in all cases their surveys of adolescent sexual activity provided conservatives with evidence difficult for liberals to refute.

Kennedy and other Democrats went along with the new legislation in order to protect services to teen mothers but also out of their own discomfort at dealing with sex. Afraid of appearing too permissive, they allowed conservatives to define the debate. Senators Kennedy and Denton worked together, a collaboration that ensured early passage of the bill. Denton agreed to omit some of the references to promiscuity, chastity, and pre-marital sex, and to reaffirm teenage pregnancy and childbearing as impor-tant concerns. In return, he retained the legislation's central focus: the prevention of sexual relations among teenagers. A small number of con-gressmen, such as Henry Waxman of California, and groups like Planned Parenthood were uncomfortable, but there were few negative speeches during the debate.

With premarital sexual behavior now an official target, more federal dollars were available to survey adolescent sexuality. NICHD and other institutes funded more national surveys than ever before and firmly estab-lished the federal government as having the right to know what teenagers did sexually. They even added questions about sexual behavior to other surveys like the National Survey of Children and the National Longitudinal Survey of Work Experience and Youth. In 1982 the National Center for Health Statistics added the never-married to its National Survey of Family Growth, the first time the government asked unmarried women about their sexual behavior. They justified this by referring both to history and to the sexual behavior of teenagers:

> The first survey, in 1955, was based on interviews with currently married white women aged 18–59. By 1973 and 1976, formerly married women and single mothers were also interviewed and black women were sampled at higher rates so that separate statistics for them would be reliable. Since then it has become clear that interviewing only women who have been married or had children is now inadequate for a full picture of U.S. fertility. Two reasons for this are a substantial rise in premarital inter-course among teenagers during the 1970s and the steady increase in births to unmarried women since at least 1940. Information on *all* women aged 15–44 is necessary to identify the number of women "at risk" of preg-nancy—those who have ever had or are currently having intercourse, and who are not sterile.

Thirty years earlier Ronald Freedman and his colleagues had cited the national interest to justify the first national fertility survey. Now the goal was more humanitarian: estimating "the population in need of contracep-tion and of family planning, infertility, and other reproductive health services."[34]

NICHD also funded the first national survey of the sexual behavior of unmarried women aged 20–29, a group that accounted for a larger propor-tion of births than teenagers. And it funded numerous small-scale studies of adolescent fertility-related sexual behavior in an attempt to solve the seemingly intractable problem of adolescent sexuality and pregnancy.[35] In contrast, the Office of Adolescent Pregnancy Programs began funding programs to promote chastity and evaluating abstinence curricula designed to delay young people's sexual activity.

Most of these surveys included few questions on sexual behavior, but the size and random quality of their samples made their results hard to argue with. In addition, their questionnaires were competently designed and pretested and the surveys were conducted by professional survey research organizations using experienced, trained interviewers. Analyses of the 1982 National Survey of Family Growth showed that women were spending a decreasing proportion of their total reproductive lives married. With less marriage, sexual intercourse was now commonplace among the unmarried. Over half of the oldest cohort of women interviewed (40–44) had become sexually active while unmarried, and the rates rose for each successively younger cohort. But stigma apparently remained. Sexually active unmarried women used less contraception than their married sisters, and this difference was more pronounced among blacks.

Since the majority of unmarried American adults engaged in sexual intercourse, chastity seemed an unattainable goal. The family planning community argued instead for more information and a greater availability of contraceptives. Yet the 1982 National Survey of Family Growth showed that two-thirds of those aged 15–19 were already receiving formal instruction about pregnancy and contraception.[36] Abortion rates in America were higher than in comparable countries, and half the unmarried respondents said they would abort if they became pregnant. Why unintended pregnancy remained so high was not clear, but it seemed related to a general discomfort about sex.

Koray Tanfer and Marjorie Horn, reporting in *Family Planning Perspectives* on the NICHD-funded 1983 National Survey of Unmarried Women, the first national survey of adult unmarried women, repeated and expanded these findings with evidence that women were postponing marriage but not necessarily pregnancy and childbearing.[37] Because these women were old enough to make their own decisions about sex, Tanfer could focus on contraceptive use. He and Horn did not write with the ambivalence of other researchers but addressed the family planning community directly in their explanation of why some women did not use contraception.

In the 1980s researchers of adolescent sexuality took a more conservative problem-oriented tack. Some emphasized the relationship between early sexual activity and problem behavior such as drug abuse, or suggested that sex education encouraged the young to experiment. Such claims even appeared in *Family Planning Perspectives*. In addition, racial differences began to be discussed freely. Some authors even suggested that young, poor girls were not simply victims but, like others, made the best of their circumstances. In an evaluation of a much-lauded program for pregnant and parenting teens called Project Redirection, Denise Polit concluded that teenage mothers had more children after completing the program than the comparison group who were not enrolled because they were less likely to terminate a pregnancy. The program provided positive rewards for mothering skills, and the babies were showered with love and attention; Polit suggested that this might have lessened participants' interest in contraception or in terminating an unintended pregnancy. Frank Furstenburg and his colleagues in a survey of the children of a group of black teenage unwed mothers also found the problem of teenage childbearing difficult to resolve. These children appeared to repeat the childbearing patterns of their mothers by becoming sexually active and pregnant at young ages.[38]

Such findings increased the pressure on researchers to find ways to prevent early sexual activity just as the framers of the AFLA had intended. Surveys evaluating AFLA's abstinence and other sex education curricula provide a contrast to the well-researched national surveys and illustrate the difference in ideology between the established research community and Congress. Most demographers did not believe programs that promoted abstinence alone could solve the problems of adolescent sexuality and pregnancy. And they had the support of government researchers both in funding and in joint research articles. Researchers on the evaluation studies were not demographers but faculty members in departments like family resources or human development at state universities in Utah and Arizona or psychologists working for corporations. With less survey expertise and few ties to academically trained policy experts in federal funding agencies, they could not aspire to the research quality of the demographers. Most of their funding came directly from OAPP or from state welfare agencies rather than NICHD. As the Deputy Director of NICHD, a demographer, put it: "The Office of Adolescent Pregnancy Programs felt chastity initiatives should be one of the emphasis areas. The chastity discussion got much more polarized than it needed to. The choice began to sound like abstinence or contraception. The polarization was not constructive—perhaps these two issues should be linked together more closely. It made it harder to create messages about delaying sex."[39]

Some evaluations questioned the effectiveness of chastity education. Marvin Eisen of Sociometrics and Gail Zellman of the Rand Corporation reported on two sex education programs for the Texas Department of Human Resources. They found no relationship between program participation and the delay of intercourse, although participants' knowledge of contraception and their communication with parents increased. And some who undertook OAPP evaluations also concluded that abstinence curricula did not work. F. Scott Christopher and Mark Roosa evaluated Latino and black students attending an abstinence-only middle school program called Success Express at twenty-eight sites. Designed to prevent the initiation of sexual intercourse among virgins, the program provided no information on contraception, focusing instead on the negative consequences of sexual intercourse and on ways to decline sexual advances. The program provided no support for those already sexually active, and it suffered from a high drop-out rate. Christopher and Roosa concluded: "After two years of implementation and evaluation of program effects with over 800 adolescents, the conclusion remains the same: The results of the Success Express Program provide no support for the notion that this type of primary prevention program will be successful in achieving its ultimate goal, reducing teenage pregnancy rates in the communities served."[40]

These arguments that abstinence-only programs did not reduce sexual activity came as no surprise to government demographers who supported a more comprehensive approach such as a two-pronged program (funded by the Ford Foundation) for low-income eighth-graders in Atlanta that combined abstinence education with contraceptive advice. In contrast, Brent Miller, a professor of family and human development at Utah State University, and Terrance Olsen, a professor of family sciences at Brigham Young, studied an abstinence curriculum in twenty high schools in Utah, New Mexico, and California and found that, in the short term, participants' permissive values decreased and discussion with parents increased. Although it was hard to generalize from this heavily Mormon student body to the rest of the population, Miller and Olsen's work provided conservative legislators with ammunition to expand the program.[41]

In more than fifteen years of research into the sex lives of teenage girls, and regardless of their political stance, the predominantly male investigators assumed that becoming sexually active was a young woman's own decision, albeit a naive one, even among the very young. Not until 1987, when Kristin Moore at Child Trends, a Washington-based policy organization, included two questions on nonvoluntary intercourse in the longitudinal National Survey of Children (whose respondents were by this time aged 18–22), did survey data appear showing otherwise. Moore asked:

- Was there ever a time when you were forced to have sex against your will, or were raped?
- How old were you the first time this happened?[42]

Two-thirds of those who became sexually active at age 14 or younger described nonvoluntary sexual intercourse, as did half of those who started at age 15. These findings suggested that many sexually active young teenagers might indeed be victims, but in a quite different sense than previously imagined. Now their victim status could not be cured by condoms.

Yet the Planned Parenthood Federation continued to promote a picture of adolescent sexuality consistent with AGI's 11 million teenagers campaign. Planned Parenthood also remained committed to its long-held belief that while poor teenagers might be most affected by the epidemic, all were at risk, although the emphasis began to shift toward the poor. In 1986 the Federation hired the Harris Poll to undertake a survey of American teens that included some questions about sexual behavior. The report on this survey started with findings reminiscent of arguments of fifteen years earlier: "The survey documents the scope of a national problem: many teenagers are sexually active, and yet many do not use birth control. High rates of teenage pregnancy are the inevitable result. And those results will fall heaviest, the survey shows, at those levels of society where teenagers and their parents have the least resources to cope with the problem."[43] Given the number of federally funded large surveys of sexual behavior among teenagers, the Planned Parenthood poll seemed unnecessary. But stating the issue in clear and simple terms helped keep the country focused on the problem.

Another publication was even more instrumental in keeping teenage sexuality and pregnancy at the forefront of national concern. In 1984, soon after the enactment of AFLA, the National Academy of Sciences established a panel of experts to evaluate the Act's causes and consequences and to evaluate alternative programs and policies to ameliorate the problem of teen pregnancy. Funded by several foundations led by the long-supportive Rockefeller Foundation, the panel included a mixture of government research funders, academic researchers, and policy advocates who had played key roles in defining the problem. These included Wendy Baldwin of NICHD; the researchers Richard Jessor, Kristin Moore, and Frank Furstenburg; and Jacqueline Forrest of AGI. The panel's 1987 report, appropriately entitled *Risking the Future,* restated the issues and cited volumes of research. It reiterated the themes that had pervaded research on adolescent pregnancy, beginning with the assertion that "Adolescent pregnancy and childbearing are matters of substantial national concern."[44]

Like Planned Parenthood, the panel focused on the dangers not to society but to the young women themselves: "No human experience is at once so transiently private and lastingly public as an unintended pregnancy. When the mother herself is a young adolescent, only partially educated and almost wholly economically dependent, the pregnancy is inevitably enmeshed in a ragged tapestry of personal, interpersonal, social, religious, ethical, and economic dimensions." In case the reader had not yet got the message, this was quickly followed by a description of the never-changing magnitude of the problem: "Adolescent pregnancy is widely recognized in our society as a serious and complex problem. Regardless of one's political philosophy or moral perspective, the basic facts are disturbing: more than one million teenage girls in the United States become pregnant each year, just over 400,000 obtain an abortion, and nearly 470,000 give birth."[45] By now the image once predominant among researchers, that young women were victims who would pay for their naïveté for the rest of their lives, was in sharp conflict with a more punitive one, that pregnant young women needed punishment, not the encouragement of a permissive society that allowed them to indulge in sexual pleasures without fully facing the consequences. And the panel could not ignore this view.

To allay the fears of the various constituencies, the panel listed somewhat contradictory recommendations. While panelists argued for enhanced life options, increased access to contraception, and no restrictions on abortion for the young, they also recommended delaying sexual initiation (noting that prevention programs were ineffective but endorsing them anyway) and better access to adoption. Finally, the panel called for continued support of a broad-based program of research, commenting that the availability of data had helped their deliberations immeasurably.

In the early years of sex surveys researchers had been able to control the interpretation of their findings and define the meaning of sexual events in the company of other sexologists. After Kinsey the media began to simplify and reinterpret findings to sell newspapers. When demographers started surveying fertility, they got the federal government interested in the intimate lives of the populace. While this led to more funding and improved the quality of surveys, it also meant that researchers lost some control over their message. Now funders began to determine what information was needed, and politicians began to select from results to argue for legislation in line with their political agendas. No matter how widespread unmarried sex and pregnancy became, no politician could publicly suggest it was acceptable. Sometimes this meant that conservative social scientists had the loudest voices or that researchers found themselves following the interpretations of others in deciding what their data meant. The voices of respondents became even harder to hear now that researchers had been joined by a cacophony of professional interpreters. This was especially true for young women, a group that had historically been talked at and not listened to.

6

Coupling and Uncoupling

The impact of sexual behavior on the development of close, male-female relationships is not well understood. Social scientists have carefully scaled sexual attitudes and counted the frequency of various sexual acts . . . Seldom, however, have researchers explored the psychological meaning of sex for participants or the effects of sexual behavior on interpersonal relationships.

—Letitia Anne Peplau, Zick Rubin, and Charles Hill, 1977

IN 1970 Leon Jaroff, a senior editor at *Time* magazine, attended a weekend group session at the Personal Growth Lab in Cleveland. Led by the Gestalt therapist Sylvia Evans, the students talked, touched, and embraced as they took turns sharing their experiences as a camera filmed the session. Frances sobbed convulsively after revealing her husband's suicide. She found relief in being held aloft by the rest of the group, rocked back and forth, then lowered and comforted by their hands. Bob learned something about handling his long-suppressed anger at his father's brutality, and Linda gained reassurance about her femininity. Finally attention turned to Leon: "I stood up, and under the encouraging eyes of the group members whom by now I knew so well, stepped forward, with little self-consciousness. I was actually looking forward to an experience that only two days before I would have approached with a sense of dread. The camera swung to me." America was in the midst of what the psychologist Carl Rogers called "the most significant social invention of this century," a movement in which the release of emotional and libidinal feelings would help successful individuals like Jaroff learn how to reach their fullest potential.[1]

If pubescent girls were too young to handle their sexual feelings, adults needed to embrace theirs. The new movement saw heterosexual sex as a life-enhancing pleasure which all deserved, and indeed needed, whether married or not. Sex provided endless opportunities for the experiential learning that was essential if individuals were to get in touch with themselves. This perspective originated in the 1950s and early 1960s in the writings of Abraham Maslow, a psychology professor at Brooklyn College and Brandeis. In Maslow's best-known work, *Toward a Psychology of Being*, he summarized the basic tenets of the human potential movement, which he founded with Rogers and Curt Lewin.

Maslow argued that each person's biologically based inner nature was part unique and part common to all; that it could be subjected to scientific study; that it was basically good but weak; and that it could be easily suppressed but never abolished. Those who denied this essential nature grew sick and needed to hurt others. Emotional development, "self-actualization," was a lifetime task involving a sometimes painful process of discovery and nurture of one's inner nature. Self-actualized individuals were more successful in every way, in their careers as well as their personal lives. Where marital adjustment researchers of the 1930s and 1940s had emphasized selection and adjustment as the bases of a healthy relationship, now growth and change became the goals. The architects of the new movement urged those involved in a relationship to struggle with each other rather than to accommodate, and to discover themselves in the process.[2] Those undertaking this journey should constantly try new activities and ideas, including new sexual experiences. To help those involved in the search for personal perfection, sex researchers, starting with Maslow, began to use surveys to document ways individuals and couples could enhance sexual pleasure.

The research that emerged from the human potential movement was, like the movement itself, staunchly focused on the educated middle classes. When family researchers had concentrated on this class, they had seen the couple as composed of gendered halves, each incomplete without the other, and marriage as a basic building block of social stability. In contrast, Maslow and other humanistic psychologists saw two equal individuals whose relationship existed for personal pleasure and growth. The couple, as such, could be sacrificed if it interfered with self-actualization. Now individuals, not families, provided the basis for a strong society. Self-actualized individuals needed only small doses of love, were above selfish love, and were capable of giving large amounts of unselfish love. Freud had argued that society repressed individual desires in order to maintain social order, but Maslow described societies as either growth-fostering or growth-inhibiting.

Social problems resulted from the unexamined, repressed desires of normal individuals produced by societies that denied rather than enhanced human potential. One should "accept and enjoy one's needs and welcome them to consciousness."[3] Sex was a basic human need, and self-actualized individuals satisfied it just as they satisfied other appetites in a non-exploitative way, negotiating with their partners to increase their experience and expand the boundaries of what each was willing to do.

Since men and women did not need each other to be complete, in theory, gender would no longer determine a person's life course. Thus the movement appeared to liberate middle-class women from the demands of femininity. Where family researchers had seen women's pleasure as dependent on men's ability, the new movement made "dependence" a psychological state to avoid. In Maslow's vision, power came from a person's inner resources, not from external ones. Self-actualized individuals would be able to get what they wanted regardless of personal wealth or social standing. Some were richer and had higher status, but this was not the source of their power. Status and wealth did not cause self-actualization, they demonstrated it. In the negotiations involved in any relationship, such individuals would not be self-sacrificing. Self-sacrificing acts were not altruistic because they created obligations on the part of recipients.

In practice, this caused problems for women. It was a male model of success. It valued self-confidence and personal advancement but not nurturance and emotional attachment. To succeed, women had to become like men. If they did poorly in negotiating with men, this was because they were less self-actualized, not because of their economic dependence on men or their socialization into caregiving. In the terms of humanistic psychology, they manipulated others into feeling obligated rather than going through the inner struggle necessary to become powerful individuals. This self-serving viewpoint of privileged men came into conflict with the reality of women's lives. Not only were they historically disadvantaged compared to men, women were the primary caregivers of children, and children necessitated self-sacrifice.[4]

Furthermore, Maslow himself was ambivalent about women who freely expressed their sexual "needs." In 1942 he interviewed "normal" (as opposed to "neurotic") female graduate students and measured their levels of "dominance-feeling," which he defined as "good self-confidence, self-assurance, high evaluation of the self, feelings of general capability." He concluded that high-dominance-feeling women were more "promiscuous," more likely to masturbate, had a greater frequency of homosexual experience, and were more likely to enjoy being on top during sex. They preferred "straightforward, unsentimental, rather violent, animal, pagan, passionate, even sometimes brutal love-making." Thus he depicted sexually active women as masculine and deviant. He even suggested that, for women, self-actualization brought mixed rewards: "The best marriages in our society (unless both husband and wife are definitely secure individuals) seem to be those in which the husband and wife are at about the same level of dominance-feeling or in which the husband is *somewhat* higher in dominance-feeling than the wife." Although Maslow blamed this on "our insecure society," his mixed message for women continued as his ideas spread, and it informed a large number of surveys over the next several decades.[5]

Maslow's position that the self-actualized were more sexually liberated did not really become influential until the 1970s and 1980s, when many "sexological" surveys appeared. But the 1960s saw precursors of these. From the beginning many were undertaken by psychologists like Maslow. Psychologists are less interested than sociologists in the social and cultural context of respondents' lives, and the human potential model proposed the development of the inner self as the appropriate path to social change. Their resulting lack of interest in differences in the external conditions among groups led psychologists to select easily available respondents rather than to use probability samples. These tended to be middle-class people like themselves, a group that seemed to be the most amenable to self-actualization. Where sociologists usually provided information on nonrespondents, including nonresponse rates, and often published their questionnaires, psychologists rarely discussed issues of data. Often they did not even note the year in which they collected their data. For them such factors were less important than personal attributes.

When Terman and Burgess surveyed marital happiness in the 1930s, they did so out of a profound concern for the future of marriage as an institution. Sexological surveyors in the 1960s continued to believe in marriage, but rather than defending it on the grounds of social stability they saw it as promoting personal development. They considered sexual problems treatable with psychological help. Some ceased to view sex as the glue to hold marriages together, seeing it instead as an appetite that the successful satisfied as needed. Others surveyed extramarital relationships and described the positive experiences these brought for individual members of couples.

And the most important theme of sexological surveys of the 1970s and 1980s, female sexual response, had already been apparent in the 1960s. Maslow's disciple Manfred DeMartino tried to replicate Maslow's findings about high-dominance women in three studies; in each he described such women as resembling the profile of successful men: high self-esteem, above-average sex drives, and positive feelings about sex. He was not alone in arguing that sexual response was less problematic for successful women. The sociologist Robert Bell interviewed college-educated married women and found that their expectations for sexual pleasure were higher than those of earlier generations. Most of his respondents reported that their sexual adjustment and frequency of intercourse were "about right." In fact: "A number of married couples may find that the sexual interests and desires of the wife have increased to a point greater than that of the husband. But because of biological limitations on the male, he cannot normally function as a sex partner without some sexual interest (as women can and often do)."[6]

In spite of the call to throw off their shackles, women appeared to be having difficulty adapting to sexual liberation. In a study funded by the U.S. Public Health Service, Seymour Fisher and Howard Osofsky asked women these questions:

- How would you describe your own sexual responsiveness?
- I am very much more responsive than the average. ☐
- I am above average. ☐
- I am average. ☐
- I am slightly below average. ☐
- I am considerably below average. ☐

Few respondents pondered the absurdity of the question, and the majority scored themselves "average," probably because it was closest to "normal." Fisher and Osofsky wanted to find which psychological variables correlated with sexual responsiveness:

In an initial session, two body image measures were administered which were designed to evaluate intensity of body awareness and clarity or definiteness of body boundaries. In a second session five days later the subject removed all of her clothing; was examined gynecologically for 30 minutes; moved to a desk with only a sheet wrapped about her; and responded once more to the two body image tests. It was considered that the experience of the gynecological examination combined with the fact of being nude except for a sheet during the response to the tests created a situation in which the subject was forcefully confronted with her body as possessing sexual attributes.[7]

They theorized that women who were comfortable in this situation would be more sexually responsive than those who were uncomfortable. Women's unresponsiveness was no longer the result of early socialization or incompetent husbands. For humanistic psychology, with its focus on the individual and its deemphasis of context, the problem and its solution lay within the woman herself.

If self-actualization was a lifetime task and self-actualized individuals enjoyed sexual pleasure, how could sexual activity decline with aging? During the 1960s surveyors attempted to find a cure for this "problem." In contrast to surveys of sexual responsiveness, these surveys involved men. While the sexuality of young men was straightforward, in a world where a vibrant sexual drive signaled psychological health older men needed scrutiny, since "sexual interest and activity have a normal place in the life of the older individual." Furthermore, researchers posited that the best preparation for a sexually active old age was a lifetime of practice. For example, there was a positive correlation between continuing to masturbate and engaging in sexual intercourse. The only disagreement came from a former Kinsey researcher, Clyde Martin. In spite of similar findings, Martin stated that men who were "not fully potent" were also free of anxiety about this, and so he disputed the notion that sexual functioning was essential to health.[8]

It was not until the media took an interest that researchers' ideas about human potential reached a mass audience. By the 1970s the media began promoting a plethora of self-help movements, such as est and Esalen, which translated humanistic psychology, and sexual liberation, for mass consumption. Messages directed at a growing urban singles population appeared in books, television, newspapers, and magazines. Adulthood, writers opined, did not require the negation of the child within; in fact, the goal of adult life was fun, and sex was part of this fun. Sex manuals replaced marriage manuals as sources of advice, and explicit sexual images and commodities abounded.[9] Conventional marriage seemed on its way to becoming one of several available lifestyles, the one for the fearful who craved security and intimacy rather than self-actualization. Previously firm walls protecting privacy and decorum were falling. Films like *Deep Throat* crossed over from porn houses to mainstream movie theaters. Television sitcoms and dramas such as the highly successful situation comedy *Three's Company* featured sexual plots. And magazines displaying explicit sexual images appeared in every neighborhood drugstore, no longer confined to the back.

In this picture of modern life portrayed by the media, taboos remained. Only adults could participate; the sexuality of the young was, as we have seen, a cause for concern. Mutual consent was a requirement, but this issue was complex. While all agreed that people should not do anything they did not want to do, experience became a badge of honor. This created pressure to experiment and to enjoy a variety of sexual practices regardless of personal taste. Homosexual pleasures, for example, could be explored in order to broaden experience, but this lifestyle was still taboo. The increasingly open sexuality of gay male society might be admired, but the appropriate object of desire for a "normal" sexually open and free adult was still a member of the opposite sex.

The best-known advice magazine for hedonists, *Playboy,* was founded in the 1950s, and its circulation peaked at 6 million in the early 1970s. *Playboy*'s ideal, the man who was not tied down by marriage, loved women, especially beautiful women. They should be wonderful, sexual playmates, but not wives. In response, some women's magazines, such as *Cosmopolitan,* urged women to conquer their sexual inhibitions, become equals in the bedroom, and rely on themselves.[10]

The books *Human Sexual Response* and *Human Sexual Inadequacy,* by William Masters and Virginia Johnson, also located sexual pleasure in technical competence rather than in love. These authors more than any others helped create the field of sex therapy, a field that greatly influenced and was influenced by the human potential movement.[11] They also firmly and with great fanfare disputed the Freudian notion of the superiority of the vaginal orgasm and established the clitoris as the site of female sexual pleasure. Kinsey had made the same argument decades earlier but had been largely ignored. Even though their findings implied that women did not need men for sexual pleasure, Masters and Johnson believed in marriage and insisted that sexual problems caused the majority of divorces. Yet they used surrogates to treat sexual disorders and insisted that women were capable of multiple orgasms. While their "discovery" of the clitoral orgasm deemphasized penetration and the goal of simultaneous orgasm, thus making it potentially easier for women to achieve orgasms, their emphasis on technical mastery helped create new expectations for female sexual performance. The media popularized their work, distilling it to two ideas: that women had greater sexual capacities than men, and that sexual problems were treatable. Those whom sexual bliss had previously eluded could now join in.

Surveyors of sexual behavior responded to these ideas and also helped create them. They focused their research on sexual liberation from societal repression and provided information about the progress of the middle class toward this goal. And, as they helped shape appropriate sexual activity, they actually created possibilities and pleasures. Sexual enthusiasm involved risks, even for tenured faculty, and researchers learned to manage their results carefully. Many sexological surveys appeared in the *Journal of Sex Research*, the official journal of the Society for the Scientific Study of Sex, founded in the 1960s. Although the Society advocated liberation, it claimed a rigorous adherence to the scientific method. This rendered research results serious and safe. As a demonstration of "science," esoteric survey titles abounded: "A Self-Report Investigation of Two Types of Myotonic Response during Orgasm"; "Relationships among Sexual Arousability, Imagery Ability, and Introversion-Extroversion."

Most sexological surveys published during the 1970s were positive about sex and permissive in orientation, although a minority, published in journals not devoted to sex research, noted problems with the new lifestyle or represented a rear-guard, more disapproving viewpoint. And in spite of their claims about science most of these surveys did not use probability samples but relied on volunteers or took advantage of the captive audiences in professors' classes. What little information researchers chose to share with their audience suggests that many of the surveys were administered by the investigators themselves, a practice long held in disrepute.

The 1970s saw the emergence of women researchers in the previously male-dominated field of sex surveys. They were a minority, most co-wrote articles with men, and they did not challenge the fundamental tenet of a strong, autonomous sex drive. Many subscribed to the male model of sexual pleasure, which emphasized orgasm as the only goal. They discussed the issue that concerned them most, so female orgasmic inadequacy came under even greater scrutiny. But they also examined power differences between men and women that interfered with women's pleasure.

This increased fascination with every facet of female sexuality resulted not only from the advent of women researchers but also from long-standing beliefs that men, but not women, possessed a powerful, ever-ready libido. Any heterosexual goal—marriage, relationships, and now sexual liberation—apparently required a better understanding of the mysteries of female sexuality if women were to perform as men desired. The human potential movement blamed female inadequacies on repression of the inner nature, making the attainment of sexual satisfaction a matter of technique, attitude, and practice. The solution to this was for women to work harder at sex.

Many surveyors interviewed only women. The implication was that men were an unproblematic source of comparison. Sometimes these researchers taught women about their sexual functions in an attempt to improve arousability. Others debated the issue of control. Did women who felt they had some control over sexual feelings enjoy sex more, or did women need to lose control to enjoy sex? Alcohol, some argued, released sexual inhibitions, increasing women's sexual activity or level of enjoyment. Most believed that practice made perfect. Instead of stigmatizing a woman, sexual activity belonged to the successful. Practice might include masturbating or having sex with a number of partners.[12]

Researchers measured women's "sexual arousability" using an inventory, the SAI (sexual arousability inventory), and reported that women with more sexual experience were more readily aroused. Thus treatment for sexual dysfunction "might include the gradual expansion of the variety and frequency of erotic experiences."[13] This widely used scale, developed by the psychologists Emily Hoon, Peter Hoon, and John Wincze, illustrates the way psychologists rendered the intrusive process of asking women explicit sexual questions into "science."

The SAI consisted of twenty-eight items, each describing a potential activity. Respondents scored each item from minus one (the only level of negative arousal) to plus five (the highest level of positive arousal), indicating the extent to which they thought they would find each activity sexually arousing. Minus one indicated "adversely affects arousal; unthinkable, repulsive, distracting"; zero was "doesn't affect sexual arousal"; five was "always causes sexual arousal; extremely arousing." The items were as follows:

1 When a loved one stimulates your genitals with mouth and tongue.

2 When a loved one fondles your breast with his/her hands.

3 When you see a loved one nude.

4 When a loved one caresses you with his/her eyes.

5 When a loved one stimulates your genitals with his/her finger.

6 When you are touched or kissed on the inner thighs by a loved one.

7 When you caress a loved one's genitals with your fingers.

8 When you read a pornographic or "dirty" story.

9 When a loved one undresses you.

10 When you dance with a loved one.

11 When you have intercourse with a loved one.

12 When a loved one touches or kisses your nipples.

13 When you caress a loved one (other than genitals).

14 When you see pornographic pictures or slides.

15 When you lie in bed with a loved one.

16 When a loved one kisses you passionately.

17 When you hear sounds of pleasure during sex.

18 When a loved one kisses you with an exploring tongue.

19 When you read suggestive or pornographic poetry.

20 When you see a strip show.

21 When you stimulate a partner's genitals with your mouth and tongue.

22 When a loved one caresses you (other than genitals).

23 When you see a pornographic movie (stag film).

24 When you undress a loved one.

25 When a loved one fondles your breasts with mouth and tongue.

26 When you make love in a new or unusual place.

27 When you masturbate.

28 When your partner has an orgasm.[14]

Researchers added the scores for the items to get a total score, which they used as an indication of the respondent's level of sexual responsiveness.

The experience of responding to the SAI, which many women must have found embarrassing or intrusive, disappeared in the reports. The language used in the items conveyed messages about appropriate female sexual behavior by listing only varieties of a loved one's embraces and impersonal sexual activities, such as going to strip shows or using pornography. Absent, for example, were such items as sex with a long-time acquaintance and sex with a one-night stand. In addition, the authors did not describe the administration of the test. Did women take this test in an impersonal environment? If so, could they anticipate arousal from the listed activities, especially those they had never experienced? Researchers endorsed the scale, because it correlated with reported frequency of orgasm under different circumstances and because they got similar scores when they tested and retested it on groups of middle-class volunteers. While this made it seem more scientific, it did not tell the reader what the test actually measured.

A second group of researchers interviewed men as well as women to show that women fell short of the new standards of sexual liberation. And researchers sometimes distorted findings to highlight difference. David Sue interviewed undergraduates about their erotic fantasies during sexual intercourse.[15] His data revealed striking similarities by gender: about 60 percent of both men and women fantasized, the majority to enhance their own arousal or their partner's appeal. According to his tables, about 50 percent of each sex fantasized about forced sex, with the men only somewhat more likely (a ratio of three to two) to imagine themselves as the aggressor. Of each sex, about 40 percent imagined a former lover and just over half fantasized that others found them irresistible. In fact there were significant gender differences in only three out of thirteen types of fantasies. Yet instead of discussing this, Sue focused on difference. Men, he noted, were twice as likely as women to fantasize about an imaginary lover, and one-third of women but only one-fifth of men fantasized about being forced to have sex.

The popularity of studies of gender differences in sexual response conveyed ambivalence about women's liberation, both sexual and otherwise. A movement premised on the idea that women could do anything men could seemed to challenge the established portrayal of female sexuality as complex and multifaceted. One reaction was to reinvent the stereotype by arguing, for example, that only a certain type of women responded like men. One study found that extroverted women became sexually aroused more easily than introverts, but that among men no such differences existed. Female extroverts, the researchers explained, "may be less stereotypical in their sexual roles than their introverted counterparts." Another survey examined gender differences in responses to erotica. While women were less willing than men to watch pornographic films, especially hard-core films, this was true only for men and women who were stereotypically sex-typed. That is, men with high masculinity scores on a sex-role inventory were especially likely to volunteer to see erotic films, while women with high femininity scores were especially unlikely. Those with more androgynous scores did not differ by gender. Such research gave women the mixed message that while it was good to be sexually assertive and easily aroused, feminine women did not do these things. They were unable to make demands.[16]

In a third group of studies, of the relationships between couples, female sexual response could be seen to depend on more than learning or practice. Some women had incompetent or insensitive partners. Like other surveys in the 1970s, studies of couples examined the relationship in terms of the benefit to each individual. Because of this, an assumption that mature adults would engage in serial relationships was common.[17] These surveys portrayed the sex drive as powerful and individual, a view consistent with Maslow's concept of the innate inner self. Some surveys undertaken by women accepted the human potential perspective but also revealed ways in which women saw things differently. Caroline Waterman and her associates, for example, correlated self-actualization with sexual pleasure, which they measured by counting orgasms. Low self-esteem did not hamper men, who all claimed orgasms whenever they had sex. But women with highly self-actualized male partners reported less sexual pleasure than did those whose partners had lower scores. As the researchers explained, "self-actualization sometimes involves high levels of self-centeredness."[18]

This finding highlighted an unacknowledged aspect of sexual liberation. The human potential movement assumed individuals would use their equal resources to obtain what they wanted. If women did not bargain as well as men, they should redress the balance by becoming more selfish. Yet, given gender inequities, men could use these arguments to justify getting their way. After all, they owed it to themselves and their psychological growth to do what they wanted without obligation to their partner. It was up to the partner to be self-actualized enough to demand her own pleasure. While most surveyors noted the difficulty women had with this, a few described successful women who coped with inadequate partners by having affairs.[19]

A decade earlier, when surveys had investigated who was having sex, questions on sexual behavior had been few and straightforward. Now, as they began to examine the actual activities couples engaged in, they needed ever more explicit questions. Revealing the results made even liberated researchers nervous. Specific acts disappeared from many accounts, replaced by scales intended to show that sexual activity and response were measured scientifically. Although scales had appeared in earlier sex surveys, their use exploded and their items became more sexually evocative in the 1970s and 1980s as psychologists dominated the discipline of sexology. Scales provided answers to sets of questions about whether respondents had ever engaged in various sexual acts, how often, whether they found them pleasant or unpleasant, and how they would respond to those acts they had not engaged in. For example, one of the rare studies of married couples involved testing a self-report inventory, the Sexual Interaction Inventory, designed to diagnose sexual problems among heterosexuals. It included explicit descriptions of the sexual acts listed on the more innocent Bentler scale, which had been developed to measure premarital sexual activity. Now respondents were asked to rate how much each act aroused them.[20]

Even surveys of couples that took a less individualistic perspective described the couple as consisting of two autonomous individuals, not two incomplete ones. One of the few large sex surveys of the 1970s not conducted by demographers was undertaken by Philip Blumstein and Pepper Schwartz of the University of Washington. As sociologists, the authors located their study in the tradition of marital adjustment surveys, modernized to include both gay and heterosexual couples who were living together.[21]

Blumstein and Schwartz were interested in social context, but their methodology undermined the value of this approach. Rather than using probability sampling they recruited respondents in a variety of ways.[22] Heterosexuals heard about the study quite differently from gay men and lesbians, resulting in noncomparable groups. The sample suffered from volunteer bias that overrepresented those more interested in sex and more tolerant of diversity. Such methodological weaknesses, common in smaller studies, were unusual in a large survey with federal and foundation funding. The researchers erroneously estimated their response rate to be 50 percent by using the ratio of those who filled out a questionnaire to all those who asked for one. The true response rate was much lower, since everyone invited to participate, including every viewer of the *Today Show,* was a potential respondent. The questionnaire raised additional concerns; for example, it used the undefined term "sexual relations," which probably had different meanings for heterosexual and gay respondents.

Blumstein and Schwartz took it for granted that the individuals' own needs were paramount in any relationship, but they also assumed that good relationships had a high level of sexual activity. Yet they also understood that sexual relationships exist in a social context. They were especially concerned with the unequal power of men and women, which they described as particularly marked among married couples, in which husbands usually initiated and wives had the right to refuse. Cohabiting heterosexual, lesbian, and gay male couples were all more egalitarian. Power even dictated sexual position; women with little power were subjected to intercourse "in the missionary position." But the researchers ignored other contexts. They reported, for example, that children made having sex more difficult and that disagreements over raising them had a negative impact on sex lives that husbands, in particular, did not like; but they did not consider whether parents found having children so rewarding that they were willing to temporarily sacrifice their sex lives somewhat.

Blumstein and Schwartz's book about their survey, *American Couples,* attracted media attention, and as a result the authors influenced the public's understanding of relationships in America and helped spread the idea that serially monogamous, egalitarian partnerships were becoming the norm. While they helped make gay and lesbian relationships seem more normal, they portrayed gay men as less monogamous than other groups; the only group in which less than half believed in monogamy.

By the end of the 1970s a counter-movement against sexual hedonism began to develop. It was focused on ambivalence about perceived changes in female sexuality away from modesty and reticence and toward sexual freedom. This change was spearheaded by the media, which had actively participated in creating and disseminating permissive ideas about sexual liberation but now began to raise questions. Attacks on sexual freedom came from two seemingly unrelated sources. Some groups in the women's movement believed that sexual liberation was a way of disguising as pleasure a long-standing oppression of women. And an attack on hedonism by conservatives received wide media attention. Surveys began to incorporate these themes.

Two books by conservatives published in the early 1970s provided ammunition for the attack: Midge Decter's *The New Chastity and Other Arguments against Women's Liberation* and George Gilder's *Sexual Suicide.* Decter charged feminism with encouraging the sexual downfall of women. Gilder agreed and, using sociobiology to repackage old ideas, asserted that whereas men were naturally sex-obsessed and promiscuous, women were not slaves to their libidos. They were civilization's caretakers, exchanging sexual favors for men's domestication and support of children. Both writers wanted to return to a mythical past in which sex occurred only within marriage for the purpose of reproduction. Anything else left women unhappy and society in ruins.

By the end of the 1970s these ideas began to infect political debates. Conservatives attacked unconventional lifestyles and ideologies, including gay liberation, sexual activity among the young, the *Playboy* mentality, women's liberation, unmarried pregnancy, and pornography. They increased public anxiety by selectively interpreting demographic evidence. Since young women no longer confined sexual activity to marriage, conservatives concluded that, encouraged by sexual libertarianism, young women had no guilt about having sex.

Conservatives blamed the women's movement for these changes. But many feminists were ambivalent about the effects of liberated sexuality on women. Some thought that although problems of female sexual response were a natural outcome of male-dominated sexual activity, sexual liberation still benefited women. Others disagreed, arguing that female sexual pleasure could not exist as long as men controlled women. Male-dominated sexuality actually harmed women; for example, pornography provoked men to abuse women.[23]

Both feminism and conservatism tempered the liberationist ideology of the 1970s, and while some surveys of the 1980s retained a permissive viewpoint, others signaled concern about the dangers of sex. Of major importance in setting the new tone were surveys documenting the incidence and effect of sexual abuse. Earlier surveys of sexual behavior had

assumed consent, although evidence that couples' sexual activity was sometimes coercive was not new. Eugene Kanin and his colleagues had reported
high rates of sexual assault in college students' dates during the 1950s.
Feminist concerns made such evidence harder to ignore. Kanin's data were
rediscovered in the late 1970s, when writers drew attention to rape in
general and date rape in particular as a danger of sexual freedom.[24]
Women's groups pushed prosecutors to change their handling of rape cases
and demanded the right to walk in safety with Take Back the Night marches
in American cities. Rape cases began to hit the national headlines, beginning with Joan Little's 1974 murder trial for killing a prison guard who tried
to rape her. This attention, greatly increased by the publicity surrounding
the 1982 gang rape at Big Dan's Tavern in New Bedford, Massachusetts,
caused prosecutors, ever mindful of the electorate, to take rape seriously.

In 1975 Congress established the National Center for the Prevention and
Control of Rape, located in the National Institute of Mental Health, and, in
the decade before it was dismantled, researchers completed more than
thirty surveys concerning sexual assault. These received wide attention, and
the media rarely questioned the surveyors' point of view. A depiction of sex
as dangerous and deviant sold papers. Some surveys focused on victims;
others were of perpetrators.

Among the most-cited studies were those of Mary Koss, who was instrumental in drawing attention to date rape. Koss received an early NIMH
grant to survey more than 2,000 college women and over 1,800 men using
a self-administered questionnaire. Acknowledging that rape was partly a
matter of definition, she divided her female respondents into four levels of
victimization: 13 percent, the "highly sexually victimized," were forced
against their will to engage in intercourse; 24 percent, the "moderately
sexually victimized," were subjected to forced fondling or attempted intercourse; 18 percent, the "low sexually victimized," engaged in undesired
sexual intercourse as a result of "extreme verbal coercion"; 38 percent were
"not sexually victimized" at all. (The remaining 8 percent had no sexual
experience.) These were Koss's definitions, not those of the victims. In fact,
almost half of the highly victimized did not define their experience as rape.
Few rape victims reported the incidents: of the highly victimized, only 8
percent went to the police, 13 percent to a rape crisis center, and half
discussed the experience with no one. And, in a finding with great implications for "normal" male/female relations, Koss found that most victims
knew the perpetrators. Koss tested several existing models of rape, all of
which suggested that the woman's behavior or personality precipitated the
attack, and concluded that there was little evidence of this. Instead, she

adopted a feminist position that rape victims were no different from non-victims. She saw rape as endemic in normal heterosexual relationships, and all women as in danger of being raped.[25]

With her portrayal of all women as equally at risk, Koss provided a way to understand rape and took the blame from the victim. However, she conveyed the idea that women could do nothing to prevent sexual assault, and her inclusion of verbal coercion as victimization told women to be wary of all sexual encounters. Answering yes to any of the following questions indicated that a woman was "sexually victimized":

- Have you ever:
- Had sexual intercourse with a man even though you didn't really want to because he threatened to end your relationship otherwise?
- Had sexual intercourse with a man when you didn't really want to because you felt pressured by his continual arguments?
- Found out that a man had obtained sexual intercourse with you by saying things that he didn't really mean?[26]

Koss's label implied that women had no choice in these situations. She might have asked why some women continued relationships with men who insisted on sex whenever they wanted or why so many agreed to unwanted sex when no force was threatened or implied. Koss could have interpreted the gray area between assault and full consent to the benefit of women everywhere. By labeling everything that was not fully consensual as sexual victimization, she missed this opportunity. Campus after campus adopted these oversimplifications, incorporating discussions, seminars, and films about date rape into student life. While this informed young women and men of the serious nature of the issue, it assumed that an improved sexual climate could be achieved by the teaching of definitions. It omitted serious discussion of relationships and the meaning of consent.

Koss's data analysis was flawed. Her numbers did not always total correctly, and she used multivariate analysis of variance, a procedure that assumes random samples, not convenience samples. But the most important shortcoming of her work was that she presented women as powerless. Koss asked the "highly victimized" how they defined the incident, and if the attack met the legal definition of rape she labeled women who did not so define it as mistaken. She did not give their reasons for defining it differently. Furthermore, she did not acknowledge that all women were not equally at risk of rape. There was no recognition that some women did put themselves in vulnerable situations. The issue needed discussion, especially if women who believed they had done this were reluctant to label the event rape. Certainly irresponsible or risk-taking behavior did not make women accomplices to sexual assault, but young women needed to learn how to lessen the possibility of sexual attack or harassment.

A 1990 study by the National Victim Center similarly estimated that 13 percent of women had been raped. Of these, 40 percent had been raped more than once. One-third of rapes had occurred before the victims were 11 years old, and only one-fifth had been perpetrated by strangers. These shocking numbers, presented in a glossy pamphlet, received a great deal of press attention. The *New York Times* reported the data along with Koss's comment that the numbers, like hers, were higher than the Justice Department's official ones. Yet this study contradicted the picture of all women as equally likely victims, since if this were so, only 13 percent of victims would have been raped more than once.[27]

While some researchers labeled all women as potential victims, others began to create a more complex picture. Their studies were also marred by problems of data quality, but their findings were worth verifying and understanding. For example, in F. Scott Christopher's interviews of undergraduate women at Arizona State, almost all said they had been pressured into unwanted sexual activity, in most cases involving persistent physical attempts but not physical force or threats. Most women stated that sexual pressure made a relationship worse. In a small survey of college women in New York State, Sarah Murnen and her associates also found high levels of unwanted sexual activity, mostly sexual intercourse. Many of her respondents felt responsible for the incidents, especially those who knew the man involved. These women seemed to consider men's desires more important than their own.[28]

If all women were potential rape victims, were all men potential rapists? Men did not escape the researchers' gaze. In 1985 Eugene Kanin published the results of a survey comparing "self-identified rapists" with men who said they did not commit rape. The rapists claimed more heterosexual experience, spent more time pursuing sexual activity, and were more exploitative in this pursuit. Kanin concluded that rapists lived in a world of aggressive sexuality. This idea was adopted by the best-known researcher on male sexual aggression, the psychologist Neil Malamuth, who argued that because of traditional sex roles and widespread misogyny in society a large proportion of men were potential rapists. In this scenario, the familiar portrayal of normal desire as urgent and insistent was problematic. He set out to demonstrate this in a series of studies in Canada and the United States.[29]

Malamuth described a substantial percentage of men as indicating that they would commit rape if they could get away with it.[30] These potential rapists fit the model of aggressive sexuality with "callous attitudes" about rape, identifying with rapists rather than victims when viewing depictions of rape, and believing other men would rape if they would not get caught. They were more likely to subscribe to myths about rape, such as "victims cause assaults and derive pleasure from them" or "women secretly desire and enjoy rape." Many potential rapists found depictions of rape arousing and said that actually raping someone would be arousing. They were also more aggressive toward women in general. Malamuth measured whether respondents might commit sexual assault by administering a five-point "Likelihood of Rape Scale." Over one-third indicated they would or might rape. Malamuth believed that cultural factors, especially pornographic depictions of rape showing victims who enjoyed being raped, encouraged these rape-prone men to act out their fantasies. These men tended to believe such images, since they confirmed their beliefs about women. Such depictions had increased during the liberationist 1970s. This contention was a further blow to heterosexual masculinity, which had long been seen as straightforward and not worthy of study. It now appeared that the most "normal" men had the worst problem. The men who most embodied the masculine values of aggressive sexuality were the most pathological.

Malamuth collected his data by exposing students to hypothetical situations. For example, he reported that most male undergraduates found stories in which rape victims became involuntarily aroused to be more exciting than ones where victims reacted with abhorrence. Men with high scores on the Likelihood of Rape Scale were more aroused than other men by the second type of story. He also found what he called an "educational effect." If respondents heard stories of victims reacting with abhorrence before other kinds of sex stories, they were less sexually aroused by the subsequent stories. Malamuth did not claim that pornography caused sexual aggression, only that it increased men's callous attitudes and hostility toward women and was a trigger for men already predisposed to rape.[31]

While Malamuth was engaged in this research, Koss was analyzing her data on men to see who would admit having committed sexual assault. She placed her male respondents in groups comparable to her four victim groups, but men did not report sexual assault as frequently as women did. Of the men admitting to an assault, none had faced legal repercussions. All had committed the assault in the context of a social relationship. Perpetrators did not differ from other men on psychological tests, although they held more beliefs that Koss saw as supportive of rape, such as believing rape myths or gender stereotypes. Koss supported the image of normal male sexuality as harmful with her conclusion that rapists differed from their peers only in their commitment to "the oversocialized masculine belief system."[32]

When Malamuth used Koss's questions to determine which men had sexually assaulted women, he found the assaulters similar to his potential rapists: aggressive toward women and sexually promiscuous. Ten years after beginning these studies Malamuth reinterviewed some of his male respondents and their current partners. Men who were sexually aggressive toward women while in college continued this pattern of behavior in later life, and hostile masculinity and sexual promiscuity remained the best predictors of this path. Malamuth believed that most perpetrators got away with rape. Since only fear of discovery deterred these men from acting out their desires, potential rapists could and would rape with impunity, and women were powerless to change this.

This research, with its new portrayal of male sexuality as problematic, presented a convincing picture of rapists, but it had problems. Readers could not judge the quality of the data collection and analysis. No information was provided about sampling techniques, little about interview schedules, and none about who had collected the data and how. The limited information available suggested that sample size was often too small for the number of independent variables. Malamuth typically used regression analysis, a technique that requires random samples, something he did not apparently use. His predictor variables correlated highly with one another, creating uncertainty as to whether each actually measured a different attribute. Since he measured attitudes and beliefs at the same time, Malamuth could not show cause and effect, only that certain attitudes were associated. Finally, he told readers nothing about the men's backgrounds, unintentionally supporting the idea that some men just naturally had uncontrollable sexual proclivities. Apart from the trigger of pornography, he did not explain why some men became potential rapists when others did not. Nor did the many other psychologists who conducted similar surveys.[33]

Koss and her associates finally undertook a large survey of students across the country using probability sampling. This produced rape data of a higher quality than any up to this point. More than one-quarter of women reported having been victimized by behavior meeting legal definitions of rape or attempted rape. Only 8 percent of men reported perpetrating such an act.[34] Similarly, over half the women acknowledged some sexual victimization, but only one-quarter of the men confessed to any comparable activities. Koss assumed that the discrepancy resulted from men's lies and

denial, but at least some of it might have been caused by different definitions of coercion. The importance of definitional problems is exemplified
in the few surveys delineating men's experiences as victims of women's
rapacious sexual desires. In these, almost as many men as women received
unwanted sexual demands, although the men were rarely victims of physical force and were not usually traumatized by the event unless the initiator
was male.[35] This type of research trivialized the serious issue of sexual
assault and its causes. But part of the problem lay in definitions. No survey
included questions that would make it possible to unravel tangled issues of
consent and power.

Rape was not the only sexual danger surveyed during the 1980s. Some
researchers located sexual abuse in families whose members or friends
perpetrated it against unprotected children.[36] They described such behavior
as rampant. These experiences were not confined to women, but, again,
men were less likely to find them traumatic. Men, it seemed, almost never
had the same problems women had. Even though these surveyors varied in
how negatively they portrayed childhood sexual experiences, their portrayal
of out-of-control sex and inappropriate objects of desire supported the
arguments of writers on the right.

By the 1980s even sexologists writing on less inflammatory topics began
to retreat from their liberationist stance. Their goal of releasing sexuality
from societal repression had seemed achievable during the 1970s. Now a
conservative counter-attack, which demanded a return to repression, made
many of them nervous. Some researchers began to hold families responsible
for the sexual behavior of their children, claiming, for example, that "young
adolescents from intact families are consistently less likely to report substance use and sexual intercourse." Surveyors found irresponsible families
to be numerous. In one study one-third of the mothers and over half the
fathers did not know their children's level of sexual experience. It seemed
the sexual revolution had gone too far, encouraged by neglectful, tired, or
overly permissive parents. Such ideas were underscored by writers decrying
the preponderance of students who chose role models from the media
rather than their parents, or reporting that most students preferred to
marry, and even to date, sexually inexperienced partners.[37]

In addition to this conservative trend, new scholarly work began to have
an impact on surveys, work that questioned many of the assumptions of
liberationist sexology. Pro-sex feminist scholars, social scientists influenced
by John Gagnon and William Simon's theory of sexual scripts, and gay and
lesbian scholars all argued that sexual desires and behaviors were produced
within society, not in opposition to it. If women were less responsive than

men, this was not because society repressed their innate sexual desires but because men and women in a particular society created different sexual personas. These researchers recognized that one had to study sexuality in a social and historical context.

In the 1970s the government, usually NIMH, had funded a few sexological surveys, but in the more conservative 1980s research funds were restricted to surveys about the dangers of sex, especially AIDS, and to studies with a more traditional bent. Researchers with federal funding achieved a higher quality of research design, and some even used probability samples, which, aside from fertility surveys, had been rare in sex research. Often these surveys considered social context to a greater extent than in the previous decade. Lynn White and Bruce Keith, in a survey funded by the National Institute on Aging and based on a probability sample of over 2,000 married persons, demonstrated that shift work increased married couples' sexual problems "because the sexual aspects of marriage may be particularly vulnerable to different work and sleeping schedules." This acknowledgment that sexual pleasure might be more affected by one's life than by one's individual predispositions also appeared in a 1984 study of sexual dysfunction; Patricia Morokoff and Ruth Gillilland found that unemployed men had more problems with achieving and maintaining erections than employed men. Similarly, Cathy Greenblat, using random sampling techniques in a 1981 NIMH-funded study, found that the long-accepted decline in couples' sexual activity over time was more a function of children, work, and exhaustion than of a declining male libido. Respondents were not concerned about this decline, because they had other ways to express their feelings.[38]

With this inclusion of the social context, gender became an important explanatory variable. Lillian Rubin studied married couples of all social classes and found that women used emotional attachment to create sexual desire but men did the opposite. These sociological studies were influenced by the liberationist research of the 1970s but recognized the complex forces shaping sexual relationships. Some researchers, for example, acknowledged that marital sex was not always the most rewarding, an admission rarely made before 1970. Using data from the NICHD-funded National Survey of Families and Households, a probability sample of over 13,000 couples undertaken at the University of Wisconsin, Denise Donnelly examined the 16 percent of marriages in which the couples had not had sex in the previous month. These couples had higher than average levels of marital problems but lower than average disagreements about sex.[39]

In the post–Masters and Johnson world, interest in sexual technique as a solution for marital problems was still strong. Sometimes an emphasis on technique served conservative purposes. The sex therapist Edward Eichel trained monogamous married couples in his "coital alignment" techniques. He then interviewed the couples and claimed a rise in simultaneous orgasm while in the missionary position. In spite of increased caution, many studies stayed firmly within the self-actualizing tradition and provided even more explicit guidelines for an improved erotic life. In these studies non-monogamous relationships during courtship were common and those engaging in them thought them not particularly harmful; persons with high levels of physical activity wanted and had more sex; and people with low levels of guilt had fewer sexual problems and more kinky sex fantasies.[40]

And researchers continued to use scales to render their increasingly explicit surveys scientific and therefore neutral. A scale developed by Paula Nurius and Walter Hudson illustrates the lengths to which serious scientists would go in their search for sexual understanding. Their scale contained seventy-eight descriptions of what students currently did and/or would like to do. Items on the list had the tone of soft-core pornography:

- I rub my penis around the lips of a woman's vagina until I become very sexually excited.
- I slide my penis in and out of a woman's vagina very gently until I become very sexually excited.
- I rub a man's penis around the lips of my vagina and clitoris until I come.
- I become sexually aroused when I cover a man's penis with my vagina.[41]

Virtually all the items concerned the genitalia. Volunteers were told to read the questionnaire before agreeing to participate, probably because the researchers feared many would find the survey offensive. Its publication in the *Journal of Sex Research* in 1988 testified to the persisting enthusiasm of scientific sexology for liberating Americans from their sexual hangups, even in the face of increasingly hostile opposition to this agenda.

By the 1980s surveys of the unmarried usually assumed that sexual activity would take place early and often. And in spite of the more nuanced understanding of gender and sexuality in feminist and gay writing, gender was still the ultimate explanation for sexual difference. In spite of the convergence in men's and women's behavior, these surveys reported no convergence in motive. Men wanted sex for pleasure and physical release whereas women sought love and emotional commitment, and men still sought sexual experiences without commitment while women tried to avoid sex until they obtained love. Furthermore, although most men were satisfied with their relationships, "men desired to a greater degree than women that their partner be more rough, more experimental, more willing to engage in fast, impulsive sex, initiate more sex, play the dominant role in sex more, talk more dirty during sex, be more wild and sexy, be more variable in where sex is had, give more instructions, and be more willing to do what 'I want.'"[42]

Women continued to fall short of experts' hopes, and interest in female sexual response persisted. But it would have been difficult for any woman to learn from the results of surveys. Clarity was sacrificed to scientific pretension in such statements as "Sexual Daydreaming Scale values were obtained from 12 items of the retrospective 344-item Imaginal Processes Inventory," and "utilized in this study was the Sexual Arousability Inventory, a Likert-type scale designed to measure self-reported sexual arousal in women."[43]

Orgasm remained the premier goal of sexual liberation, and in this women still failed. Most researchers posited a female sexuality that was problematic but curable in those with a good attitude and a willingness to practice. These surveys largely ignored external factors such as incompetent partners, power differentials, or past socialization as explanations for women's continued inability to achieve orgasm easily. Women and their bodies were the problem and were subjected to obsessive scrutiny only limited by authors' imaginations. And the women of interest were young. The sexuality of old women was invisible even though old men were seen as in need of help.[44]

Among the often contradictory "discoveries" about young women in surveys of the 1980s were these:

1. Experience increased the likelihood of orgasm during intercourse.[45]

2. Women who had infrequent orgasms blamed themselves for this perceived failure and did not take credit for the times they succeeded, while those who were more frequently orgasmic took personal credit for this and did not blame themselves for occasionally failing to reach orgasm.[46]

3. Sexual fantasizing neither improved nor harmed a woman's satisfaction with her current sex life.[47]

4. Sexual fantasies increased sexual satisfaction.[48]

5. Sexually experienced women "with strong sex drives" read erotic romances to enhance their pleasure.[49]

6. Pain at first intercourse might be "endorphin mediated," so women who were happy rather than guilty the first time should experience little pain.[50]

7. Swedish women had far fewer negative reactions to their first intercourse than American women.[51]

8. Women who were easily carried away by hypnotic suggestion or drinking alcohol were more likely to have frequent coital orgasms.[52]

9. Moderate drinkers reported less problem with orgasm than heavy drinkers or women who rarely drank.[53]

10. Women with physical disabilities tended to be less satisfied with their sex lives.[54]

11. While nocturnal orgasm might have a biological basis, cultural factors like sexual liberalism influenced frequency.[55]

12. Those mature enough to be concerned with others had more interest in interpersonal sexual activity.[56]

13. Women who were "oriented to" law and order felt more guilt about their sex lives than those who were at the higher "social contract" stage of moral reasoning.[57]

14. Women who had had several partners were more likely to experience orgasm before their partner ejaculated.[58]

15. "The earlier that the respondents became aware of the existence of female ejaculation, the greater the likelihood that they had experienced ejaculation."[59]

By the end of the 1980s the human potential movement and the related sexual liberation movement were confronted with a paradox. The right to pursue one's own interests even at the expense of others was reasserting itself in political and economic life as anti-tax and anti-welfare sentiments swept the country. Yet the apostles of this view blamed "the sexual liberation crowd" for all or most of America's ills and argued that the government must regulate the sexual activities of consenting individuals. In spite of this official disapproval, interest in sexual matters was unabated in almost all sectors of American society. As Lillian Rubin concluded in *Erotic Wars*:

It makes no difference whether or not we personally experience our sex lives as deficient. We find ourselves grappling with a set of impossible expectations, with some standard "out there" against which we measure ourselves. For we live now with a new sexual dogma that allows for as little deviation as the old one did, one that calls us to a relentless preoccupation with the content and quality of our sexual interactions. Paradoxically, our absorption with what's wrong and how to fix it creates its own problems. And sex becomes another issue that needs time and attention, another obstacle to be overcome, instead of a time out for gratification and pleasure.[60]

Because sexologists feared being charged with prurience, they cloaked their explicit research in obscure language and supposedly scientific terms. To alleviate the problems Rubin described, the public had to look elsewhere.

7

Excising the Experts

From studying the numbers we learn that, no matter whether we make love once a day or once a year, there are other women like ourselves.

—*Cosmopolitan*, 1988

D URING the 1970s and 1980s public interest in sexual behavior intensified. Sex research remained firmly in experts' hands, and their jargon, complicated data analyses, and publication in professional journals made their findings inaccessible to general readers. And readers wanted answers to questions rarely asked in academic surveys: how others felt about sex, whether they were fulfilled sexually, whether they had "good sex lives." The media had delivered the human potential movement's messages that Americans had the right to a vibrant sex life and that women should be as satisfied as men. But it was unclear what these messages meant. How were readers to know if their sex lives were vibrant? Magazines and books began to fill this information gap by presenting readers' own descriptions of their sexual activity. These allayed anxiety by conveying the message that Americans were sexually up to par. In contrast to academic surveys, such commercial surveys were easy to understand and exciting to read. Their audiences could learn directly from people like themselves without struggling through an expert's translation. At least it seemed that way. With their use of ordinary voices, commercial surveys appeared as the unvarnished truth not distorted by the expert. But they lacked most of the safeguards of survey research, from random sampling to pretested questionnaires.

Commercial sex surveys originated in the 1960s, and from the beginning they strove for maximum appeal by combining entertainment and encouragement. Most concentrated on women, since, not surprisingly, women seemed to be the group most worried about their sex lives. The first commercial survey, Gael Greene's *Sex and the College Girl,* published in 1964, posed the titillating question of what young women were *really* doing on campus. Greene visited 102 colleges and interviewed young women along with the occasional young man. Although she did not specifically ask about behavior, concentrating on the safer topics of attitudes and beliefs, many respondents "told all" anyway. Greene presented herself as a teller of truth: "At first I was uncertain how to get at this truth—what sort of language to use with teenage girls who showed up in response to an unexpected phone call from 'A Miss So-and-So who says she's writing a book' . . . Often by mid-interview the gloves were torn to shreds, four-letter words were flying freely . . . They answered my questions freely, with sometimes painful frankness." Respondents' actual words gave Greene's work authenticity. At the same time, she delivered the report in a tongue-in-cheek style that conveyed her irreverence toward the project. She described female students at an urban commuter campus, for example, as "all sexy packaging, but the rule is—no free samples."[1]

College women could be sexually active and a little wild, but when teenagers were the subject, entertainment took a back seat to proselytizing. In 1967 *Seventeen* magazine fielded a survey of the sexual behavior and attitudes of teenage girls. To avoid the stigma that might result from describing actual readers, especially if they confessed to sexual experience, the editors chose not to publish the questionnaire in the magazine. They mailed it to 2,000 teenage girls, giving no information about how they obtained the names, and 1,500 responded. This assured readers' parents that sexually active teenagers were part of the generic group "teens" but not readers of *Seventeen* like their own daughters.

The magazine showed its seriousness about the issue by presenting the survey results in the form of a sermon to young readers: "You've seen the statistics: one in six teen-age girls is pregnant when she marries; over 100,000 teens bear illegitimate babies each year; a shocking 200,000 have criminal abortions. You've heard the worried talk: young people are rejecting society's ethical standards; sexual experimentation is rampant in our high schools."[2] Alice Lake, the author of the article, noted that those who responded to the questionnaire were eager for more knowledge about "birth control, sexual intercourse, sex drive." A small but significant minority were sexually active; 15 percent were no longer virgins, and this number was increasing. But Lake told readers that most teens were not like this. Three-quarters of respondents disapproved of sex before marriage, and those who approved tended to be older and to approve only for engaged couples. Furthermore, many of those who had engaged in sexual intercourse had had serious doubts afterward. *Seventeen*'s young readers could go on being good girls without fear of being out of step.

It was not until 1969 that *Psychology Today* invented the readership sex survey that became the model for subsequent commercial sex surveys.[3] By publishing first the questionnaire and later the results in the magazine, it created respondents from its audience. Whereas most academic researchers did not publish their questionnaires even as they slowly adopted other tenets of good survey practice, the commercial surveyors, who violated most of those tenets, did publish their questionnaires. This technique produced a sample as large as Kinsey's with little effort. Even though 92 percent of *Psychology Today*'s readers did not return a completed questionnaire, many would have read it and thought about their answers. They could compare their putative answers with those of actual respondents. Finally, the large number of respondents (20,000) gave a false impression of representativeness and of scientific fact.

The survey enhanced its scientific aura by using two survey experts from the University of Michigan, Robert Athanasiou and Phillip Shaver, to write the questionnaire and analyze the data. Then the psychologist and writer Carol Tavris produced a reader-friendly report. She and her colleagues placed quotations in boxes beside the many numeric facts in the text to illustrate their points. This presentation of the facts in respondents' voices became typical of commercial sex surveys. Their rationale for undertaking the survey was familiar to sex research aficionados:

Hoggamous, higgamous, men are polygamous.
Higgamous, hoggamous, women monogamous.
  We know that this brilliant summation of the state of the sexes has held true for many years. Would it be true, we wondered, of young, well-educated, fairly high income people? Or would a group of self-defined sexual liberals really reflect major changes in the sexual behavior of men and women?

Psychology Today set the standard for other reader-response surveys by presenting its subject seriously while simultaneously titillating audiences. Sex surveys were designed to sell magazines, and readers of this survey were treated to an article bluntly entitled "Sex." To the right of the headline was a quotation from a self-actualized, pro-sex woman who must have delighted male readers and who provided a role model for female readers: "All my life, dear sir, I have, I think, been a kind of Slinky Toy female emotionally . . . going from loving step to loving step, one at a time, in relationships with men. I love them all, and I mean this, and were I to be exiled to a desert island anywhere, I'd take four or five along with thousands of books, swim fins, and no other women at all."[4]

The twenty-eight boxed quotations throughout the text painted a varied picture, but none was as strikingly libidinal as this first quotation. Most came from women. Although women seemed to be "inching closer" to men in their behavior and standards, the authors concluded that men were more permissive than women, a finding similar to those of academic researchers. Women had been the major audience for sexual and other self-improvement advice throughout the twentieth century. They remained the gender with the malfunctioning libido.

During the 1970s, as sexological surveys increased in number, commercial sex surveys became a fixture of magazines and books. Designed as moneymakers, they responded to readers' interests, and their themes provide insight into what these were. Three approaches predominated. One type of survey, often written with men in mind, exposed the sexual practices of the liberated to provide voyeuristic thrills for the older or less daring. These surveys both entertained and reassured audiences about their own sexual prowess and sophistication. A second more serious type expressed concern about the behavior of teenagers, although here too explicit content increased sales. The third and largest group, reader-response surveys, were designed to tell readers what people like them did sexually. Most of these were published in the magazines that advise women on many aspects of their lives, which have no male counterparts. And there were books in the same genre. This type of survey also entertained by describing some lives that were wilder than the typical reader's. Even surveys of men's behavior seemed to be written for women.

In spite of the ambivalence of experts, the American public believed there had been a sexual revolution and that the sexually liberated were to be found on college campuses. The media reinforced this by presenting American campuses as places where students got stoned, listened to rock music, and engaged in wild, uninhibited sex. Sexologists in academic journals provided the media with sympathetic accounts of the changing sexual activity of students, but public attitudes toward college students combined anger and envy. Magazines like *Playboy* picked up on those feelings. *Playboy* portrayed college men as no longer restrained in their natural raunchiness by coeds but as surrounded by female lust. In 1970

Playboy published a survey of nearly 200 campuses that underscored these stereotypes:

> An image of the seventies student as a freaky radical haunts the American mind: His hair is down to his shoulders and there's a psychedelic gleam in his eye as he tosses a tear-gas canister back at a thick olive line of Guardsmen protecting the R.O.T.C. Building. After the confrontation, he splits for an apartment where he spouts Ché and Mao, smokes dope and then tears off his clothes and leaps into a tangled erotic pile. Later, he wearily plans the revolution—to overthrow mom, the flag, Agnew, and apple pie—while the Jefferson Airplane sings "Up Against the Wall, Motherfucker."[5]

Playboy's success lay in its ability to convince Caspar Milquetoast that he was really Don Juan and, thus, more interested in overthrowing sexual mores than the government. The magazine concluded that, except for the issue of Vietnam, students were quite politically conservative, and that hedonism reigned. Students were more sexually permissive than in Kinsey's day: four-fifths of the men and over half the women had engaged in premarital intercourse. Almost half described marijuana use; these were more likely to have had sexual intercourse, and they did so more often. A year later, when *Playboy* repeated its survey, things were looking up. The nation's campuses were quieter, use of marijuana and other drugs was increasing, and women's rates of sexual activity were catching up with men's.[6]

In 1976 *Playboy* undertook a third survey. This included fewer questions on politics and many more about students' sexual activities. The introduction showed the change in emphasis. It also signaled a spoiler of fun emerging on the horizon:

> For the past few years, we've been hearing disturbing rumors that all's quiet on the college front. According to most sources, the sexual revolution had ground to a halt; the battle between the sexes had declined into a cold war in which virginity and lesbianism were the weapons of choice . . . Here is the harsh truth we found: It is actually possible to go through four years of higher education without getting laid, though why you'd want to is beyond us. Fortunately, the odds are against it. What makes it so hard to go through school unscathed is the coeds. In 1970, about 49% of female students graduated with more than their brains intact. The figure has fallen to 26% in 1976. At the same time, the percentage of male virgins has gone up from 18% in 1970 to 26% in 1976. This magical equality of percentages means that students have arrived at that promised land—a sexual utopia where the women are just as active sexually as the men.

Playboy never questioned the existence of universal sexual adventurism on the part of men. And, lest the reader wonder about the 1970 disparity in male and female rates of virginity, *Playboy* hypothesized the existence of "a few overworked cooperative ladies." Since 1970, just as their elders feared, most good girls had begun to turn bad, a trend *Playboy* strongly endorsed. The magazine smirked at students' behavior and suggested that readers would behave in the same way if they had the opportunity. The 1976 questions were printed in the magazine and covered a range of topics including "What turns you on? Masturbation; oral sex; anal intercourse; mechanical aids; being tied up or chained in sex play; master-slave role playing; inflicting or receiving pain during sex?"[7]

Surveys of adolescents needed a different stance. Although college students seemed old enough to look after themselves, younger teens required protection and jokes would be unseemly. The solemnity of the *Seventeen* survey remained in commercial studies of younger teens in the 1970s, but the attitude became more permissive. Kantner and Zelnik's well-publicized studies of adolescent sexual and reproductive behavior worried parents, and two books responded to such fears by describing what young people of both sexes were doing. Yet they simultaneously comforted the young that their desires and behaviors were perfectly normal.

In the first, Robert Sorensen reported on questionnaires and interviews from young people all over the United States in a 1973 book intended to help parents "open up communications with their children about sex and love which have been lost to a multitude of families in recent years."[8] By reading his book parents could hear about their children's sex lives, in words their children might use, without having to actually talk to them. New York's Episcopal bishop Paul Moore Jr. set a tone of liberal sympathy in the introduction. Sorensen's survey, he said, showed that teens rarely exploited one another. To underscore this sensitivity, the survey contained hundreds of opinion questions about feelings of being understood, sexual values, and pleasure in sexual activity. This was information demographers did not provide. Interspersed with these were explicit questions about behavior: masturbation, heterosexual and homosexual intercourse, birth control, and various types of petting.

Sorensen spoke to youth as well as to parents. He never moralized, and he provided authentic-sounding insights:

> For most boys first sexual intercourse assumes its greatest significance before it happens. Boys have strong anticipations of physical pleasure; many boys anticipate that their status and self-esteem will be increased by

their first sex act . . . The usual adolescent girl does not anticipate her first sexual intercourse as an isolated experience. Few girls doubt they will have it; but they seem to fantasize about it in advance less often than boys . . . Once she has had her first sexual intercourse, a girl often feels different about herself—not deprived or bereft of her virginity, but different *within* herself.[9]

Thus the book described sexual activity as an important developmental stage. It was natural for the young to have strong desires and to need love. Young people were fortunate when their families were understanding rather than repressive. At the same time, Sorensen provided explicit and titillating descriptions of teen sex. He walked a fine line between education and reassurance on one side and prurience and exploitation on the other. The need to show concern while exploiting the commercial possibilities of sex was nowhere more apparent than in surveys of the young.

Aaron Hass, whose book *Teenage Sexuality* was published in 1979, walked an even finer line. Hass described parents as desperate to know what their teens were going through, yet unable to talk to them. Yet he also addressed the needs of youth: "One of the most common questions that adults have about their sexuality is 'Am I normal?' . . . In recent years there has been a great deal published about adult female and male sexuality . . . Until now, teenagers have not had a similar avenue to which they could turn for information or relief." To provide this information, Hass asked even more explicit questions than Sorensen's, worded to educate teens that normal people participated in such behaviors. For example, he asked students to complete the sentence "If I went out with a boy I would want him to kiss my vagina . . ." by choosing from a list of options ranging from "on a first or second date" to "only if we were married." By not making "never" an option, Hass showed that he too understood his survey's commercial possibilities. Still, he noted that many teens felt pressured into sex and did not enjoy it, thus letting such teens know they were not alone.[10]

While adults had concerns about teenagers, they were more anxious about themselves. Some of the best-known reader-response surveys of the 1970s dealt with this anxiety. These included Morton Hunt's *Sexual Behavior in the 1970's*, commissioned by *Playboy*, and Shere Hite's *The Hite Report: A Nationwide Study on Female Sexuality*. Hunt was a freelance writer specializing in love, sex, and relationships. He described himself as someone who "grew up with an immense curiosity about all those forbidden topics" as a result of "prim and proper parents." Unlike other authors of commercial sex surveys, Hunt paid attention to data collection. He gave his study academic legitimacy by citing academic experts. Yet his interview techniques violated the survey rule that interviewers should not lead respondents in particular directions: "I would sometimes offer a little bit of myself . . . by saying 'I know how you feel, I had a period when I was single in my early forties and went through many of the same experiences.' Nothing more detailed than that, but just so they knew that I was not somebody sitting judgementally far above them." To give each reader someone with whom to identify, most of the book recounted individual sexual histories and desires that illustrated a range of options. Many of these narratives informed readers that their own sexual experiments or desires were normal, while accounts of exceptionally daring, exciting, and wild sexual lifestyles hinted at a world of endless sexual potential beyond.[11]

Hunt concluded that profound changes had taken place in sexual attitudes and behavior. Americans, he said, were increasingly interested in using sex to express their feelings. Using Kinsey's findings as a basis of comparison, he told readers that normal people like themselves were becoming permissive about all aspects of sexuality and were willing to try a variety of acts that were "biologically and psychologically free from pathology." Even so, most regarded sexual activity as having profound emotional importance in their own lives. Hunt's opinions of people's lifestyles were clear from the terms he used for them: uptights, swingers, and liberals. He saw the liberal pattern as ascendant and gave readers the message that this was the pattern they should follow.

Although the sexual message was explicit, the social message was conservative and resolutely heterosexual. Homosexuality was chosen "only by persons of special needs." These needs ranged "from the purely situational (. . . the homosexuality of prisoners) to the unmistakably neurotic (. . . the homosexuality of the 'mama's boy')."[12] Hunt explained his belief that there had been no sexual revolution by postulating that most Americans wanted love and marriage. The only change was that they wanted a wild sex life behind closed doors, and this, Hunt asserted, many already had. This socially conservative message made his writing safe even while it titillated.

Hunt was at his most conservative in writing about women. In his view, truly liberated women had their most satisfying and regular orgasms during intercourse. For Hunt, as for his sponsor *Playboy,* the women's movement was the enemy of sexual bliss: "Many of the shriller voices in the women's-liberation movement portray married intercourse as male-chauvinist exploitation of the female body, with husbands being clumsy, hasty, brutal and selfish, and making no effort to delight or satisfy their wives, let alone consider, in the first place, whether their wives wish to be made love to . . .

But our survey data appear to contradict this picture of contemporary married sex."[13] By the time of Hunt's study *Playboy* had been the target of protests by women's groups across the country and had struck back vigorously. The feminist critique of marriage was not one with which the magazine sympathized. After all, most of its male readers were, or would be, married, and, as *Playboy* understood, they wanted to believe that it was women who most benefited from marriage.

Hunt was right to fear unsympathetic feminists. Even as he wrote, an active member of the National Organization for Women, Shere Hite, was collecting her own data. Most surveys told women that they were on their way to becoming sexually fulfilled, but Hite took issue with this. Most sex surveys had been done by men, she said, and nobody had asked women the right questions. She wanted "women to be the experts and to say what female sexuality was all about."[14] Hite sent questionnaires to consciousness-raising, abortion rights, and other women's groups and advertised for respondents in newspapers and magazines, including *Ms., Mademoiselle,* and *Brides.* Out of 100,000 questionnaires distributed, she received over 3,000 responses, a response rate, she claimed, that was standard for surveys of this type.

Hite's questionnaire was hard to complete. Each question contained multiple sub-questions, an elementary mistake in design. She did not introduce her delicate subject carefully but began abruptly with numerous questions about orgasm. Some required detailed responses. Others asked for imaginative projections that would be difficult for many respondents. Yet others asked for seemingly impossible details from past events:

- Do you have orgasms? If not, what do you think would contribute to your having them?

- Do you always have orgasms during the following (please indicate whether always, usually, sometimes, rarely, or never):
  masturbation
  intercourse (vaginal penetration)
  manual clitoral stimulation by a partner
  oral stimulation by a partner
  intercourse plus manual clitoral stimulation
  never have orgasms

- Also indicate above how many orgasms you usually have during each activity, and how long you usually take. Space for comments if desired:

- Please give a graphic description of how your body could best be stimulated to orgasm.

Quoting women's responses, Hite organized her results around themes. She started with masturbation "to show that women can orgasm easily." She defended her use of orgasm as the measure of female pleasure: "It's the cultural institution of what we think of as sex that means that most women don't regularly orgasm easily with their partners. If women can orgasm easily during masturbation, then that should be included in whatever we call sex."[15]

In contrast to Hunt, Hite portrayed sexual intercourse as unsatisfying to women. Many women said they never had orgasms during intercourse, and Hite, like male experts, assumed lack of an orgasm meant lack of sexual pleasure. In rapid succession Hite introduced readers to respondents' complaints about never finding a man with whom they enjoyed intercourse, respondents' admissions of faking orgasm, and their rare descriptions of achieving orgasms during coitus. Even here there were problems:

- The problem here is that both positions [I prefer] he finds uncomfortable and appears to accommodate me resentfully and passively.

- On top I prefer the man not to move at all but they simply don't pay attention and move anyway.

- Most men do "harder" too hard.

Not only was intercourse less satisfying than masturbation but men's basic technique of thrusting was all wrong, said Hite. She blamed the sorry state of female sexual pleasure on patriarchal societies, such as the United States, that glorified intercourse. She and her readers agreed that *Playboy* exemplified this, with readers stating "sometimes I think if I see another *Playboy* spread on sex in the movies I'll scream" or "if the crap in *Playboy* or *Penthouse* is anybody's idea of a sexual revolution then it's revolting all right." To make matters worse, Hite argued, male experts in *Playboy* and elsewhere caused women to blame themselves for not having orgasms during the great event.[16]

These were fighting words. When Hite's book appeared in 1976 she had no idea what to expect from the media. Responses varied. Some feminists praised the book. The novelist Erica Jong enthusiastically reviewed it for the *New York Times*. Jong agreed that men were usually the ones to describe how women felt. She also agreed that men regarded women's sexuality as a problem. She marveled at the book's detailed technical information on female sexual response, and she accepted the book's findings at face value.

Many academic feminists, in contrast, were uncomfortable with both Hite's methodology and her message. Although she purported to demonstrate the radical idea that sexuality was culturally, not biologically, pro-duced, they felt she reduced the problem to mean, incompetent, selfish men and a hesitancy to discover masturbation. On the latter point, the historian Linda Gordon commented in a review, the book "suggests that sexual ecstasy is within our grasp, and that only our hang-ups keep us from attaining it."[17] Another weakness of Hite's study, for writers like Gordon, was its orientation toward young, attractive, autonomous career women who were unencumbered by children and focused on pleasure. These women could purchase the vibrators, read the text, and undergo the self-improvement necessary for one-person sexual bliss. Women whose finan-cial survival depended on pleasing a mate could read a five-page treatise on "economics." Even here, Hite's naive solution was for readers to under-stand that they were free to explore their own sexuality, to learn whatever they wanted, and to do what they liked sexually.

In spite of such reservations, Hite's book was on the bestseller list for a number of weeks. Where other writers told women that sex was getting better and better, Hite questioned this. She told women that their sex lives were not so good, and that it was not their fault. Hite's work was poor methodologically, but her message coincided with many women's experi-ences. She described a reality they could recognize. Even though she did little to place sex in a broader social context or to explain why women felt sexually restrained, she made them feel better. Furthermore, the victim role was comforting to many women. Hite did not hold them accountable for working hard to please men, for being more interested in their partners' pleasure than their own, or for accepting unsatisfactory sexual relationships rather than risk being alone.

Hite's message may have touched a chord with many women, but it disturbed those in the media who wanted to encourage women to think that sexual bliss with a partner could be theirs. *Redbook,* a magazine for young married women, distributed a survey to its readers and produced a different picture. Carol Tavris, who had worked on the *Psychology Today* report, and Susan Sadd summarized the findings in a *Redbook* article and in a book. They explicitly compared their study population to Hite's, noting that theirs was undoubtedly more traditional. Where Hite had specifically dis-avowed experts, *Redbook* hired a sociologist, Robert Bell, to write the ques-tionnaire. Tavris and Sadd exulted in the large number who responded (100,000), which they declared to be unprecedented in sex research.

Tavris and Sadd, with insight rare among survey authors, acknowledged that readers wanted to know if their desires or their sexual habits were similar to those of others and therefore normal and permissible. The authors were nonetheless surprised at the large number of respondents who stated this explicitly. Others wrote that they had used the survey to begin a discussion with their husbands, or at least that they would try to do so. Thus Tavris and Sadd were conscious of the sex survey's power to create as well as reflect normality.

Even so, Tavris and Sadd presented their good news as if their survey had no impact on its results. They implicitly criticized Hite by complaining, "These days we hear more about the problems of sex than about its pleasures."[18] They assured their audience that most *Redbook* wives enjoyed marital sex and continued to find sexual happiness as they aged or entered the labor force. The typical wife was more likely to complain about too little sexual intercourse (38 percent of respondents) rather than too much (4 percent). And sex was getting better. Well under half of Kinsey's female respondents easily experienced orgasms. By the time of Hunt's survey this figure had grown to just over half. Among *Redbook*'s respondents, 63 percent reported that the happy event occurred always or almost always. It looked as if the problem of female orgasm might soon be over. And it seemed the cure was easy: "since I've stopped worrying about all this I've had more orgasm during intercourse, sometimes with no foreplay at all." This woman added tellingly, "When I thought I was abnormal, I never had any."

Hite had described female orgasm during intercourse as a difficult trick and one hindered by men. Tavris and Sadd took the more heartening position that men were women's allies in the pursuit of sexual pleasure. They thanked the "100,000 silent husbands" who were "an invisible testimonial to the strength of the sexual bond between women and men."[19] This echoed the findings of Hunt, whom Tavris and Sadd cited more frequently than they did Hite. This unlikely coalition between a magazine for married women and the *Playboy* empire reflected the overwhelmingly heterosexual impulse of both. *Playboy* approved of marital sex as long as it included variety. *Redbook* told readers that marriage was the center of women's lives, but that these days everyone had sex before marriage, which was good because it improved marriage. In this view, the sexual revolution encouraged new sexual appetites and freedoms, ensuring that husbands and wives would not grow tired of each other.

Shere Hite was not so easily dismissed. Her book on female sexuality outsold all the other sex surveys combined, and she quickly followed it with *The Hite Report on Male Sexuality*, a book consisting almost exclusively of quotations from her survey of men. She decided to let men "speak for themselves" with less commentary than in the first book because, as a woman, she could "speak for women but not for men." She believed quoting the respondents this way meant that the data were not mediated through the writer's cultural lens, a view common in commercial sex surveys. She did not acknowledge that selecting quotations and organizing the themes was an interpretive process: that with so much data from which to choose, she might easily choose those representing her own biases.

Hite also directed men's responses through her questions. Where other surveys portrayed women moving closer to men in attitude, Hite assumed that men and women not only differed almost entirely but strongly identified with their own gender. Since she used different questionnaires for men and women it was impossible for the sexes to make similar responses. For example, she did not ask women if they could respond emotionally because she assumed they did. But she explored the issue with men in a way that produced the finding that men shut themselves off from their emotions:

- Have you ever wished you could be a mother? How did you feel when you found out that you couldn't bear children? How did you find out? How do you feel about it now?

- Have you found the warmth and closeness in your life that you want? Where?

- Do you believe in being ruthless when you have to?

- Do you often feel hurt or sad when you don't show it? Do you force yourself to behave like a robot? Do you ever *feel* like a robot?[20]

These questions implied a masculine role that strangled men emotionally.

Hite's organization of themes furthered this perception. Where her book on women started with masturbation, she began the male book with quotations showing fathers teaching their sons brutal lessons about manhood. In the first two pages of Chapter 1 men remembered their fathers letting a companion beat a duck's brains out; telling them not to cry; instructing them that the future involved making money; and describing women as weaker than men. These quotations, and the pages that followed, showed women that they found men hard to deal with because men were imprisoned by masculinity. When she finally got to sex on page 142, Hite began the topic with "Are Men Monogamous in Marriage?" She answered this with quotations documenting their infidelity. Her men also reported that they liked marriage because they liked being looked after, even though women's economic dependence made them angry. They were especially angry at the women's movement. As for sex, they experienced performance pressure during sexual intercourse and had their most intense orgasms from masturbation, and many fantasized about rape.

A feminist writing about men made male reviewers angry. The *New York Times* editor Robert Asahina took Hite to task in a piece entitled "Social Science Fiction," a pithy phrase that caught on with other writers. Hite, Asahina contended, was a "best selling author who [had] never written a book" but had strung together quotations. Hite responded to his charges with outrage. Citing experts' praises of her book, she defended her sampling method by stating that random samples could never be confidential. If she had used one, she added, most people would not have participated. She added that this was not why she was being criticized. Noting that most critics of her work were male, she said they were angry because the book said things about men that they did not want to hear.[21]

In spite of Hite's defensiveness, the appellation "social science fiction," was unfair. Even though most commercial sex surveys were guilty of the same charge, they had not been attacked like Hite. Selecting voices to represent a group of respondents is inevitably not random, regardless of the sample type or the author's biases. These problems exist in all qualitative research and are especially egregious in commercial surveys, where the goal is to sell copy by drawing attention to outrageous answers. And Hite had a point about male critics. Asahina's critique explicitly associated social science fiction with feminism, suggesting that he was as disturbed by Hite's feminist ideology as by her methodology. Commercial sex surveys rarely offered a critique of traditional gender relations. They created a different fiction from Hite's. Their fiction, that readers had satisfying sex lives because modern men had become great lovers and women had thrown off their puritanical inhibitions, was more palatable to male book reviewers. But this fiction did not appeal to the many women who bought Hite's book. They wanted a world they could identify with. Fiction can create such a world better than methodologically sophisticated surveys, and Hite's book on men, like the one on women, became a bestseller. In addition to consoling women readers about who was really to blame, it read like a bodice-ripper, with titillating accounts of what men liked to do sexually.

Just as Hite's book on women had been followed by the *Redbook* survey, a more sympathetic account of men's sexual lives accompanied her book on men. Anthony Pietropinto and Jacqueline Simenauer started collecting data several years after Hite but rushed their book into print. Like Hite's book, theirs explained men to women. Although they charged Hite with failing to understand that American men were changing, their descriptions of men's sexual desires and attitudes mirrored hers. The men they quoted were ambivalent about women's newfound independence and wanted women who were sexually abandoned but who brought little experience into a relationship. Men wanted to communicate with women so they could tell them what to do sexually. One man appeared to summarize most men's views by stating that a woman should "act very sluttish, only with me, in bed."[22]

During the 1970s most purveyors of surveys that told readers about others like themselves had a more conservative message than academic sexologists. The academics no longer defended marriage. They saw personal development as the goal and marriage as worthwhile only if it facilitated this. Commercial authors took the safer route of telling women that sex within loving, intimate relationships, especially marriage, was the best and getting better. Hite gave her readers a different message from either of these. She said that sex was not so good for women or all that great for men either. Like other commercial sex surveyors, Hite told readers about themselves in a salacious enough way to keep them entertained, but the similarity stopped there. Where other surveys reassured women that their sex lives were vibrant, Hite told them that they were unhappy, that they had reason to be unhappy, and that this was not their fault.

The decade ended with data collection for Hite's third book, *Women and Love,* in which she pressed this theme even harder.[23] This book's concern was larger than sex. Hite asked why women suffered so much pain in love relationships with men, and she answered that sex was central to the problem. She told readers what they wanted to hear. Women, she wrote, differed from men in not considering sex to be a good way of making up after an argument. And women had difficulty deciding to agree to sex when a new relationship started. This was not surprising, since men still looked down on sexually experienced women. Finally, men took no responsibility for contraception, and date rape was widespread. Unhappy relationships were inevitable when women loved men. Even women who engaged in activities that threatened their marriages were not to blame. Many women had been driven to cheating. Indeed, 70 percent of those married five years or more had cheated, Hite charged. They did so because of the alienation in their marriages. These women no longer trusted love, because disappointment inevitably followed.

While Hite pleased her audience, she attacked mainstream American values with her claim that men had weakened the marital bond. When the book appeared in late 1987 the mood was increasingly conservative. Men already felt their sexual desires were under attack from the rape surveys. A further attack on men did not sit well with the editors of major newspapers and magazines. Hite had defended her first two books against harsh criticism, and her tone in *Women and Love* was unmistakably defensive. She never acknowledged that her surveys were flawed. Still, she could not have anticipated the fury she inspired.

The reviews started innocently enough with a story in the *Los Angeles Times* that simply repeated Hite's major points. It was followed a week later with Hite's picture on the front cover of *Time*. A letter from the publisher in *Time* described her as "at the center of a storm about some of the most contentious issues of our time," adding that the book had "sparked some skirmishes" at the magazine, with women having mixed responses and men unanimously objecting. The *Time* writer Claudia Wallis acknowledged that Hite had tapped deep feelings of dissatisfaction among women, but complained that the book's "unrelieved bitterness and rage against men" were hard to swallow. These early stories reflected the country's concern and confusion over the women's movement, gender roles, and the state of the American family.[24]

The men's objections won the day. A few weeks after its first article the *LA Times* cited Warren Farrell's statement that "the Hite Report is exaggerated and methodologically enormously flawed." While these charges were true, Farrell, a writer known for his hostility to the women's movement, used similar techniques in his own work. Many other articles followed, and these fell into a predictable pattern. There were hostile headlines: "Hite of Folly; Shere Hite's Latest Is Insipid, Infantile and Altogether Insulting to the Women It Purports to 'Study'"; "The Shere Hite Report—Sheer Hype?" Stories quoted criticism from experts, usually men, such as Donald Rubin, chair of the department of statistics at Harvard ("So few people responded, it's not representative of any group, except the odd group who agreed to respond"), or Robert Groves, a professor of sociology at the University of Michigan ("the functional equivalent of malpractice for surveys"). Buried somewhere in the stories would be a critical discussion of her findings.[25]

Yet the findings were what most annoyed the critics, and the methodological criticisms simply provided a venue for attack. That this was so can be seen in *Playboy*'s critique of her work. The writer, James Peterson, interspersed criticism of her methods with outrage at her ill-treatment of men. Asserting that "in this culture . . . it is the anti-sex message that sells," he rewrote several of Hite's quotations about men's cruelty. For example, an account by a woman whose boyfriend slapped her when she tried to get him to talk about his recent personal crises became "this woman, the moment her lover was preoccupied, responded to the sudden drop in attention by trying to push him over the edge." Peterson described Hite's respondents as disturbed women who hated men. He added that their opinions were no more representative of all women than interviews with the Klan would be of American race relations.[26]

Feminists were, again, divided. While many defended Hite, others recognized the concerns to which she gave voice but were troubled by the quality of the data collection, the analysis, and the oversimplified noncontextual diagnosis of the problem. Writing in the *New York Times,* the sociologist Arlie Hochschild acknowledged both the methodological problems and the lack of attention to power but argued that the findings were useful. She praised "the moving stories of women, and the continuous stream of deep probing questions Ms. Hite raises about them."[27] Hochschild advised Hite to acknowledge that her respondents represented only the large number of women who had serious emotional troubles with men. What this group had to say could enlighten the rest of the population, if they could be encouraged to listen.

Thus Hochschild understood something that the critics of Hite's survey methodology did not. In describing how many men and women felt about heterosexual relations, Hite had provided insights not possible in a more structured, methodologically sound survey. Unfortunately, Hite, like Kinsey, was unable to distinguish friends from enemies. Instead of accepting her work's limits and focusing on its contributions, she replied to Hochschild with insistence that her sample represented all women. This led Hochschild to admonish her by noting that the best social science makes modest claims and willingly doubts and reexamines itself. Hochschild added that if Hite adopted this more modest stance she might prompt her critics to relax their suspicions and listen to her.

But it is unclear that Hite's critics could have listened. Most of the criticisms of Hite's work were correct, but the press distorted her problems and vilified her. Groves and Rubin could have made the same criticisms of many other samples, if newspapers had bothered to ask. Other writers who made similar errors, like Hunt, were ordained as experts and frequently quoted. Singling Hite out for attack deflected attention from her troubling message about the state of heterosexual relationships. Hite was an incredible commercial success, selling over 20 million copies of her books, and ironically she came to stand for the idea of sex surveys almost as much as Kinsey did. Her popularity served to increase the intensity of attacks on her. In contrast, most commercial sex surveys did not challenge the sexual status quo, so the press reported their findings as fact and rarely questioned their data.

While this controversy unfolded, writers continued to produce other commercial surveys. A few were published as books, often targeted at special groups, but most were readership surveys from magazines of all kinds. These presented their readers' responses in ways that promoted the particular magazine's image. In the tradition of Kinsey, moreover, normal was defined as what people did, so its meaning varied from one magazine to another. In spite of the more conservative atmosphere of the 1980s, these surveys sought to entertain, and their message combined a libertarian mixture of information and snickers. Almost all the major women's magazines undertook sex surveys during the decade. Each survey reassured its particular audience about normal behavior and the attainability of sexual bliss, and each reaffirmed heterosexuality as the norm.

Cosmopolitan was particularly prolific during this time. Its first survey appeared in the magazine and as a book. In the book's introduction, the editor and *Cosmopolitan* Girl *par excellence* Helen Gurley Brown took pains to legitimate the results with the claim that it was the biggest sex survey ever. The book's author, Linda Wolfe, added that the results provided a reliable sexual barometer because "the *Cosmo* woman may, in fact, be quite representative of young American women as a whole."[28] *Cosmo*'s report contrasted sharply with Hite's. Using leading questions, it produced a portrait of young American women as living sexually exciting lives. *Cosmo* did not ask if the reader had ever had sex, merely how old she was the first time. Questions covered exotic sexual practices, including sex and aggression:

- When making love, which of the following do you like? (check all that apply)
  Have your man undress you
  Pinch, bite, slap him
  Be pinched, bitten, slapped
  Have someone beat you
  Pretend to fight physically with the man or try to get away.[29]

A segment entitled "The Wilder Shores of Love" included questions about lesbian experience, sex with homosexual men, incest, orgies, sex clubs, partner swapping, and group sex. In this way *Cosmo* defined each of these behaviors as just another sexual experience their libidinal readers might try.

Cosmo's results promoted the sexually free and wild woman of the magazine's carefully marketed image, a woman with significant orgasmic capacity and many partners. For readers in bed with the magazine rather than a tangle of bodies, *Cosmo* presented a sexually exciting life toward which they could and should strive. The magazine's portrait of the *Cosmo* "girl" created and reinforced expectations for how real *Cosmo* girls should behave sexually. Yet, in spite of the direction in which the questionnaire pushed them, *Cosmo* respondents did not quite respond as intended. In particular, it was difficult to ignore a disturbing undertone of confusion and pressure. Many respondents, for example, said that the sexual climate made men's advances difficult to reject.

Cosmo made its owner's fortune with its permissive views about sex. Even the *Ladies' Home Journal* survey two years later had a positive tone toward sex. The *Journal* described the typical respondent as "reassuringly mainstream" and the survey as "a valid indication of the state of married love in America today." Ellen Frank of the University of Pittsburgh gave the study legitimacy by analyzing the data. She and Sondra Forsyth Enos claimed that no previous researchers had examined sexuality within marriage to see how it was "kept vital." The survey asked about premarital sex, extramarital sex, orgasm, and whether their readers made love anywhere but the bedroom. It did not inquire about such practices as sadomasochism or group sex. Still, *LHJ* informed its readers that they had vibrant sex lives. As with *Cosmo* readers, almost half made love three to five times a week. These were women who knew their pleasure depended on the skill of the men in their lives. As one respondent commented: "He gets better every year. So does our marriage. And sex is super!" Frank and Enos supported their version of the sexual revolution, which they described as strengthening heterosexual, monogamous marriage. *LHJ* readers could be nice girls while giving themselves permission to be sexual and to do things as daring as making love with the lights on. One-fifth had even had extramarital affairs, but the magazine told readers that this figure was low compared with wives in *Redbook* or *Cosmopolitan*'s surveys.[30]

In spite of the cheerful tone, orgasm remained elusive. *LHJ*'s respondents reported frequent intercourse and great pleasure in lovemaking, but 40 percent did not have orgasms very often and 7 percent never did. As one woman characterized the problem, "during 'normal' sex, I never have an orgasm, but my husband is patient while I bring myself to orgasm before or after we make love."[31] Orgasms did not seem to be difficult, but orgasms during vaginal penetration were. Since women had been told for almost a century that this particular type of orgasm was the height of sexual bliss, their continued "orgasmic inadequacy" caused them concern. *LHJ* had to acknowledge this, while continuing to tell wives that their sexual happiness was greater than ever before and was creating stronger and more stable marriages and families.

Cosmo and *LHJ* took their sex surveys seriously and assumed that their female readers genuinely wanted information as well as entertainment. In contrast, *Playboy*'s first readership survey excited its male audience with snickering and boasting. The authors did make claims to accuracy, finding the over 100,000 responses "astonishing," and they used experts to give the survey credibility, but here the similarity with other magazine surveys ended. *Playboy* assumed that men's needs were sexual, not emotional, and the magazine published the results in a five-part series that did not spare readers a single detail. And, in case the results were not exciting enough, it spiced the articles with quotations from famous erotic descriptions of men's sexual activity. Twenty percent of the responses came from women, and *Playboy* gleefully reported that men and women were similar in their attitudes and behavior. They meant that women were like men, that is, that the "zipless fuck is alive and well."[32]

Playboy's portrayal of its readers' sexual behavior celebrated sexual liberation. Liberation meant engaging in frequent and varied sexual activity and sexual talk. What was normal for others was not normal for *Playboy* readers, the magazine jubilantly claimed, because its readers had greater sexual capacity and experience. *Playboy*'s libertarian philosophy even made the magazine more tolerant toward lesbians, gays, and bisexuals, who seemed to have the kinds of sex lives *Playboy* admired. The magazine declared that gay men and lesbians were much like other men and women: "It's worth noting that the terms heterosexual, homosexual and bisexual ought to be used as adjectives, not as labels. There's a whole spectrum to sexuality; contemporary sex is too colorful to be thought of as a three-position game . . . when you call someone a homosexual it's like calling him a left-hander. It's only part of what he is."[33]

But *Playboy* also denied that gender determined sexual attitudes and practices, since straight men and lesbians were less sexually adventurous than those with other orientations. This implied that homosexual men were, in fact, different. No doubt the largely heterosexual male readership did not want to be confused with gay men. The article took a middle ground, educating *Playboy* readers that homosexuality was not a sin. It was different but not too different. Along with *Cosmopolitan*, *Playboy* presented same-sex sex as approaching "normality." This partial legitimation coincided with the pathologizing of heterosexual male desire found in Hite and the rape surveys. These combined trends seemed to undermine long-held views about gender and sexuality and, in turn, helped stimulate the conservative backlash toward sex that arose during the 1980s.

Playboy, in reality, had stereotypical opinions about men and women.

Responding to readers' concerns, the magazine devoted one article to the female orgasm. In spite of the female respondents' supposed sexual bravado, most had the same difficulties as other women. The article's author, Kevin Cook, had advice for his male readers. Both male and female respondents described orgasm as the best moment in intercourse, so Cook gave men a list of recommendations about helping female partners achieve this. The list ended by telling men to lighten up. Men, Cook said, should not be so willing to make sacrifices in order to produce a female orgasm. After all, "women are looking for experimental, considerate, patient partners, not sacrificial lambs."[34] Cook was not questioning the primacy of the orgasm, he was taking a position reminiscent of writers of the 1930s like Ernest Burgess and Lewis Terman. Men, he stated, should be a little more selfish and focus on their own bodies. Hite would have said they already did this, and that their anxiety about sexual prowess simply pressured women into lying.

Playboy instructed men on female desires, but a more typical pattern was for surveys to tell women about men. *Cosmopolitan* undertook two such surveys in the late 1980s. The first simply asked readers about the sexual performance of the men in their lives and concluded that good men were hard to find. In the second the urologist James Gilbaugh Jr. questioned financially successful male patients about their sexual activity and desires. He was pleased to reveal that these men experienced little change in their attitudes or prowess since they were 25. Half claimed to be able to climax in two to five minutes after starting, and almost all said their erections were as big as ever. Sex, moreover, was high on the list of these professional men's pleasures, ranking second only to golf.[35]

As the 1990s approached, some women's magazines documented the changes of the 1980s by repeating earlier surveys. While surveys were expensive to produce, magazine audiences wanted and listened to advice. The surveys were ideal for advising women about this topic of great importance and for telling women that things were better than ever. *Redbook*'s 1987 survey found that married women's sexual satisfaction had increased. *Redbook* had been telling its readers this for some time now, so it is not surprising that readers agreed. Almost two-thirds of the respondents said that they experienced orgasm every time they had sex. Most women loved sex. Most said they would have sex more often if they were not so tired from doing other things, such as raising children, or if they did not feel so bad about their weight.[36]

Even *Seventeen* got into the act. Its survey more than twenty-five years earlier had admonished its readers to stay chaste. By 1991 the very young readers of *Seventeen* were treated to the results of a new sex survey. The magazine's readers were still not allowed to be the respondents. These were "a nationally representative group" of teens aged 14–21. But the magazine explicitly told its readers that they themselves were having more sex than teens in the past. Even so, it added hopefully, "The real news is that you are apparently thinking about and having sex more responsibly." Since this survey's audience had to be treated gingerly, the few behaviors discussed were presented in the negative, for example, "49% of you have not had sex, and here are the two top reasons why . . ."[37]

In spite of this serious tone, commercial sex surveys were rapidly becoming frivolous entertainment for magazine readers. In 1989 *Redbook* poked fun at its own efforts with a story about the responses to a list of questions about sex that it had mailed to a sample of its readers. These questions and the readers' answers appeared in the magazine, prefaced by an exhortation: "Ask yourself. Ask your husband. Ask your friends and family the same provocative questions. You'll have fun—and learn a lot about each other too. Perhaps more than you bargained for." Many questions consisted of hypothetical choices:

- Suppose you couldn't avoid an accident that would result in nerve injury. Would you rather suffer an injury that numbed your entire genital region, or one that made you completely deaf?

- If you could have $500 a day for every day that you had no physical contact at all with your partner, how long do you think you could last?

This explicit use of sex surveys as entertainment was at odds with *Redbook*'s more serious presentation of sex as important for marital happiness, satisfaction, and longevity. Such presentations helped create an image of sex surveys as naughty and trivial.[38]

A survey in a magazine for young women, *Mademoiselle*, pushed the idea of sex survey as entertainment to its extreme while still attempting to inform its audience. Magazines for the unmarried had been reluctant to undertake sex surveys, and *Mademoiselle*'s survey demonstrated the tremendous change in the content of young women's magazines during the 1980s. The editors removed married respondents from the analysis and took pride in their single readers' active sex lives. The survey was sent to a random sample of subscribers to *Mademoiselle* and *Details*. Like *Playboy*, *Mademoiselle* told its readers that they were more experienced than other people. The editors wondered if this was "because they read *MLLE*? Or are sexually experienced women attracted to *MLLE*?" The headlines told readers that they were like the "unembarrassed women and shameless men, single and between 18 and 30, [who] go all the way in our ultimate sex survey." The visual presentation of results combined brash jokes with information. Boxes on every page summarized important points with headlines like "Bad News for Girls," or "In Your Dreams." Diagrams made visual points: a cracked mirror illustrated the answers to the question "Would you enjoy sex more if your body was different?" and a bar graph used penises instead of bars to document men's feelings about the size of their penises. In spite of the jokes, the magazine also included the usual depressing report that women felt bad about their bodies, did not experience orgasms every time, and often faked them to gratify men.[39]

In the thirty years since the first commercial sex surveys, magazines had become far more comfortable with them. Until the 1960s popular magazines had been nervous discussing sex. When they first did so, they used experts to give their studies credibility but kept them in the background in the interest of clarity. In this way, they gave their readers scientific evidence of their own normality, told in the lucid voices of others like themselves. This meant that for the first time women's own words appeared, seemingly without tampering. Endlessly fascinating to readers, sex sold magazines, and over time the media became less modest. By the 1990s sex surveys were staple fare, and when they were too expensive to produce, magazines could dispense with data collection and analysis altogether and instead present questionnaires with codes at the back so readers could interpret their own answers to such questions as "How sexy are you?" "Are you a right-brained or left-brained lover?" and "What's your love-making IQ?"[40] Actual sex surveys were not as numerous in magazines as they seemed, largely because of the prevalence of these pseudo-surveys.

Commercial sex surveys and pseudo-surveys helped create desires and behaviors among their readers with their reassurance about normality and their willingness to embrace variety. Their faulty sampling, leading questions, and mistakes in analysis did not prevent them from providing fodder for a confession-hungry public. Commercial surveys could be dismissed as merely sensationalist entertainment. Unfortunately, they created an image of sex surveys as sensationalist and trivial in the public mind. In the 1980s AIDS intensified the debate about whether the government should ask Americans about private sexual activities, and commercial sex surveys provided an important but misleading reference point.

8

Gay Men and AIDS

It is critical to identify factors that reliably differentiate homosexual males who maintain safer sexual practices from those who persist in risky behaviors in the face of the epidemic.

—Karolynn Siegel, Frances Palamara Mesagno, Jin-Yi Chen, and Grace Christ, 1989

ALTHOUGH some of the earliest surveys focused on men, for most of the twentieth century researchers of sexual behavior concentrated on women. It was not until the early 1980s that men's behavior again caused consternation among more than a few feminists. And this concern arose, as it had in the early part of the century, because a deadly disease was striking men. This time around, panic in the general population was not as great, at least in the beginning. The new disease did not seem to threaten the family as venereal disease once had, since it appeared to strike gay men only. As a result the response to the crisis started slowly. The disease spread rapidly in cities with large gay populations, and its cause was at first unknown. While medical researchers struggled to identify the nature of the illness, social scientists began using surveys to understand its transmission.

The new disease attacked the immune system and led to outbreaks of rare ailments like Kaposi's sarcoma and *Pneumocystis carinii* pneumonia. The Centers for Disease Control (CDC), which had an obligation to trace all infectious diseases, created the Kaposi's Sarcoma and Opportunistic Infection Task Force. This group pursued the possible explanations proposed in the media, in the scientific community, and by politicians, pundits, and religious leaders. Some writers wondered if the disease was related to the use of nitrite inhalants to increase sexual stamina, or of other drugs. Or perhaps gay men's lifestyles had overloaded their immune systems. Others, including many members of the task force, believed that the disease was sexually transmitted, but in the absence of any known virus, demonstrating this was difficult.

Surveys were a promising way to proceed, and the first organization to undertake one was the CDC. The CDC had a history of studying infectious diseases, such as syphilis or tuberculosis, among marginalized segments of the population such as prostitutes or poor blacks. It had already conducted interviews with gay men on exposure to hepatitis B, and it now began to interview gay men about their sexual behavior and partners. The rest of the country, including the media, may have been indifferent to the fate of "sexually deviant" men, but by 1982 the CDC had two surveys under way: a cluster survey tracing the partners of men with the disease, and a case-control survey matching men with the disease to men without. The researchers soon concluded that the new disease, which they now called AIDS, was sexually transmitted. Furthermore:

> Although the cause of AIDS is unknown, it may be caused by an infectious agent that is transmissible from person to person in a manner analogous to hepatitis B virus infection: through sexual contact; through parenteral exposure by intravenous drug abusers who share needles; through blood products, particularly in patients with hemophilia who received clotting factor concentrates; and perhaps through mothers who are Haitian or intravenous drug users to their infants. The existence of a cluster of AIDS cases linked by homosexual contact is consistent with an infectious-agent hypothesis.[1]

Sex research, for all its imperfections, had diagnosed the existence of a virus before medical research had isolated it.

In demonstrating that AIDS was spreading via sexual activity, the CDC relied on and reflected the viewpoints of two types of earlier research. First, a number of surveys had gathered details about gay sexual practices and lifestyles. Second, several surveys had focused on sexually transmitted diseases. The latter surveys became the model for how to think about and ask about the new disease. In order to understand the CDC discovery, it is necessary to trace these two bodies of research.

The few surveyors of gay men and lesbians before the 1950s had justified their work as providing a clearer lens through which to examine heterosexual Americans. In these surveys homosexual behavior was sometimes pitied and sometimes explained, but it was always seen in comparison to "normal" sexual behavior between men and women. Even when Kinsey described homosexual sex as normal, he meant that it was not very different from heterosexual sex. After World War II things began to change. The war had created a new awareness and openness among those whose sexual tastes involved others of the same gender. Although under siege during the Cold War of the 1950s, lesbians and gay men took advantage of the increased sexual tolerance and political activism of the 1960s. As part of a growing militancy, the new Gay Liberation Movement began to press for surveys to enhance their own understanding of who they were, instead of simply being the target of the research agendas of others. Surveys began to appear both from within the gay community and from organizations sympathetic to gay concerns.

From the start, activists considered homosexuality an identity. In this scenario, persons were born gay and remained so throughout their lives, even if they did not recognize this or even denied it. Kinsey's outlook, that homosexuality was simply a behavior to which anyone might be drawn, seemed outmoded. Yet in its pursuit of identity politics the movement made political use of Kinsey's data. In 1977 Bruce Voeller, the executive director of the newly formed National Gay Task Force, decided to demonstrate the movement's potential political strength. By averaging Kinsey's estimates that 13 percent of men and 7 percent of women had predominantly homosexual "outlets" for at least three years between ages 16 and 55, Voeller produced a gay population of 10 percent. Thus he transformed Kinsey's data on sexual behavior during three years of adult life into a measure of unchanging sexual identity. Arguing explicitly that "gays were a huge voting block," since "the voting booth is the world's safest closet," he concluded that gays lived "in every extended family in America."[2]

Two surveys undertaken at the Kinsey Institute in the late 1960s are important in understanding the history of surveys of gays. For the first, conducted in about 1966, the sociologists Martin Weinberg and Colin Williams obtained funding from the National Institute of Mental Health (NIMH).[3] This was the first government-funded survey of homosexuals and helped NIMH stake out a territory it has continued to hold. Weinberg and Williams interviewed members of the somewhat staid Mattachine Society, the oldest political organization of gay men, as well as men attending homosexual clubs in New York, San Francisco, Denmark, and the Netherlands. They cautiously included few items on sexual behavior, and their portrayal of gay men as relatively uninterested in sex was in line with an impression widely accepted up to this time and one the assimilationist Mattachine Society had promoted. Because they expected this result, the surveyors did not ask about number of partners. Even when they asked about sexual behavior, their respondents sustained this image. Only one-fifth of the men reported having sex three time a week or more.

In 1969 Weinberg undertook a second survey, this time with Alan Bell. The increased openness in gay life after the Stonewall riots of that same year allowed a different picture to emerge; that of the "promiscuous" gay man. Weinberg and Bell's survey involved homosexual and heterosexual men and women in the San Francisco area and included many questions about sexual behavior. Insisting that their goal was to correct stereotypes about homosexual lifestyles, Bell and Weinberg interviewed those at the forefront of the new lifestyle—San Francisco respondents who were openly gay. They were recruited from a variety of locations such as bars and bathhouses, and through advertisements. Bell and Weinberg asked about number of partners and one-night stands.

Bell and Weinberg presented gay men as promiscuous and lesbians as faithful, a picture based more on gender than on sexual identity. These have remained the standard portrayals of gay sex since that time. The male homosexuals Bell and Weinberg described measured their personal worth in terms of how much sex they had. Sex was the centerpiece of their lives; they continually cruised for partners, and almost half reported lifetime totals exceeding 500. Over half these partners were one-night stands. In contrast, lesbians were less interested in sex than in love and were faithful, romantic, and emotionally committed. The majority reported fewer than ten lifetime partners, with half having no one-night stands. It was as if men unfettered by women and women unfettered by men developed unbalanced sexual personas.[4]

This survey and others like it gave support to an emerging public image that women who had erotic relations with other women remained sexually undeveloped in warm, romantic, loving bonds. Since men had the responsibility for teaching their partners sexually, the manless lesbian remained untaught. If the opportunity arose, straight men might even convert lesbians. This portrayal helped explain the somewhat more tolerant public attitudes toward lesbians than toward gay men. Heterosexual men, who wanted to have nothing to do with "faggots" for fear of contamination, might find "dykes" sexually exciting and bisexuals even more so. By this time lesbian sex was a staple in mainstream pornography, whereas gay male pornography existed in a highly segregated market. Similarly, surveys of swinging during the 1970s and 1980s frequently reported that men liked to watch female-to-female sex but were careful to avoid physical contact with other men.

The gay activism that grew out of the 1960s and 1970s led to a mini-explosion in surveys of the sexual behavior and adjustment of gays. Some surveys continued to show gays as abnormal. These emphasized high rates of deviance in gay backgrounds, with, for example, more experience of incest and more tolerance for and experience of such behaviors as rape and prostitution. Most surveys, however, addressed the interests and concerns of the gay community. These replicated the gender distinctions found by Bell and Weinberg. Researchers described the men as having frequent anonymous sexual activity, childhood sexual experience, and multiple fleeting relationships. They portrayed lesbians as self-confident and psychologically well adjusted, and as sexually content and reaching orgasm more easily than other women, though they did not have sex often. These messages told young homosexual men and women what kinds of people they were, how their desires were constituted, and what kind of sexual behavior made one gay.[5]

The gay rights movement actively promulgated these images, particularly that of the promiscuous gay man. Bruce Voeller argued that homosexual men were not more promiscuous, but that they were more often successful in their pursuit because their potential partners were men and therefore equally interested in sex. The message about lesbians was more varied and reflected the feminist split over sexuality discussed in Chapter 6. Some researchers described lesbians as faithful and nurturant in love relationships, but others portrayed a less gendered, more gay-identified sexuality. The latter group included the gay activists Karla Jay and Allen Young, whose book *The Gay Report* was published in 1977.[6]

Jay and Young described the sexual practices of about 5,000 lesbians and gay men, drawing their respondents from personal networks, gay newspapers, and the National Gay Task Force. This nonrandom sampling technique overrepresented those most public about their sexuality and most eager to discuss it. Jay and Young described the goal of the survey as to allow heterosexuals to hear gay voices, but their book spoke directly to the gay community. They asked many detailed questions about sexual activity, and these produced descriptions of exotic, and shocking aspects of gay sex that probably offended some heterosexual supporters. Breaking the rules of survey research, Jay and Young plunged into sensitive questions from the beginning of the interview without any desensitizing introductions. They did this because of their untested assumption that gays would not be shocked by explicit questions about sex.

Jay and Young portrayed homosexuals as inherently different from heterosexuals from childhood on. Their questionnaire communicated the message that lesbians as well as gay men *were* their sex lives. In contrast to earlier surveys, the questionnaire for lesbians disputed the centrality of love in their lives and invited the finding that lesbians, like men, were more focused on their genitals than on their hearts. The questionnaire's only concession to gender was in a curious change of language from explicit vernacular on the men's survey to scientific terminology on the women's. Even so, the authors had to conclude that gay men were indeed more interested in sex and less romantic than lesbians. When asked to describe good sex, lesbians wrote about the ambiance, about their partners' pleasure, and about love. The men's shorter descriptions focused on penises, power, and submission.

Surveys like this, undertaken from within the gay community, helped gay men and lesbians in search of an identity. These surveyors told readers that sex was central to gay identity, and they created a vision of gayness as fixed, unchanging, and "true." They assumed that desire, behavior, and identity would correspond once the "true" gay person emerged, and they provided guidance about what gays and lesbians should do. Sexual experimentation was good, as was variety in acts and partners. Yet their female respondents resisted Jay and Young's apparent desire to create a picture of sexually active lesbians.

This positive evaluation of sex predominated in the gay community until AIDS. When AIDS appeared, researchers built on the descriptions of gay men found in surveys like Bell and Weinberg's and Jay and Young's. AIDS turned the sexual licence of gay men into a killer. But even in the decade before AIDS was discovered, a few surveys of sexually transmitted diseases (STDs) portrayed gay male sex in negative terms. Because they reported high rates of STDs, gay men were targeted in such surveys. Although the CDC had not undertaken behavioral sex surveys before the 1970s, it had used a modified version of Kinsey's interviewing technique for contact tracing of the sexual partners of syphilis cases. In 1968 William Darrow became director of the CDC behavioral unit. A sociologist who had learned contact tracing techniques at the New York City health department, Darrow began to survey venereal disease prevention when he moved to the CDC. He had to move slowly, because the federal government was leery about sex surveys and the CDC would not approve protocols. Darrow's doctoral dissertation, completed in 1973, was a survey designed to explain the increases in STDs in the United States in the late 1970s. He explored the relationship between number of partners and STD infections, and also the infection-preventing power of condoms. His questions became the prototype for surveys on AIDS.[7]

In the early 1970s public health officials became concerned about increases in hepatitis B (HBV), because this virus could be transmitted through blood transfusions. To learn about transmission, Wolf Szmuness and his colleagues at the New York Blood Bank interviewed a number of potentially high-risk groups. They concluded that the role of heterosexual intercourse in transmission was unclear. Although heterosexuals who had many partners seemed at high risk, spouses of HBV-infected persons did not contract the disease at unusually high rates. An "unexpected finding" was the high prevalence of hepatitis B among homosexual men, but only among those who frequently engaged in anal intercourse. The researchers explained this by two factors: that the mucous membrane of the rectum was often damaged during anal intercourse; and that "the mucosa of the rectum may be a better portal of entry for virus than the digestive tract."[8]

Even though anal intercourse is only one way HBV is transmitted, this research placed the disease firmly in the ranks of STDs. It also inadvertently introduced the notion that gay sex was disease-prone sex. But it was a particular sexual activity, anal intercourse, that increased the chance of infection, not gay sex in general. While Szmuness and his colleagues did recognize that only some gay men engaged in anal intercourse, they did not note that since their gay sample was recruited in part from patients at gay health clinics, it almost certainly overrepresented those who did so. And with the emphasis on the population at risk and not the risky behavior, their clarification was subsequently lost, and all gay sex became suspect.

Darrow further implied a connection between gay sex and disease with an analysis of the STD histories provided by the gay men in Jay and Young's survey. Calling sexually transmitted diseases a "serious problem" for gay men, Darrow noted that almost two-fifths of the men reported having had gonorrhea, almost one-sixth reported syphilis, and one-tenth reported HBV. Those who had had one of these diseases were more likely to have had the others. Many partners, anal intercourse, and "furtive" sexual activity, such as going to prostitutes and having sex in bathhouses, increased the chances of STDs.[9] Jay and Young had intended their survey to demonstrate the joy of gay sex, and it did this, but it also supported the idea that gay sex was unhealthy. It contrasted greatly with sexological surveys among heterosexual adults, which presented sex as healthy and good for the participants. And once STDs became the focus of research, lesbians disappeared from view. Their low rates seemed to sever their connection to sexual activity even more sharply.

Toward the end of the 1970s the CDC undertook an HBV survey that, in retrospect, would seem prescient. This survey was prompted by a need to test promising new HBV vaccines. The CDC wanted to verify clinical trials of the vaccine by interviewing and vaccinating a high-risk population. Because of the earlier survey findings, they chose to study gay men. Darrow and Don Francis, a CDC epidemiologist who worked on the vaccine, collected interviews with gay male patients at clinics in five major U.S. cities that had reported high numbers of cases of HBV. By using these high-risk gay men to study the sexual transmission of HBV, the CDC not only performed much-needed research but also unintentionally confirmed the emerging stereotypes about gay male sex. Researchers erroneously assumed that incidence rates for gay men attending STD clinics could be generalized to all gay men, an assumption that would also inform responses to AIDS in the early 1980s.

The questionnaire conveyed the image of gay men as consumed by their sexuality. Like Jay and Young, the surveyors abandoned the accepted practice of preceding intimate questions with less intrusive ones. Detailed questions about "frequency of exposure" to various sexual activities followed brief questions about demographic events and HBV history. The survey findings were shocking. Almost two-thirds of the men had been exposed to HBV, and the survey confirmed that this higher-than-average incidence resulted from "passive anal-genital intercourse with nonsteady partners" and from rectal douching. Anal intercourse was beginning to be seen as an activity in which all gay men, and only gay men, routinely engaged. About half the respondents who had no HBV serological markers agreed to test the new vaccine, which proved safe and effective, possibly even after exposure to HBV.[10]

At the annual STD conference in May 1981, where this was triumphantly announced, James Curran, the head of the CDC's prevention services, also described an unprecedented five cases of *Pneumocystis carinii* among gay men in Los Angeles, thus heralding AIDS. This led to the early CDC surveys and helped establish AIDS as sexually transmitted. In the CDC's cluster study, Darrow and others interviewed nineteen of the earliest Los Angeles cases and traced their sexual partners to find seventy-eight men connected by sexual activity.

Suspicious that a scientifically rigorous survey, with interviewers who asked questions in a nondirective manner, would elicit incomplete answers from men who might hesitate to tell the truth, Darrow used a version of Kinsey's interview technique:

I always felt that our job was to find the truth as quickly and efficiently as possible. So, when I interviewed patients, I did ask leading questions.

When I went to interviews with gay men as part of the cluster study, I wanted them to know that I knew as much about the gay lifestyle as they did. I would ask them, in ways Kinsey might suggest, not "Have you ever been to a bath," but "When you were in New York and you wanted to go to the baths, did you go to St. Marks or some other place? . . ." And if they'd been to certain parties or events, I knew about those. I'd say "What did you have on? Did you see anybody who had a certain flower patterned shirt?" They'd be absolutely amazed.[11]

The epidemiologists at the CDC mirrored Kinsey in other ways. They wanted to amass as many cases as possible and paid little or no attention to sampling. They assumed that the terms "homosexual" and "bisexual" were synonymous with people who engaged in sexual activities with others of the same gender as themselves. But not all people who had sexual experience with same-gender partners considered themselves gay or homosexual. And it was possible to be sexually inexperienced, celibate, or sexually involved with someone of the opposite gender, and to consider oneself gay. Conflating behavior and identity confused the issue.[12]

For the thirteen men for whom the researchers obtained complete information, nine had had sexual contacts with other known AIDS patients, some with more than one. Four men had had sex with the same patient, whom researchers named Patient Zero. Patient Zero was able to name seventy-two of his estimated 750 partners over the previous three years, and Darrow clustered forty known AIDS cases in circles around him. With this information plus evidence from the case-control survey, CDC social scientists were able to conclude that AIDS was probably sexually transmitted. And, with HBV transmission as a model, they quickly focused on anal intercourse as the most likely avenue of transmission.

Preconceptions about the sexual lifestyle of gay men combined with the discovery that the new disease was sexually transmitted led to the association, in the public mind, of AIDS with a highly promiscuous lifestyle. In this view gay men, without women to civilize their sexual urges, were dangerous. This message was communicated by the first name given to the new disease, Gay Related Immune Disease. And when eleven of the first twenty-four cases in San Francisco turned out to have participated in the HBV vaccine study, data collected from them reinforced this belief.

Since the CDC already had blood samples from 1978 and 1980, Paul O'Malley, who had run the study in San Francisco, proposed to reinterview these men and to take new blood samples. This was not possible until 1984, when the CDC obtained funding. Researchers reinterviewed a sample of the men from the City Clinic in San Francisco, reanalyzed their earlier data, and tested blood samples using the newly available HIV test. They were able to pinpoint when the men in the study had become HIV-positive. Comparisons of blood samples from 1978 with those from 1984 provided evidence of the rapid spread of HIV in this cohort and of the long incubation period between seropositivity and full-blown AIDS. In 1978 fewer than 5 percent of the men in the sample were seropositive. By 1984 two-thirds were, although fewer than one-third were symptomatic. Infection progressed so quickly in this high-risk population that by September 1985 the CDC's *Morbidity and Mortality Weekly Report* reported that almost three-quarters of the study population had serological evidence of HIV infection.[13]

The CDC researchers concluded that, in the days before AIDS was discovered, high levels of anal intercourse with many different partners helped explain why HIV spread so quickly through the gay male population.[14] But the men in their survey had been recruited at an STD clinic in the city with the largest and most "out" population of gay men in America. They had no doubt been to more bathhouses, picked up more strangers, had more anonymous sexual partners, used more drugs, drunk more alcohol, and had more anal intercourse than most gay men in San Francisco and certainly than most gay men in the rest of the country. Given the paucity of national data, it is not possible to know how rapidly AIDS spread in the entire gay male population of America, but it could not have been as rapid as it was for this segment.

This group of men included one-sixth of all AIDS cases in San Francisco, and San Francisco's rate was among the highest in the country. By using, as a proxy for all gay men, a group whose sexual conduct was most repugnant to mainstream American sensibilities, researchers unintentionally supported the image of deviant male homosexuals whose lifestyle was fatal. Although the CDC researchers cautioned against generalizing from their incidence data, they also communicated that these men represented the vanguard of what would happen to others. For the next decade, studies quoted the level of infection in the City Clinic sample as evidence of the high levels of HIV infection among gay men, even though no other survey produced such a high rate.

In spite of these inadvertent distortions, the importance of CDC research in providing early information about the spread of the disease cannot be understated. CDC researchers noted that their understanding of how HBV transmission occurred had provided a model for the transmission of AIDS; in particular, their knowledge of the role of receptive anal intercourse had enabled them to make quick discoveries.[15] Furthermore, these CDC surveys helped define the main research goals of the many surveys of AIDS among gay men that were beginning to pour forth. These goals were to measure the incidence of AIDS and to understand the mode of sexual transmission; to document behavioral changes among gay men to more closely resemble heterosexual lifestyles; and to promote such changes. In working toward these three goals, researchers built on stereotypes about gay male sexuality found in the surveys of the 1960s and 1970s. The CDC surveys helped make these stereotypes a dominant part of the public discussion of sex after the discovery of AIDS. They linked the sexual practices of gay men to the transmission of the disease and encouraged gay men to conform to hetero-sexual sexual norms. In doing so they helped define AIDS as a sexually transmitted disease rather than as a blood-borne virus transmitted in sev-eral ways, only some of them involving sexual activity.

Gay social scientists were quick to join the fight against AIDS. One of the first groups to embark on AIDS-related behavioral research consisted of the San Francisco psychologists Leon McKusick, William Horstman, and Thomas Coates. Their longitudinal survey, the AIDS Behavioral Research Project, began in 1983 with the specific goal of promoting behavioral change among gay men. McKusick and his colleagues wished to capture evidence of a variety of lifestyles. They had little knowledge of sampling and little survey experience but had a great deal of knowledge about the sexual and social practices of the gay community. With limited funds from the city and county health departments, they interviewed men in different types of locations. To obtain a mixture of high- and low-risk behaviors, they chose a range of respondents including men leaving bathhouses and gay bars and those who had not recently visited such places. All were "out" enough to respond to an advertisement in the paper or visit a gay bar or bathhouse. Under half of those receiving the questionnaire completed it, and this low response rate became even lower over time, in part because many did not give their names and addresses when first interviewed.[16]

Like other surveyors of gay men, McKusick and his colleagues did not lead up to probing questions with more neutral ones. They moved quickly to questions about sexual orientation and about how "out of the closet" the respondent was. From there they proceeded to detailed personal questions. This approach reflected both the sense of urgency surrounding the research and the assumption that gay men would be comfortable discussing their sexuality. Coates defended this bluntness: "Gay men are much more open about their sexuality. They are identified by their sexual orientation, and as a group they celebrate sexuality, enjoy it, and enjoy talking about it. For these reasons, it was less difficult to ask about sexual behavior . . . there was a great deal of motivation to get involved, because they were the ones getting killed by the disease."[17] More experienced surveyors might have tested these propositions rather than assuming their truth.

Even in the early years of their survey, McKusick and his colleagues asked detailed questions designed to pinpoint the transmission of the disease. They asked about both passive and active anal intercourse, with and without a condom. They asked about other activities like "fisting" because many at the time thought its association with rectal trauma would facilitate AIDS transmission. Since they wanted to measure behavioral changes, they also asked about frequency of these activities a year earlier, questions that, given the unreliability of memory, produced doubtful results. They included questions on number of partners, drug use, and other STDs, and they asked men about their experiences with and responses to AIDS. The state of knowledge about the transmission of AIDS shaped these questions. At the time of this first round of the survey, considerable uncertainty existed about how the virus was transmitted. The CDC had shown the importance of receptive anal intercourse, but this did not rule out other sources of transmission as yet undetected, and it was appropriate for the researchers to pursue them.

If experts were unsure which behaviors were dangerous, gay respondents were even more confused. In analyzing the first year of their data, McKusick and his colleagues documented reductions in oral-genital sex, but reported that many men still engaged in other behaviors such as unprotected anal intercourse. Some men even believed they were less susceptible than others or that they had made all the necessary changes in their behavior. Coates, a faculty member in internal medicine at the University of California Medical Center in San Francisco, had expertise in promoting behavioral changes to reduce the risk of illness. He persuaded NIMH to fund follow-up interviews with the same men every six months as a more accurate way to document behavioral changes in the gay community than by relying on memory. He also examined the correlates of behavioral risk-reduction. NIMH's early involvement was appropriate, as it was the only one of the National Institutes of Health with a history of funding surveys of homosexuals.

Over time these repeated interviews began to provide evidence that gay men in San Francisco, in response to AIDS, were abandoning the newly self-destructive aspects of their lifestyles. Condom use increased fourfold between 1984 and 1988. Not only did individual gay men change, but the entire community's response was heroic. Much of the behavioral change was initiated and supported through gay networks. Their community was overwhelmed by the need to support the dying, the HIV-positive, and the merely terrified, yet gay men continued to receive better support from this source than from elsewhere. Unfortunately, since many men dropped out of the survey, and since these men may have been less proud of their progress, these positive results may have merely meant that those most responsive to the message were also most likely to remain in the survey.

Two other Bay Area surveys were among the most important in creating and documenting the AIDS story: the San Francisco Men's Health Study, a longitudinal survey of sexual practices and HIV infection; and a series of annual surveys evaluating an AIDS-prevention campaign. Both studies involved random samples of gay men, but even with better sampling than the other surveys, their location in the city most associated with gay men meant their results could not be generalized to the rest of the country.

The San Francisco Men's Health Study began in 1984 at the University of California, Berkeley, with funding from the National Institute on Allergy and Infectious Diseases. Warren Winkelstein Jr. and his associates took a probability sample of single men aged 25–54 in those census tracts of San Francisco with the highest reported AIDS caseloads. Respondents agreed to twice-yearly interviews, to physical examinations, and to HIV testing. Forty percent of the eligible men refused, and more dropped out after the first round. Still, the study produced interesting results. Almost half the homosexual and bisexual men in the survey were HIV-positive. While high, this rate was lower than found in previous surveys based on nonrandom samples and much lower than that of the CDC's City Clinic cohort. Furthermore, the study conclusively confirmed receptive anal intercourse as the major source of sexually transmitted HIV infection, thus clearing gay men's other sexual practices as causes of the disease. Rectal douching before sexual contact was the only other activity to increase risk of infection.[18]

The Berkeley researchers also confirmed what others had found, a positive relationship between number of partners and HIV transmission. This was a confusing finding. The HIV risk from having many partners depended on the level of infection in the population from which the partners came. If rates were high, then many partners would not be much more risky than one. While Winkelstein and his colleagues noted that the risk from number of partners applied only to men who had receptive anal intercourse, they nevertheless recommended that all men decrease their number of partners. Their data showed that a man who did not practice receptive anal intercourse but had many sexual partners of unknown infection status was safer than a man who regularly practiced receptive anal intercourse with only one partner of unknown infection status. Men who practiced receptive anal intercourse with many partners probably had the greatest chance of infection, but this relationship was not demonstrated. Number of partners mattered only for those engaging in risky behavior, but survey-ors implied that number of partners was a causal variable independent of all others. They argued that gay men should become monogamous, stop having anal intercourse and other activities associated with rectal trauma, and use condoms.

Some activists disagreed. Taking the position that AIDS did not require a major change in gay sexual practices, they viewed arguments to the contrary as promulgated by a homophobic, anti-sex society intent on forc-ing the sex-celebrating gay culture into the heterosexual mode.[19] From their perspective, gay men could engage in any sexual activity with anyone they desired as long as they practiced it safely, that is, used condoms. While technically correct, this position ignored the correlations among various practices and the evidence that men needed supportive social networks to make behavioral changes. Some respondents in the AIDS Behavioral Re-search Project were gay men who knew better but still could not resist dangerous activities once they entered the bar and bathhouse culture. Both points of view misinterpreted the evidence.

Like others who undertook AIDS surveys of gay men, Winkelstein and his colleagues wanted to create behavioral change. In their reinterviews they found their recommendations had been effective. Their respondents re-ported marked declines in both anal intercourse and number of partners. They may have felt the need to report more behavioral change than they were actually achieving, but the findings were reinforced by reports that rates of new infection had declined dramatically. In addition, men who were already HIV-positive reported decreases in insertive anal intercourse, thus lessening the number of "receptors" they put at risk.

Much of the credit for these changes belonged to the other major survey that used sampling. Commissioned by the San Francisco AIDS Foundation with funding from the city's department of public health, this survey was intended to collect data for a public relations campaign promoting behav-ioral change and for evaluating the campaign once it started. Research and Decision Corporation, a market research company, used random-digit tele-phone dialing to obtain respondents. Gay male interviewers then screened households in San Francisco for self-identified gay and bisexual men using the following introduction:

This survey is sponsored by the San Francisco AIDS Foundation, a local non-profit foundation that is responsible for AIDS prevention in San Francisco. For the rest of this survey, we are interested in speaking with one group of people who are at highest risk for AIDS: men who have sex with other men, or who identify themselves as gay or bisexual. Would you include yourself in one of these groups? *(If hesitant, continue:)* We are also interested in speaking with men who may only occasionally have sex with other men. If you fall into one of these categories, we would very much appreciate it if you could complete the survey . . . In no way will your name ever be associated with this survey, and your answers will help the AIDS Foundation in their prevention campaign.[20]

Only 3 percent of those identifying themselves as eligible refused to participate, but one-third of households in the contact area had no phone, so poor men, many from minority groups, were underrepresented. If interviewers suspected that a respondent was eligible when he denied it, they called him back, and the study's director, Larry Bye, believed the use of gay interviewers increased response rates. The questionnaire included questions about a variety of sexual practices and changes in those practices but did not distinguish between types of anal intercourse until 1989, possibly because of ignorance about transmission.

The first year's survey provided the data to design a campaign to increase safe sex practices among gay men. It revealed that a significant proportion of gay men in San Francisco were not monogamous and engaged in behaviors that researchers defined as risky: "fisting," "oral-anal contact," "anal intercourse with exchange of cum," "oral sex with exchange of cum," and "sex with different partners." Men were more likely to have reduced their total sexual activity than to have shifted from what the authors considered unsafe behavior to what they labeled "possibly" safe: "anal intercourse with a condom," "anal intercourse without a condom but with no exchange of cum," "oral sex, but no exchange of cum," "deep french kissing," and "mutual masturbation."[21] There was, in particular, a great resistance to condoms. For Bye and his colleagues, part of the problem was that gay men saw oral and anal sex as inseparable facets of gay identity and perceived much of the "safe" behavior as sexually unsatisfying. While men understood that AIDS was preventable, they told the interviewers that contradictory information about the best strategy for prevention was confusing.

These San Francisco surveys demonstrate the reasons for this confusion. During the same period in the same city, one group of researchers was demonstrating that oral-genital sex was not a great risk for gay men, while another group campaigned to reduce this practice, putting it in the same category as anal intercourse. This piecemeal approach to AIDS research conveyed mixed messages to those whose behavior it targeted. By trying to change so many behaviors simultaneously instead of concentrating on the few that accounted for almost all cases of HIV transmission, these well-intentioned researchers made behavioral change harder to achieve. Part of the social scientists' confusion occurred because the medical literature itself was unclear and nonstatistical in its approach. Physicians could not say that oral-genital sex had *never* produced a case of HIV transmission, so they included it as a risk factor without noting that it was considerably less risky to a gay man's health than, for example, driving a car. But even members of the gay community often accepted the belief that sex without women was hard to control. Many urged their community to adopt the heterosexual model.

In spite of this confusion, three-quarters of respondents, when reinterviewed a year later, remembered the advertising campaign and reported fewer partners and less sex, both safe and unsafe. The 1989 report described three groups of men: one was careful about risky sexual practices; a second was careful but had occasional lapses; and a smaller but sizable group took frequent risks. Many of the last group were substance abusers, poor, and with low education. This group would have been larger had this not been a telephone survey.

Social scientists, many of them gay, were heroes in their willingness to abandon other research interests, to learn new survey skills, and to begin fighting this new and terrifying disease. Some would die of AIDS during the next decade. They did not consider the gay sexual lifestyle inherently evil or revolting. In fact, they valued the celebration of bodily pleasures. But they forged ahead without carefully questioning the urgent need for behavioral change. They unintentionally participated in creating the image of AIDS as a sexually transmitted gay plague. The plethora of AIDS-related behavioral surveys of gay men conducted in the following years further confused the picture. They were diffuse, repetitive, and based on convenience samples, and they were a poor use of limited resources. Yet they filled an information vacuum and helped save lives. The relationship between anal intercourse and HIV transmission was so strong that the many poor-quality surveys obtained the same results about anal intercourse even though, in other ways, their data were misleading.

The Bay Area dominated sex surveys after the appearance of AIDS, but by 1984 surveys had begun in other cities, contributing to the emerging national consensus in the gay community and elsewhere about the risky nature of certain sexual practices. New York and other northern cities had the largest number of AIDS cases, the majority of which were transmitted through shared needles during drug use or by sexual transmission to the partners of intravenous drug users. But during the 1980s more AIDS surveys focused on gay men than on drug users, partly because AIDS was seen as an STD but also because the gay community was well organized and demanded data. When NIMH funded a New York survey by medical sociologists at Sloan-Kettering Cancer Institute, they targeted gay sex. The surveyors aided understanding of the role of number of partners in HIV-transmission:

> When virus prevalence was low, decreasing the number of partners with whom one engaged in risky acts was an effective way to reduce (although not eliminate) one's risk of infection. Now that the prevalence is high, participation in risky sexual acts even with a few partners presents a high probability of HIV exposure. Therefore, in order to assess the degree to which HIV infection may continue to be spread, research on the sexual practices of at-risk groups must focus not on extent of reduction of risky practices but on extent to which men continue to expose themselves to the risk of infection.[22]

The pattern of concentrating on gay men rather than other groups occurred in other cities, and it reinforced the view that AIDS was caused by gay male sex.

But new findings, even if they were not always reliable, continued to add to the picture of gay men and AIDS. A Boston study funded by the National Institute on Alcohol and Alcohol Abuse and the CDC added two details: having had partners from California was positively associated with becoming HIV-positive, as was engaging in a "high period" of sexual activity, when, presumably, risk-taking increased.[23] Since California was associated with a pleasure-seeking gay lifestyle, this survey and others like it increased the pressure on gay men to turn away from its temptations.

One other important study, the Multi-Center AIDS Study, began in 1985 in Los Angeles, Chicago, Baltimore, and Pittsburgh. Funded by the National Institute on Allergy and Infectious Diseases and the National Cancer Institute, it had goals and methods similar to those of other studies. Respondents were tested and reinterviewed at six-month intervals to see who became seropositive for HIV, whether anal intercourse was the most important predictor, and whether condoms prevented infection. The survey replicated other findings, a necessary undertaking given the danger of the disease. Unfortunately, a second round of the study confused the picture somewhat with a finding that men who practiced both insertive and receptive anal intercourse had an even higher risk of HIV infection than those who practiced only receptive anal intercourse.[24]

The most likely explanation for this unique finding was the use of small volunteer samples whose results were unreliable. To paraphrase John Tukey's criticism of Kinsey, all the many studies combined did not tell as much as researchers would have learned from one national probability survey of the gay community by an experienced survey organization. Such a survey would have made it possible to generalize the results to the gay male population as a whole. The project would not have been easy. It would have been much more expensive than any of the individual surveys. Furthermore, statisticians had not solved some of the methodological issues of taking such a survey. There are difficulties in defining the population, since men who define themselves as gay are not coterminous with men who engage in sexual activities with other men. There are problems of measurement, since men with same-sex sexual experience often do not admit to it. And taking a sample of the relatively small number of gay men in the total population would involve screening out many ineligible men.

If the various National Institutes of Health that were funding AIDS surveys by 1985 had pooled their resources, they could have financed the research necessary to develop a sample and funded a reliable national survey of men who had sex with other men. Estimates of the size of this population were based on a few relatively small national samples of sexual activity in the entire adult population, that is, on samples in which the number of men who admitted to sex with other men were tiny and therefore subject to serious sampling error.[25]

In spite of these flaws, behavioral research on gay men had a great impact on their behavior and lessened the spread of the disease to younger members of the community. Even if risky activity was not eliminated, its reduction greatly lowered rates of HIV transmission. AIDS had a low probability of transmission from each single act of receptive sexual intercourse with an HIV-positive inserter. Because of the severe consequences of HIV infection, men who continued to have occasional lapses took tremendous personal risks, but changes in behavior by most gay men greatly reduced the rates of seropositivity in the total gay male population.

By the end of the 1980s the focus of society's concern about HIV had shifted from gay men to the sexual transmission of HIV among the heterosexual majority. Experts in survey research, particularly demographers, who had largely ignored gay men now rushed to address the issue of whether AIDS was a danger to all Americans, including heterosexual men. These men had been the standard for normal sexual behavior throughout the century, and no one anticipated the consequences of finally turning the spotlight on their sexual activities.

9

Politics and Sex Surveys

The vital need for data to help in designing, implementing, and evaluating programs to curb the epidemic's spread transcends numerical tallies of people infected and lives lost.

—National Academy of Sciences Committee on AIDS Research and the Behavioral, Social, and Statistical Sciences, 1989

ALTHOUGH the evidence indicated that gay men were reducing their risk of AIDS, by the mid-1980s the United States was in the midst of a panic about the disease. This panic was fueled by experts of all sorts. In 1985 the Institute of Medicine of the National Academy of Sciences commissioned a group of distinguished scientists to describe the statistical dimensions of the AIDS epidemic and make recommendations. Overstating the incidence among gay men by stating that up to 70 percent might be infected in some cities, the report sounded an alarm about the future course of the disease: "Infected bisexual men and IV drug users of both sexes can transmit the virus to the broader heterosexual population where it can continue to spread, particularly among the most sexually active individuals . . . The committee believes that over the next 5 to 10 years there will be substantially more cases of HIV infection in the heterosexual population and that these cases will occur predominantly among the population subgroups at risk for other sexually transmitted diseases."[1]

According to this model, AIDS would spread to "promiscuous" heterosexuals and from them to their more innocent partners. Scientists were thus reinventing AIDS as a threat to the future of the American family and the health of its young people. Over the next few years they urged the government to make AIDS a priority, a cry loudly echoed in the media. Among the proposals of scientific panels were high-quality large national surveys of sexual behavior to document the ways in which the disease might be spreading. Only the federal government had the resources to do this research.

As long as gay men were the ones who became HIV-positive, experts had not recommended large-scale national surveys. But by the mid-1980s epidemiologists started challenging the view that AIDS was "confined to high-risk and socially stigmatized groups," calling it "a kind of complacency that simply cannot be supported by the currently available evidence."[2] The implication of this was that anyone could die from having sex. For the first time, gender seemed to play little or no role in defining those with problematic sexual behavior. The threat of AIDS came at first from the lower orders and the socially marginal. In addition to gay men, known victims of AIDS now included intravenous drug users, bisexual men, and female prostitutes. All these groups had the potential to spread the disease to heterosexuals. Prostitutes' middle-class clients might transmit the virus to their wives, and a bisexual man might transmit it to a woman unaware of his double life. This woman might then pass it on to other men, as might the female partners of intravenous drug users.

Researchers began to examine these possible routes of transmission. In 1985 Nancy Padian of the University of California at Berkeley's School of Public Health began monitoring ninety-eight women with HIV-positive male partners. Over half the women had bisexual partners, and about one-quarter of these women were HIV-positive. But two-fifths of the women with intravenous drug–using partners were HIV-positive, even though none injected drugs themselves. As with gay men, anal intercourse was the most common transmission path and repeated sexual events increased the risk. Similarly, in a 1987 survey funded by the National Institute for Drug Abuse, intravenous drug users transmitted HIV to sexual partners at a rate exacerbated by high levels of anal intercourse and little use of condoms.[3]

These studies involved groups of heterosexuals who were isolated from the mainstream and did not pose much risk to the rest of society. Still, they showed that heterosexuals were becoming HIV-positive from sexual encounters. Since few adults claimed to know all the sexual partners of all their sexual partners, the potential was frightening. These fears increased as researchers began promoting the idea that behaviors, not groups, were very risky. This was technically true and was appropriate when educating groups with high levels of risky behavior. But it was easily misinterpreted. Researchers took this position to remove HIV transmission from its association with sin. They wanted to remove the stigma from groups with a history of HIV infection, but they also wanted to garner support for research. Funds would be more readily available if AIDS was not "merely" a disease of social outcasts. A 1986 report from the New York Blood Center of a survey of blood donors who tested HIV-positive took the position that public health messages should state that anyone might easily become infected with HIV if engaging in high-risk behaviors, and this theme took hold among researchers interested in HIV transmission.[4]

Researchers first considered prostitutes the most likely source of the spread of the disease among heterosexuals. With the discovery of antibiotics that cured gonorrhea and syphilis, prostitution had lost its reputation as a dangerous threat to the family, but researchers were quick to name prostitutes as likely culprits in the transmission of this modern scourge. Reports began to filter out that many prostitutes were HIV-positive. In 1986 the Centers for Disease Control (CDC) began a study in several areas of the country. It recruited about 1,400 prostitutes, paying little attention to issues of representativeness. Over half the women showed evidence of past hepatitis B infection, and while the HIV rate was much lower, 12 percent, it caused great alarm. Still, most of the prostitutes who tested HIV-positive were intravenous drug users, and they reported using condoms with clients, thus minimizing the risk of transmission.[5]

In spite of fears about HIV in the heterosexual population, it seemed that few of the truly "blameless" would get AIDS. Had prostitutes infected large numbers of men who in turn infected their families, something widely believed about gonorrhea and syphilis a century earlier, a truly innocent cadre would have been available for researchers and policymakers to highlight. Except for a few babies and the occasional middle-class spouse unknowingly married to a drug abuser, most persons who became HIV-positive could be held guilty of sexual misconduct.

AIDS was a deadly disease, apparently leading to a certain, horrible death. Its association with "illicit" sexual activity rendered its victims shameful in the eyes of many. Massive outbreaks would cause chaos, and scientists wanted to warn the public and to advise about prevention. And so in the mid-1980s a significant change occurred in the focus of research. Surveys of gay men measured which men *contracted* HIV. Now the focus became the *risk* of its contraction. Actual cases remained rare, "as yet," among drug-free heterosexuals. But even demonstrating "risk" necessitated conflating higher-risk and lower-risk activities.

Researchers sympathetic to the plight of gay men were also not about to let heterosexuals off the hook. For example, in 1987 Ron Stall and his colleagues at the Center for AIDS Prevention Studies in San Francisco studied riskiness of behavior among gay men and heterosexual men and women recruited in singles bars. They defined the celibate as "no-risk." "Low-risk" individuals either were monogamous and used a condom during anal or vaginal intercourse or had more than one partner but did not engage in intercourse. "Modified high-risk" meant anal or vaginal intercourse either with no condom and a monogamous partner or with a condom and more than one partner. "High-risk" people did not use condoms and were not monogamous. By this time rates of HIV transmission were known to be many times lower for vaginal intercourse than for anal intercourse, especially for female-to-male transmission, and gay men were more likely to meet HIV-positive partners than were heterosexuals. But by treating heterosexual and homosexual intercourse as equally risky, Stall was able to portray the heterosexuals in his study as taking more risks than homosexual men. These surveys began to portray sexual intercourse between men and women as just as dangerous as sexual intercourse between men.[6]

Since anal intercourse was the primary means of sexual transmission, researchers needed to know its frequency during heterosexual intercourse. In 1987, in a letter to the editor of the *Journal of the American Medical Association,* the physician David Bolling and the gay activist Bruce Voeller cited data from Bolling's 1974 survey of his gynecological patients. Twenty-five percent had said they "occasionally" engaged in anal intercourse, and about 10 percent said they did so "regularly," so Bolling and Voeller argued that the number of heterosexual women engaging in this practice equaled the 10 percent of men who were gay. They warned that "as HIV and other sexually transmitted diseases become epidemic among heterosexuals during the next few years, this pool of women is increasingly endangered." By including heterosexuals in the at-risk population, they made homosexuals seem more like heterosexuals and therefore more normal.[7]

In spite of these dire warnings, there was little actual evidence that AIDS was expanding into the general population, at least in the United States. Almost all new reported cases occurred in groups already known to be susceptible. But predictions that AIDS would eventually spread to heterosexual men and women influenced AIDS-related surveys of sexual behavior. The lack of reliable data was apparent. A number of components needed better measurement if estimates of HIV transmission were to be improved. There were no reliable data on what proportion of men were gay. Some thought that the 10 percent figure derived from Kinsey's data was too low, while others argued it was too high. Nor were there reliable data on gay men's sexual behaviors. Data on bisexual men were also needed to assess their risk to heterosexuals. There were practically no data on the proportion of women who engaged in anal intercourse, the frequency with which they did so, or who their partners were. Was this practice confined to "sex-crazed dope addicts," as some thought, or was it widespread? Both the National Institutes of Health and the CDC needed reliable incidence data on the risk factors associated with HIV transmission. Other government entities, such as the Office of Management and Budget (OMB) at the White House, were also pressuring the Public Health Service (of which the CDC is part) and the National Institutes of Health (NIH). These were questions for social scientists, and when a number of academics began discussing contributions they might make to understanding the spread of the disease, they pushed the National Academy of Sciences to take the lead.

The National Research Council, which is part of the National Academy of Sciences, empaneled the Committee on AIDS Research and the Behavioral, Social, and Statistical Sciences, and pressure began to mount for a national survey. Wendy Baldwin, the head of the population division of the National Institute of Child Health and Human Development (NICHD), became liaison to the committee. She quickly realized that demographers could apply their extensive knowledge of surveys, including their experience asking sexual behavior questions, to the study of the types of behavior that increased the risk of AIDS. Survey expertise had been in short supply in the research on this problem. Many AIDS surveyors had limited survey training, and survey research centers had so far ignored the problem. The AIDS surveyors rarely used probability sampling, created poorly designed questionnaires, provided limited training of interviewers, and sometimes did questionable data analysis. In December 1986, at a meeting of the directors of the NICHD-funded population research centers, Baldwin announced funding for a large national survey of the sexual behavior of adults. Since quick results were crucial, funding would be provided through contracts rather than grants. To ensure the best possible survey in this new field of government research, a contract for the survey design alone would be issued first.

The winners of the competition for this first contract were Edward Laumann, dean of social sciences at the University of Chicago, and the economist Robert Michael, director of Chicago's National Opinion Research Center (NORC).[8] Neither of these men had expertise in the study of sexual behavior, so they invited John Gagnon, an experienced sex researcher, to join them in writing the proposal and conducting the research. Gagnon and Laumann had met in early 1987 at the National Research

Council and, despite ideological differences, developed a rapport. This team won the contract partly because NORC had a history of research on risky behavior, including sexual behavior. Most centers preferred less controversial topics, but NORC had collected data for the only previous national survey of sexual behavior, a 1970 study by the Kinsey Institute. This survey's results had never been published because of a disagreement over who should be credited as the leading author, and interviews with more than 3,000 men and women had languished unseen.

A second source of NORC expertise was research by Norman Bradburn and Seymour Sudman, who, in 1974, had asked a series of questions that respondents might find threatening, including questions about sexual behavior. Bradburn and Sudman concluded that, of all the topics mentioned, masturbation made respondents most uneasy, and other questions about other sexual behaviors were nearly as disquieting. Income, long claimed to be the most difficult topic on surveys, and even drug or excessive alcohol use did not make respondents as uneasy as sex. Bradburn and Sudman also demonstrated that questionnaire wording and context affected whether respondents admitted to engaging in practices like masturbation. In a second survey in 1976 they showed the importance of confidentiality in increasing responses to questions about sex.[9]

In January 1988 the University of Chicago research team began work on designing a national survey. Laumann, Michael, and Gagnon agreed to spend several years working on AIDS research. Like generations of male researchers before them, they were confident of their ability to understand the sexual behavior of women as well as men. To begin learning the truth even before the national survey took place, they added questions on sexual behavior to the General Social Survey from 1988 on. This is an annual NORC survey covering a variety of topics, funded by the National Science Foundation. The team used data on sexual behavior from this survey to provide baseline estimates for segments of the population and to explore a number of methodological issues.

The team did not make the common mistake of assuming that sexual behavior results largely from individual biology or personality. Instead they used sociological theory to develop hypotheses about sexual behavior. In modeling AIDS transmission, for example, they applied Laumann's earlier work on social networks. AIDS could not be transmitted randomly, they argued, because individuals are sorted into sexual networks based on social background as well as sexual interest and identity. Since these networks are not well connected with one another, the researchers hypothesized that people's sexual relationships would be confined to their own networks, and that AIDS introduced into a social network would spread easily among members but not freely among networks. The team combined Gagnon's experience with sexual behavior surveys with that of the NORC methodologists to develop a questionnaire based on these ideas and on theoretical contributions from Gagnon and Michael. With this work the stage was set for a sex survey superior to any undertaken previously. Such a survey would have helped allay fears about an explosion of AIDS cases while identifying high-risk groups.

But this did not happen. Instead, one of the most bizarre chapters in the history of federally funded research ensued. A fight over the survey spread to a survey of teen fertility also funded by NICHD and pitted a number of groups against one another, including researchers, funders, politicians, and lobbyists of the right and left. In the process, the researchers' freedom to manage their surveys was severely curtailed and almost lost altogether. The media, with its interest in stories that sell, exacerbated the fight. A sex survey that put Uncle Sam right in the bedroom provided great copy and crude headlines. The public's knowledge of surveys of sexual behavior had been shaped by popular magazines and books with their promises to tell all, and survey opponents used this to raise public anxiety. The controversy culminated in 1992, with an unprecedented 51–46 vote by the U.S. Senate to ban forever these two planned national surveys.

Those who fought the survey had several motives. Members of the resurgent Christian right wing of the Republican party believed that sex outside of marriage was dangerous and destructive, and that liberals had deliberately encouraged it. These beliefs had surfaced during hearings on the Adolescent Family Life Act of 1983. At that time concern had focused on teenage girls, a group long the subject of sex surveys. Such fears gained new momentum and direction from the homophobia unleashed by the AIDS scare. Now boys appeared to be in danger of recruitment into the homosexual army. Lesbians, it should be noted, were invisible in this debate.

An at least equally important agenda of the surveys' opponents was the federal budget. Many conservatives opposed all federally funded research and saw this survey as a chance to garner support for this view. As Bob Knight of the Family Research Council later put it:

> I tend to think that massive doses of federal funding have the exact opposite effect on a problem than what they are intended to do. They tend to slow down progress because it becomes more necessary to protect the federal grant than to achieve any progress in the field. I know a friend who worked in a cancer lab in Bethesda that was fully dependent on federal

funding, and he would give a dog and pony show once a year . . . And he said they completely snowed the federal investigators who were looking to see if the grant was worthy . . . This goes on a hundred-fold all around Washington.[10]

Liberals were used to conservative attacks on spending, but the anti-sex rhetoric made them ambivalent. Defending sex was dangerous for middle-aged men, particularly for senators with shaky reputations. The braver took the position that they preferred silence except when speaking about sex would save lives. Others dodged the issue altogether. Almost no one argued that sex was a legitimate topic of research.

While researchers saw themselves as neutral scientists going wherever the data took them, they too had agendas. They ignored the evidence that in the United States and other Western countries AIDS was spreading to certain powerless groups who were desperately in need of help. Funding complicated matters. The chances for obtaining funding were increased by portraying an equal-opportunity disease that put the innocent at risk. And they were unaware of their own history of problematizing the sexual behavior of women, and even gay men, while portraying heterosexual men as having uncomplicated sex lives. Others, including the federal research bureaucracy centered in NIH, had a larger agenda to protect, since controversy over this study might initiate a general attack on research funding. They tried to handle things quietly and silenced lobbyists who wanted to organize support for the survey. This strategy permitted those on the attack to shape the rhetoric.

In retrospect, the fight over the adult survey might have been anticipated. Sex research has always been controversial, and no large survey had ever included heterosexual men, since their sexual behavior was above suspicion. Most of the researchers believed in science as a value-free activity, and they had become involved in sex research as a result of the urgency of the problem of AIDS. Thus, in spite of the controversial history of sex surveys, they and their funders expected that this survey would proceed quietly, as was the norm for most federally funded surveys. In addition, instead of being allowed to plan the survey slowly, funders and researchers faced pressure from a variety of groups, including the OMB, to provide better estimates of the number of new AIDS cases. This pressure pushed things ahead of schedule. The NORC research team was asked to apply for and then awarded a contract to pretest their questionnaire on 2,000 respondents before they finished designing the survey.[11] The OMB had to approve the questionnaires for all contract research, as man-

dated by the Paperwork Reduction Act. The proposed pretest questionnaire was submitted in November 1988, and the study directors soon
received unofficial word of approval for their pretest, which was to be
referred to by the acronym SHARP (Survey of Health and AIDS-Related
Practices).

 With the country in a panic about AIDS, the media did not stay silent.
They too wanted data. Some months earlier, in the March/April 1988
issue of *Science,* the journalist William Booth had disclosed the existence of
the never-published 1970 Kinsey Institute survey, which had been conducted by NORC. Calling it "The Long, Lost Survey on Sex," Booth complained that publication had been delayed while "the investigators fought
over whose name would appear first on the manuscript." In the wake of his
article a group headed by Charles Turner of the National Research Council's AIDS committee obtained access to the data set and analyzed the data
on male-to-male sexual contact. In January 1989, while the NORC pretest
awaited official approval, they published their findings in *Science.* The
authors focused on sex between men because of the need to project the
growth of the AIDS epidemic. Since 21 percent of male respondents had
refused to answer all or some of the relevant questions, Turner and his
colleagues imputed values for the missing data based on the experiences of
men who were similar to these men in other ways. Their estimates ranged
from over 20 percent with at least some homosexual experience to under 2
percent with an experience in the previous year, figures closely comparable
to those from the 1988 General Social Survey. The authors noted that these
were probably underestimates, since men with something to conceal would
be likely to resist answering the questions. This survey had many problems:
the sample was not truly random, the data were two decades old, and the
questions about behavior used Kinsey's terminology "sexual activity to
climax" rather than "sexual intercourse."[12]

The *Science* article might have been largely ignored had Booth not added
a sidebar. Headlined "Asking America about Its Sex Life," it began by
noting that "the first truly representative survey on the sexual life of America" was awaiting clearance and that it would ask very sensitive questions
including ones on homosexuality. Booth quoted Gagnon on the need to
understand not only what people do but why, and he applauded the larger
$15 million survey expected to follow. Gagnon was a coauthor of the article,
so the two surveys appeared to be linked. Even so, readers might not have
made a connection between the flawed data on male-to-male sex and the
proposed new survey, but a photograph from the 1969 movie *Bob and Carol
and Ted and Alice* accompanied the piece. It showed two men and two

women all in one bed and implied that the government had a prurient interest in citizens' lives.

The conservative *Washington Times* picked up this story. This paper, like much of the radical right, saw homosexuality as a direct attack on the sanctity of the family. Sex should be confined to husbands and wives, a view that seemed outmoded but nonetheless had the power to reverberate throughout the land. The article misinterpreted the methodology Turner and his colleagues had used to adjust for nonresponse and claimed that it intentionally overestimated the rate of homosexuality. This charge attracted the attention of Paul Mero, press secretary to the Republican congressman William Dannemeyer of Orange County, California. Like Dannemeyer, Mero strongly believed that the heterosexual, monogamous family was threatened by liberal values. A Mormon who home-schooled his children to avoid the pernicious effects of public education, Mero was especially incensed by homosexuality. He had heard similar charges about distorted data from the writer Judith Reisman, whose book *Kinsey, Sex and Fraud,* written with the sexologist Edward Eichel, was about to appear. Reisman charged Kinsey with fabricating his data on homosexuals, and she conflated homosexuality and pedophilia, a technique used repeatedly during the fight over the surveys to play into public fears.[13] Mero, the self-described "Dirty Harry of the office," obtained a copy of the pretest proposal, and, by February 1989 the battle over SHARP had begun.

Dannemeyer's first salvo (written, like those to follow on this topic, by Mero) attacked both the survey and the research community. Dannemeyer described the recently published report of the National Research Council's AIDS committee as a "preface to a $15 million proposed sex study funded by the National Institutes of Health." Expanding his charges in a twelve-page congressional "backgrounder," Dannemeyer described the study as attempting to indoctrinate Americans into "the Kinsey mindset." By this he meant the promotion of homosexuality and pedophilia. Using arguments developed by Reisman, Dannemeyer put Kinsey's mantle on Gagnon's shoulders with erroneous statements like this: "the heart of the study will rest on the shoulders of John Gagnon. Gagnon has been an advisor or board member of such organizations as the National Organization for the Reform of Marijuana Laws, the National Sex and Drug Forum, and the Institute for the Advancement of Human Sexuality." The plan, Dannemeyer charged, was twofold: to spend large amounts of tax money under the pretext of containing the spread of AIDS, and to reduce the social stigma associated with sexual deviance. He further charged that sex surveys were unreliable, with refusal rates of 40–60 percent, since ordinary, upstanding Americans would not agree to such invasions of privacy.[14]

To counter these arguments, NORC wrote its own background piece. It acknowledged "Americans' historic love of privacy" but added that since AIDS had no known cure it had to be controlled by behavioral change. Invoking former President Ronald Reagan, who had called AIDS "Public Enemy Number One," NORC provided assurances about confidentiality, about interviewer training, and about members of the research team.[15] The argument was accurate but missed Dannemeyer's point. A large, high-quality survey would have calmed fears about the rapid transmission of HIV. It would have estimated the prevalence of those at risk and identified which groups might yet succumb. And it would have shown the necessity of targeting particular groups for prevention rather than scattering limited funds everywhere. If successful, it would have helped contain the disease and thus allowed the continuation of what the Christian right saw as sinful ways.

In debating the aims and quality of the survey the two sides revealed entirely different visions of morality and nature. The sociologist James Hunter has characterized these differences as "culture wars," which he sees as fueled by fundamental disagreements over the source of moral authority, that is, how individuals should determine right from wrong.[16] Central to this is a disagreement over sexuality and gender. For the anti-survey forces, the only legitimate family was "naturally" composed of a husband and "his" wife and children. Sex, they believed, was nature's way of ensuring the family's survival, but this already besieged family could be destroyed by surveys of sexual behavior that encouraged girls to have out-of-wedlock babies and boys to have sex with men. Women who demanded their sexual rights, rape surveys that turned male sexual pleasure into a problem, and homosexual men who demanded sexual freedom all threatened the family as they saw it. Those opposing the research also argued that surveys were not reliable, but this was a side issue. These opponents saw nature as belonging to God, not science. For them abstinence and monogamy were the only solutions to the problem of AIDS.

In making these arguments, they could not turn to science for help. Instead they used the power of moral outrage. Christian groups organized a massive letter-writing campaign to the head of the OMB, Richard Darmon, and to NICHD. Darmon was an attractive target with George Bush newly installed in the White House and eager to retain right-wing approval. A Christian radio station in North Carolina broadcast Darmon's phone number, tying up his line for a week. Mero had circulated anti-survey material to the press, and headlines like "Get Set to Lie—New Sex Survey Is Coming," "Uncle Sam Wants to Probe Your Sex Life," and "Who Loves Ya Baby? And How?" told Americans that the government was overstepping its boundaries.[17]

For the survey's advocates, the argument rested on an entirely different base. They too defended the family, but they had a different vision of what this meant. They actively promoted monogamy among gay men, arguing that gays should form strong family bonds. In their view the family could coexist with women who had careers and freely took sexual pleasure, and homosexuality merely demonstrated the great variety to be found in nature. For them science was free of value judgments. Its methods could be used to understand a problem and create a solution. If AIDS demonstrated the importance of monogamy, this was for technical reasons, not because monogamy was morally superior. Yet most researchers were more comfortable with monogamy and relieved that it seemed to be the solution for gay men. These researchers and their funders were most comfortable with AIDS as an equal-opportunity disease, and the adult survey was an important start in this direction. And, unlike conservatives, they ignored differences in gender.

The pro-survey forces used expertise in making their case. NORC's background piece was serious and unsensational where Dannemeyer had engaged in hyperbole. And by February 1989 Bill Bailey, the AIDS lobbyist at the American Psychological Association, was coordinating pro-survey activities among scientific organizations. Bailey was familiar to research personnel in the federal government. He had pushed the Presidential Commission on AIDS, which had been appointed by Ronald Reagan as a result of pressure both from AIDS activists and from Congress, to acknowledge the need for reliable data on sexual behavior. But he had worried that the survey might become a hot issue. Bailey also enlisted members of Congress to write to Darmon.[18]

This was to no avail. On April 6, 1989, Darmon wrote to Louis Sullivan, who as Secretary of Health and Human Services (HHS) had authority over NICHD, and asked him to reexamine the survey's purpose. By now, worries that the government could get into trouble by asking Americans about their sexual behavior had led to a narrowing of the topics covered. The survey as originally conceived included questions about a wide range of behaviors, including masturbation, which caused OMB particular "difficulty." But questions on any behavior not directly linked to AIDS were deleted, thus transforming the survey from a study of sexual behavior to one more narrowly focused on AIDS. Even so, Darmon indicated that he understood the conservatives' attitude by charging that the proposed survey was still much broader than an AIDS survey. Shortly after Sullivan received Darmon's letter he received a "Dear Colleague" letter from Dannemeyer listing some of the proposed questions, including explicit ones on oral sex and anal intercourse. He also claimed that names of partners would be documented. Then he revealed what he saw as the study's true purpose: "Imagine the political landscape if any one demographic grouping were to increase their rank from 10% of the population to 15% or 20%. This is the exact reason why the purveyors of laissez-faire sexual attitudes want to use tax dollars and the federal cloak of scientific legitimacy to produce this work. AIDS had nothing to do with it except as a thinly veiled excuse." In this passage Dannemeyer revealed his concern that homosexuals threatened America.[19]

While Dannemeyer and Mero were ideologically committed to their position, they showed considerable cynicism. They pursued their objective of persuading Americans of the dangers of these surveys, regardless of the truth. In Dannemeyer's letter he banished Laumann and Michael from the story and instead claimed that the graduate student and NORC researcher, Stuart Michaels, whom he called a "prominent homosexual rights activist," was in charge of survey design and development. He elevated Gagnon to the central figure, and vilified him. When asked later why he believed Gagnon wished to inflate the percentage of homosexuals in the population, Mero responded: "Because of his writings, and he was a Kinsey disciple. That was good enough for us. We didn't have to be 100% accurate. We just needed to create an imagery that helped us win politically. We thought the real issue was not Gagnon, was not Stuart Michaels, not anybody. The real issue was whether tax dollars were going to go to this . . . When you deal with a Congress that will spend anything on anything, you can't say 'Well I don't think it's an appropriate use of tax dollars.' You have to create a whole campaign."[20]

Dannemeyer's letter provoked Laumann to write to Sullivan. Outraged at being reduced to a figurehead whose purpose was to deflect criticism, Laumann emphasized his own role in pushing AIDS-related behavioral research. He added that a large team, besides Gagnon and Michaels, worked on the study: "modern social scientific enterprises are large-scale projects akin to the Manhattan Project (of atom bomb fame) in their need for a wide range of talents and special skills."[21] Unfortunately this scientific defense was irrelevant to the opposition. At this point NICHD's Baldwin decided the debate was getting out of hand. She instructed the researchers not to discuss the project publicly and to leave negotiations to NICHD. She also asked the three lobbyists working to save the survey, Bailey, Lisa Kaiser at the Alan Guttmacher Institute, and Judith Auerbach at the Consortium of Social Science Associations, not to lobby Congress.

Sullivan announced that the Public Health Service would review the survey. This put the responsibility in the hands of a former CDC director, Assistant Secretary of Health and Human Services James Mason, who appeared favorably inclined toward the project. But rumors circulated that other high-level personnel were opposed. One appointee with strong ties to the political right was Nabers Cabaniss, who, as Deputy Assistant Secretary for Population Affairs, ran all federal family planning programs. Cabaniss had worked for Senator Denton of Alabama, the architect of the Adolescent Family Life Act, legislation designed to promote abstinence education for the young. As a conservative woman in charge of activities that single women should avoid, she had to walk a thin line. Nicknamed "the Princeton Virgin" since her undergraduate days, she claimed never to have heard of oral sex until she read about it in the SHARP questionnaire.[22]

Too dangerous to approve, yet equally dangerous to reject outright, SHARP remained in limbo. In April 1989 the Chicago team finished designing the original large survey with a proposal that closely linked theory to design.[23] It included a stratified sampling plan to ensure enough unmarried persons in all age/race categories to compare the unmarried and the married and also to increase the number of homosexual respondents. While prospects for undertaking this study seemed dim, the researchers still hoped for eventual approval.

The damage was not confined to SHARP. Just before the original announcement of the adult study, NICHD had announced a large survey on adolescent fertility and sexuality. The successful bidders were Ronald Rindfuss and J. Richard Udry at the University of North Carolina. Rindfuss had trained as a demographer at Princeton, where he had worked on the National Fertility Survey. Udry was an experienced sexual behavior researcher who had developed a number of the ideas to be tested in the new survey. Called the American Teenage Study (ATS), this proposed longitudinal survey of 24,000 teens in grades 7–11 was approved in June 1989 with little fanfare. By this time sexual behaviors that might lead to AIDS had been added to the list of research questions. Funded as a grant rather than a contract, its questionnaire did not require approval from the OMB. Yet as a result of the fight over SHARP, the already nervous government funders decided, only one month after approval, to put ATS on hold pending further review. Along with SHARP, it remained in limbo for the next two years.[24]

AIDS-related surveys presented funders with a dilemma. It was possible to decry adolescent heterosexual activity while sympathizing with the emotions of those involved. And it was likely that most Americans felt this way. After all, heterosexuality was the natural order of things. But in the eyes of most Americans, surveys about AIDS measured unnatural sexual activities. Yet this disease was killing many American citizens, and surveys might help save lives. Recognizing that a cure was far off, Bernadine Healy, director of NIH and a Bush appointee, made AIDS-related behavioral research a funding priority. The solution was to fund many small surveys and to use these to measure heterosexual AIDS transmission. Most AIDS-related surveys undertaken between 1987 and 1991, the period of the controversy over the national surveys, assumed that heterosexuals in the United States were at risk of HIV even though little evidence supported this assumption.

These surveys began to include questions about other STDs, such as herpes and gonorrhea. STDs had previously garnered little interest, but, with actual cases of HIV so rare among heterosexuals, STDs were something researchers could actually measure.[25] A 1989 study of condom use among male and female patients at a San Francisco STD clinic revealed that half the respondents were diagnosed with an STD on the day of the interview. But in this survey and others like it STDs were not the primary focus. AIDS was. Examining the risk of AIDS among clients at STD or family planning clinics became a common way of supporting the idea that many people were at high risk for AIDS. And since condoms prevented pregnancy as well as AIDS and STDs, one survey could include all three topics.[26]

These surveys were important in getting out the message that AIDS was an equal-opportunity killer. Still, most of their respondents were guilty of unsanctioned sexual activity or at least of sexual risk-taking. Victims who could be deemed innocent because they had not contracted AIDS through illicit sex or whose youth made them naive would justify more funding. This was the reason AIDS questions were added to the ATS. Demographers had little difficulty presenting AIDS as a serious risk for the young. They had long described the problem of sexual activity among young women. AIDS surveys differed from surveys of adolescent sexuality in that their focus was not just young women. Boys were more at the mercy of their hormones than girls, and they might be more likely to engage in risky activity. Furthermore, same-sex sexual experimentation was potentially more serious than pregnancy: it might kill boys.

In surveys of the young undertaken in the last half of the 1980s the theme of high-risk behavior predominated. This theme had roots in the studies of problem behavior of the 1970s, but now the nation's young were held blameless. In the new view, the young spontaneously took risks because their bodies were more mature than their brains. They drove too fast, drank alcohol because it was forbidden, used illicit drugs, and took sexual risks leading to pregnancy, STDs, and now to death from AIDS. Reports on surveys of adolescent sexual behavior often maximized the sense of urgency by citing data on AIDS: "As of January 31, 1989, nationwide, 84,985 cases of acquired immunodeficiency syndrome (AIDS) had been reported and 48,582 deaths due to AIDS had occurred."[27] But these numbers consisted almost entirely of gay men, intravenous drug users, and women who had had drug users as sexual partners.

There were few cases of teens acquiring AIDS through heterosexual intercourse. In creating the popular myth that teens were at high risk of AIDS, researchers distorted the data by proposing that since "one-fifth of reported AIDS cases in the United States have been in the 20–29 year age group" many must have contracted the disease during high school or soon after.[28] They did not explain that gay men accounted for most of the young adult AIDS cases. A few researchers acknowledged the lack of concrete evidence that AIDS was spreading among the young and heterosexual, and some studies of youth emphasized other STDs as much as AIDS. But all used AIDS to justify their research, and none pointed out that teens did not have especially high risks of contracting the disease. Risk-taking teens made perfect victims.

The federal research bureaucracy supported this argument and funded many surveys, while others used foundation or other support. These surveys all sounded similar themes: there was a serious shortage of data for assessing the risks, and young people's egocentrism and naïveté meant such risks were probably serious. The threat of AIDS spreading rapidly among youth changed the meaning of condoms, which a decade earlier had been evidence of irresponsible contraceptive practice. Now researchers started to promote condom use as a panacea for AIDS.[29]

A survey at the Center for Clinical and Behavioral Studies in New York is a good example of a type of survey that was common in the 1980s and beyond. Heather Walter and her colleagues conducted their research in New York City, which they considered an especially risky place for the young because it was an AIDS "epicenter." They first assessed tenth graders' beliefs about their risks of HIV infection and about the severity of AIDS. Then they measured how well students thought they could manage prevention. Many boys said they were unable to resist engaging in high-risk behaviors such as having intercourse when "high" or "drunk." Since only one-fifth of the sexually active reported a single "low-risk" sexual partner, consistent use of condoms, and no history of intravenous drug use in the past year, the researchers concluded that many young people were at risk of acquiring AIDS.[30]

But less than 10 percent of the sexually active students reported any of the following: one or more high-risk partners *and* no consistent use of condoms; intravenous drug use; a history of STDs (which in itself did not necessarily indicate danger of HIV transmission). Most of the so-called risk takers had had sex with more than one partner or did not always use a condom. AIDS was almost nonexistent in young heterosexuals' sexual networks, so neither of these activities was likely to lead to AIDS, even in a city with many AIDS cases. This survey and many others like it helped create intense concern about the young—an easy task, since their sexual activity disturbed adults anyway.

The federal agency that gave the risk to the young the highest priority was the Centers for Disease Control (CDC). Some youths greatly risked contracting AIDS, and the CDC was appropriately worried about them. These included gay male youth, intravenous drug users and their partners, young prostitutes, and those who lived on society's fringes. Yet the CDC did not expend most resources surveying these vulnerable young people, who in mainstream public opinion did not appear innocent. In 1988 the CDC began a series of health-risk surveys among high school students that asked limited questions about sexual activity and knowledge of HIV risks. It first funded surveys by state or local educational authorities, and in 1989 added a national probability sample of more than 8,000 high school students using the same questions. In spite of the greater risk of transmission from men to women than from women to men, CDC researchers presented AIDS as an equal opportunity heterosexual disease. And they did not acknowledge that most infected teens belonged to other high-risk groups. Instead, on finding that over half the young people in the 1989 national survey were sexually active and only one-third always used condoms, researchers asserted that large proportions of the young faced serious risks of AIDS. Furthermore, they added, high-risk groups like male homosexuals and intravenous drug users had modified their behavior, but adolescents had not.[31]

This charge totally ignored young people's actual experience with AIDS. Unless they were gay, most had no HIV-positive friends. The AIDS epidemic was real for groups like gay men, and they had changed their behavior. The heterosexual young needed to use condoms to prevent pregnancy or STDs, but researchers paid less attention to these real risks than to the more deadly but more hypothetical risk of AIDS.

By 1989 the CDC had established the Youth Risk Behavior Surveillance

System to monitor a variety of "health-risk" behaviors including sex, alcohol consumption, drug use, smoking, high fat consumption, and lack of physical activity. In 1992 it added a third data set by including the questions on the annual National Health Interview Survey. The CDC's repeated warnings that students were in imminent danger of HIV infection apparently had an impact on what the young reported doing, and from 1989 on CDC surveys showed declines in proportions reporting sexual activity and increases in condom use.[32]

Some researchers still used convenience samples of college students. A large study funded by Mayer Laboratories and conducted by the Center for AIDS Prevention Studies (CAPS) illustrates many of the problems with surveys of the young. A key hypothesis of this survey was that, although students understood the "facts" of HIV transmission, they took risks. But the researchers' true/false questions oversimplified the facts by presenting all of the following statements as equally true:

- Women with AIDS can infect men.
- Men with AIDS can infect women.
- You can get AIDS from vaginal intercourse.
- You can get AIDS from anal intercourse.
- You can get AIDS from oral sex.[33]

All were technically true, but some represented rare events, at least in the United States, and the first two lacked any specificity. These researchers would have learned more by asking about the relative dangers of different sexual activities. Instead, this list communicated that all these activities were equally dangerous. The researchers misunderstood that the most effective health programs aim to minimize risk rather than to abolish it.

Truly high-risk teens were not always easy to identify. The few studies that documented their existence did not involve expensive probability samples, so it was impossible to assess their incidence. For example, some youth (mostly boys) were intravenous drug users. Some (mostly girls) had partners who were. These were overrepresented among minorities, particularly blacks and Latinos. Instead of investing resources to determine their incidence and location, it was easier to assume all minority youth belonged in the risk-taking category. Studies of minority youth not only used the justification that adolescents took risks but also cited data showing high levels of HIV infection among minorities in general, raising fears about the risk to middle-class whites from these groups. Well-financed studies would probably have shown pockets of high-risk youth leading difficult lives and concentrated in some segments of Latino and black communities. But this would have damaged the image of all youth as inherently prone to take risks, an image essential to research support.

A few small studies were designed to locate those who were truly at risk. Ralph DiClemente and his colleagues administered the questionnaire from the CDC's school-based survey of 1988 to students in an adolescent detention center in San Francisco. Compared with students surveyed in San Francisco public high schools, the incarcerated youth had less understanding of how to reduce the risk of contracting HIV and took considerably more risks. Ninety-nine percent were sexually experienced, and over half had first engaged in sexual intercourse before age 12. In contrast, 28 percent of the high school youth reported sexual experience, and only 7 percent started before age 12. The detention center youth's high rates of intravenous drug use (13 percent) and low rates of regular condom use (25 percent) indicated their need for help. A study of black adolescent crack users presented an even starker picture. These truly high-risk youth had histories of STDs, of exchanging sex for drugs, and of using condoms only sporadically. Yet even though more reliable surveys targeted on such groups were desperately needed, the bulk of the CDC's funding went to surveys of all students.[34]

Even when young people's lives seemed to put them at risk, HIV was not always their most serious problem. In a CDC study of street youth attending drop-in centers in Hollywood, half the young men and one-third of the young women had a history of "survival sex," which the authors defined as "exchanging sex for anything needed, including money, food, clothes, a place to stay or drugs," and similar proportions had had sex when buying drugs. But among the two-thirds who had been tested for HIV, none of the women tested positive. The women's risks were older than HIV: almost two-thirds had been pregnant, nearly one-quarter had given birth, and one-third had a history of STDs. Of the men, 29 percent identified themselves as homosexual or bisexual, and one-quarter injected drugs. Not surprisingly, 5 percent had tested positive for HIV. Young men living on the street apparently had lifestyles that put them at greater risk than young women of contracting HIV. Yet the researchers concluded that all the respondents were at serious risk of HIV infection, with pregnancy and STDs as afterthoughts. In their article reporting on the survey they ignored the results of their respondents' HIV tests. To get this information, interested readers had to examine the tables accompanying the article.[35]

If African Americans were at particular risk of HIV infection, researchers needed to interview a sample of African Americans of all ages, not just youth. But AIDS remained, in the eyes of many members of society, a disease whose victims were sinners, and African-American communities were reluctant to receive another round of blame. This was especially true of poor communities, where researchers' attention should have focused. Furthermore, researchers needed victims that middle America would identify with. They had convinced heterosexual middle-class Americans that they were at risk. This group saw itself as the backbone of society and therefore as society's most important concern. Blacks and others whose lives this group deemed different could be portrayed as the original causes of the problem of AIDS but could not be the main focus of surveys. Thus few studies of poor African-American communities appeared.

The exceptions produced disturbing findings about the prevalence of high-risk groups in poor black communities. In the 1989–1990 round of a longitudinal survey of Central Harlem started in the late 1960s, over three-quarters agreed to be tested for HIV, and, of these, almost 8 percent (22) were HIV positive, most unknowingly. These were not just any members of these communities. The HIV-positive men had histories of sex with other men or of intravenous drug use, and the women injected drugs themselves, had sexual partners who injected drugs, and/or sold sex for money or drugs. The best-known study of the poor was the longitudinal "AMEN" study of African Americans, Latinos, and whites living in the San Francisco census tracts with the highest rates of admission to detox programs. Of the 1,770 respondents, 69 proved HIV-positive, all but three of them men. These men were homosexually active and/or intravenous drug users. Even so, in reporting the results, the researchers glossed over the real story their evidence told and warned that "given the prevalence of risk behaviors for acquiring HIV heterosexually, the potential is high for future spread of infection into currently unaffected groups."[36]

These studies confirmed much that was already known about HIV infection but was unpalatable to many researchers. Persons with serious risks of HIV infection were those who either engaged in specific risky practices or belonged to social networks with high rates of infection. Such groups often lived in poor, minority neighborhoods. Still, most people in those ethnic groups or neighborhoods were not at risk. Despite these findings, the search for evidence that AIDS threatened the non-drug-using, heterosexual population continued in earnest. One CAPS survey even described a group of affluent elderly people in San Francisco as at risk and discussed how to increase condom use in this population.[37]

Bisexual men were viewed as a more serious threat. But an analysis of the bisexual respondents in the San Francisco Men's Health Study, a study of

HIV transmission among gay and bisexual men that had begun in the early 1980s, concluded that it was unlikely they were a major source of HIV among women. Bisexual respondents reported great reductions in high-risk behaviors, especially when engaging in sex with men. While there were no reliable data on either the incidence of bisexuality in the population or the sexual practices of those who regularly had sex with both men and women, bisexual men were apparently a minimal threat. Intravenous drug–using men were a different story. Between 1988 and 1991 Stephanie Tortu and her colleagues interviewed over 5,000 women who did not inject drugs but had male sexual partners who did. Of the women tested, almost 6 percent were HIV-positive. These women were in social networks that did not endanger the whole society, and society showed little concern for them.[38]

While these small surveys kept AIDS transmission in the news, none provided much-needed estimates of the actual size of the high-risk population. Those who needed to know, like the National Research Council's AIDS committee, used whatever data they could find to fill the gap, such as a *Los Angeles Times* telephone survey in the five cities with the most AIDS cases. One reliable source of data was the NORC General Social Survey, since it was based on a probability sample, had well-tested questions, and used highly trained interviewers. Unfortunately its sample was too small to provide information on important subgroups like gay men. Starting in 1988 the SHARP team, along with the NORC researcher Tom Smith, examined the relationship between number and type of sexual partners and the risk of HIV exposure. Most respondents had little risk of HIV: over 80 percent reported having had sex with zero or one partner in the previous twelve months, and less than 7 percent had engaged in activities that put them at even some risk of AIDS. Smith also explored methodological issues. He compared different introductions, experimented with wording and question order, and analyzed nonresponses to the questions about sexual behavior. No matter what he did, on average men reported more sexual partners and more sexual activity than women, a result, Smith argued, of both male exaggeration and female underreporting. This acknowledgment contrasted with numerous studies in which researchers accepted young unmarried men's accounts of their behavior without discussing the accuracy of such reports.[39]

The General Social Survey was also used to question the accuracy of official AIDS estimates. In 1986 the Public Health Service had estimated that between 1 and 1.5 million Americans were infected with HIV, an estimate that had not been revised in subsequent years. There were numerous problems with this estimate, one of which was the use in constructing it of Kinsey's estimate of the proportion of men who had sex with other men. In addition, the CDC, which requires reporting of all AIDS cases, had about 73,000 cases documented by 1988. Edward Laumann and his colleagues produced estimates that suggested there might be an underreporting of AIDS cases among more affluent whites, whose private physicians were less likely to report cases than were public clinics. Since affluent whites with the disease were more likely to be gay than to be drug users, Laumann suggested that more gay men and fewer drug users had AIDS than officially believed.[40]

Charles Turner of the National Research Council's AIDS committee and Robert Fay, a Census Bureau statistician who was a consultant to the National Research Council, had proposed that a national probability sample, with an HIV test, would produce the best official estimates.[41] Their proposal was greeted hesitantly by agencies like the National Center for Health Statistics and the Census Bureau. These are the federal government's major data-gathering agencies, responsible for numerous surveys including the decennial census, the monthly Current Population Survey, which produces the unemployment rate, and the annual National Health Interview Survey, and for compiling birth, death, marriage, and divorce data. They resist involvement in controversial activities, since public disapproval might make it more difficult to perform their mandated tasks. Questions about sexual behavior in a survey like the one proposed by Turner and Fay might have sparked such disapproval.

Even so, pressure for more accurate estimates began to mount. In 1988 the Presidential Commission on AIDS raised the alarm about the possible spread of AIDS to heterosexuals. It repeated claims that both drug addicts and bisexual men could transmit AIDS to the "general population" and suggested that 10 percent of American men were "active bisexuals."[42] Soon after this, President Reagan called for a program to determine the national incidence of HIV. The CDC, however reluctant, had to act. Its National Center for Health Statistics designed pretests of a survey like the one Turner and Fay had proposed and promised to present a full survey and HIV estimates to the president's Domestic Policy Council by 1990.

Research Triangle Institute in North Carolina won the contract for this survey, but researchers at the National Center for Health Statistics continued to make many of the decisions about the survey, such as the location of the pretests and the design features of the research. The men at the National Center for Health Statistics were used to working with the "sober, professional enthusiasm" appropriate to research on the nation's well-being. They could not negotiate the problems associated with sex research, particularly after the two national surveys stalled. Certain scientifically justifiable features of the surveys' design increased their problems. These included promising confidentiality but not anonymity, in order to have participants' names for validation studies, and proposing an anonymous additional sample of persons from gay organization rosters, STD clinics, and drug treatment programs to ascertain whether high-risk individuals would give truthful answers. These scientific considerations ran into community opposition at the site of the first planned pretest, Washington, D.C., and the pretest had to be canceled. Already suspicious of the CDC because of the notorious Tuskegee experiment, in which the Public Health Service had withheld syphilis treatment from 400 African-American men in order to observe the disease's progress, African-American opponents argued that Washington, with its predominantly black population, was being singled out for stigmatizing with AIDS.[43] After the National Center for Health Statistics received advice from the CDC's HIV Program Office on how to obtain community support, the first pretest was moved to Pittsburgh and the controversial design features were dropped. The second pretest, in Dallas, brought threats from the Dallas Gay Alliance but little actual opposition.

The Research Triangle team that conducted the actual pretest, headed by Michael Weeks, estimated that Dallas had over 4,000 HIV cases.[44] All participants received $50, but a sample of nonrespondents were offered up to $175 each for participating. This innovative follow-up proved an important feature of the survey. Those who did not participate until the second round had higher rates of HIV than those who participated when first asked. The survey's estimates of HIV transmission in different groups indicated that, except for those in known high-risk groups, infection was rare. The researchers had reason to be pleased with their results. They found rates of risky behavior that people would be reluctant to admit to, such as intravenous drug use, twice as high as those found by the prestigious National Health Interview Survey, which by this time included questions on behavioral risks in its short module on AIDS knowledge and attitudes. A survey focusing on AIDS apparently produced more accurate reports than one with AIDS as an afterthought. Even so, Weeks's estimates of the incidence of HIV infection were lower than those of the CDC or the National Cancer Institute. The CDC estimates were based on "backcounting" reported AIDS cases into numbers of HIV-positive people by estimating the size of both the gay male and the intravenous drug–using populations. For gay men the CDC relied on Kinsey's data, which were almost certainly an overestimate.

Although Research Triangle Institute concluded that a national survey was feasible, those in charge at the National Center for Health Statistics recommended to the White House Domestic Policy Council that it not proceed.[45] They invoked nameless outside experts as disagreeing on the study's feasibility. They also cited the back-calculation estimates, which many believed were too high, as evidence that survey data would underestimate the level of HIV. Congress had limited the funding for the pretest and might not have funded a national survey, but the main reason for not proceeding appeared to be that policymakers found the experience of publicly funded sex research bruising. Furthermore, lowering the estimates of HIV infection might have lessened interest in a disease to which many agencies had made major funding commitments. It would have outraged some in the gay community, particularly those activists who mistrusted the CDC's intentions. And conservative critics would have advocated cuts in funding if evidence had been found that AIDS was not spreading beyond socially stigmatized groups. This exercise in science was undone by politics.

While the Dallas pretest was in the field, ATS and SHARP remained in limbo. Even though Assistant Secretary of HHS Mason testified on the merits of SHARP before the House Appropriations Committee in March 1990, it seemed the adult survey was a sinking ship in government waters. The discouraged NORC team made two moves. They approached foundations for funding, and they sent an unsolicited grant proposal to NICHD for a two-city survey of adult sexual behavior. This proposed survey received the highest ranking from the peer review committee and was approved for funding in July 1991.[46]

While SHARP languished, ATS began to go forward. In May 1991 the director of NIH, Bernadine Healy, received Mason's consent to approve the five-year $18 million grant, and the University of North Carolina received its first check. Rindfuss and Udry began training interviewers and arranging for further pretesting of their interview schedule. While their proposed research design was not a word-for-word description of the intended shape of their survey, it provides a guide.[47] Although their sample questionnaires included many more questions on sexual behavior than had ever been asked of teens on a national survey, they did not share SHARP's neutral approach to sexual diversity. It would have been more difficult to be tolerant of varieties of sexual expression among the young, and in the ATS heterosexual marriage was the preferred goal. Instead of SHARP's integrated theoretical argument, Udry and Rindfuss listed numerous hypotheses to explain why teenagers had sex and girls got pregnant.

In their proposed survey Rindfuss and Udry presented teenage sexual activity as both a problem to be prevented and a condition to be reluctantly managed. They suggested that a propensity for sexual activity was in part inherited and in part social. They also hypothesized that children of working mothers would be more sexually active than average and that sexually experienced girls would cause the sexual downfall of boys more often than vice versa. The sexual and reproductive behavior of black teens was a special concern, and Rindfuss and Udry proposed oversampling middle-class blacks to separate the effects of race from class. In a hypothesis reminiscent of fears that white girls might emulate black girls' sexual and reproductive freedoms, Udry and Rindfuss anticipated that white teens who had black friends would be more sexually active and would use contraception less reliably than other whites. They also hypothesized that sexually active teens would be those with liberal parents, or parents who spent less time with their children, or parents who lived in communities with high divorce rates or low church attendance. While they concentrated on the causes of teenagers' sexual activity, they also argued that sex education programs and easier access to contraceptives would improve contraceptive use among those who were already sexually active. Their portrayal coincided in many ways with the conservative view that America needed strong families with stay-at-home mothers who kept their daughters in check. Yet conservatives organized to defeat this proposed survey.

One possible explanation for the opposition is the addition of AIDS as a research topic. AIDS was added by NICHD during the research-design phase. Investigating AIDS required studying boys as well as girls, and Rindfuss and Udry had already planned to include boys; unlike other fertility researchers, Udry had long included boys in his surveys. In adding AIDS, Rindfuss and Udry were more cautious than those who designed SHARP. While acknowledging that the role of heterosexual intercourse in HIV transmission was controversial, they proposed to treat vaginal intercourse, anal intercourse, and oral intercourse as equally risky. Still, they would ask boys if they had had male sexual partners, and those who responded affirmatively would be asked about anal intercourse.

Another source of conservative ire was the sample design. Udry and Rindfuss proposed sampling 100 high schools and their feeder schools using a longitudinal design. All pupils in grades 7–12 would complete a screening interview, and from these researchers would select 20,000 students for intensive at-home interviews on sexual behavior, partners, and drug use. Parents would also be interviewed. The sample size would be larger than in any previous survey of sexual behavior; Udry and Rindfuss argued that anything smaller would make many analyses impossible because behaviors that led to HIV infection were rare among adolescents.

The most controversial feature was their intention to collect the names of the respondents' sexual partners. This made the surveyors nervous:

> Respondents in phase 2 [the at-home interview] might experience social or legal consequences from the disclosure of much of the information we plan to request from them. We recommend asking them to reveal illegal drug use, illegal forms of sexual behavior, and the names of their sex partners. Respondents might be subject to arrest, embarrassment, lawsuits, ridicule, loss of employment, student loan rights, and other problems were the confidentiality of the data breached. We recommend reducing the probability of breach of confidentiality to as close to zero as possible.[48]

This nervousness was justified, because opponents of the survey focused on confidentiality. To reduce the risk of breaching confidentiality, Rindfuss and Udry recommended allowing access only to a random subset of cases. Thus their large sample would be unavailable to most researchers, even though its size was an important design feature.

Healy took pride in having approved this survey, and a *Boston Globe* interview with her on July 7, 1991, cited her role as evidence of her independence from the Bush administration.[49] This story was premature. Funders had felt comfortable approving the research because they believed their history of asking personal questions of adolescents made a teen survey less problematic than an adult survey. Paul Mero saw things differently. Although teens might be more willing than adults to answer personal questions, parents would be outraged if they knew what these questions might be.

On July 16, 1991, Secretary Sullivan of HHS appeared on a conservative closed-circuit television show where he was questioned about the teen survey, claimed ignorance, but pledged to look into it. Two days later the *Washington Times* framed the issue in an article headlined "Surprised Sullivan Says 'Whoa' to Teen Sex Survey." The story identified those opposed, including Congressman Dannemeyer ("outraged that federal money will be spent"), Paul Mero ("the questionnaire for boys 'asks the teenager if he's ever had a penis up his rectum'"), and Gary Bauer of the Family Research Council ("a survey that offends the sensibilities of millions of Americans"). The article blamed Mason and Healy for approving the survey. It also cited NICHD's "spokesman" Michaela Richardson as saying that parental approval would be required for teenagers to be interviewed, a statement it allowed Mero to counter with "this condition ensures built-in bias in the survey. 'Just think of the people who'd allow their kids to participate in a survey like this.'" Accompanying the article was a box listing eighteen out-of-context questions on such topics as vaginal intercourse, oral sex, anal intercourse, pregnancy, contraception, forced sex, and sex in exchange for drugs.

Rindfuss learned that the study had been suspended when the press began calling him three days after Sullivan acted. Although Rindfuss considered himself naive in dealing with the press, he successfully crafted a narrative that deemphasized the sexual aspects of the study and transformed the survey of risky sexual behavior into a more general study of teen life. Stories cited his statements that out of three hundred questions only ten dealt with homosexuality, and that questions about sexual behavior would be confined to those teens who indicated relevant experience: "Rindfuss said the study goes beyond sexual behavior and intravenous drug use. 'In the teen-age years, probably more than any other years, people are subjected to a wide variety of social pressures from youth groups, school, family,' he said. 'We want to understand the extent to which schools and family, churches, communities, and so forth influence adolescent behavior.'"[50]

The survey's allies in the media were more explicit in their discussion of its goals. A *New York Times* editorial noted that the nation was uncomfortable with talk about sex even while "15-year-old mothers are common, and thousands of young men are dying of a sexually transmitted disease contracted in their teens." If survey questions involved topics that some considered unmentionable, the *Times* argued, they were necessary. Indeed, "a reduction in the rate of unwanted pregnancies and a rise in age at first intercourse" could not be achieved "without the kind of information the North Carolina study can provide."[51] Conservatives argued the opposite, contending that asking such questions would promote the behavior under study.

Within a few days newspapers began to lobby in favor of the now-canceled survey. They devoted prominent space to the Democratic representatives Henry Waxman and Patricia Schroeder, both of whom spoke knowledgeably about the topic. Schroeder, one of the few members of Congress comfortable discussing sex in public, bemoaned the know-nothing attitude that had led to the cancellation and charged that Sullivan was bowing to right-wing extremism. United Press International reported that both Mason and Healy had considered resigning over the issue. Most newspapers agreed with Schroeder that Sullivan was capitulating to the Christian right and cited similar incidents such as his appointment of antiabortion activists to top positions in the department. "Sullivan," opined the Boston *Globe*, "might as well have tape over his mouth and a button on his lapel declaring 'Just Say No to Sex.'" The pro-survey lobby was ready when Dannemeyer proposed amending the NIH Revitalization Bill to prohibit funding for future surveys of sexual behavior, and he was resoundingly defeated. Schroeder amended the bill to provide $3 million per year to survey risky adolescent behavior. And Waxman successfully substituted for Dannemeyer's amendment one allowing NIH to approve any carefully reviewed survey that was declared useful in fighting disease.[52]

Both sides in this political controversy were concerned about the behavioral consequences of talk about sex. Conservatives believed surveys would inform young people of things they might not know and tell the more knowledgeable that such behavior was permissible, and they feared a world where girls and boys had the same sexual freedoms. Liberals believed that asking such questions was essential to creating life-saving behavioral change, and they saw a threat to boys and girls alike. And both were keenly aware of the power of surveys to inform the public. It was irrelevant whether or not surveys were methodologically sound, because few would question their data. The potential for results they did not like, such as a discovery that 10 percent of the population actually was gay, was another reason for conservatives to block the survey.

During the debate in Congress, those supporting Dannemeyer's amendment stressed the dangers of sex research and described these dangers in gendered terms. Although they decried the public talk about sex represented by the surveys, they used explicit sexual talk as a tool to defeat them. Dannemeyer read what he claimed were proposed questions to be asked of boys:

- The next few questions are about sexual experiences with other males. Many teenage boys have had such experiences, and it is important to this study that we ask about them.

- One, have you ever rubbed another male's sexual organs to sexually excite him?

- Two. Has another male ever rubbed your sexual organs to sexually excite you?

An outraged Dannemeyer argued that the questions' preamble, in suggesting that "many teenage boys" did these things, was intended "to develop statistical data with a subtle inference to the interviewees that this perverse type of conduct is okay." In contrast to such innocent boys, who might become homosexual from the survey, his fellow conservative congressmen portrayed girls as having already lost their innocence in a sexualized society. In their description, girls whose mothers were raising them alone and who had "never known the love or attention of a male in their lives" were never taught about "sin" and ran around "like street prostitutes."[53] No wonder they got pregnant and had half a million abortions a year.

This use of gender was intended to frighten the public into believing that the heterosexual family was threatened by the surveys. Liberals understood this and therefore avoided discussion of gender. The Democrats and Republicans who supported Waxman's amendment argued that sex surveys would save lives, and they described three "epidemics," AIDS, STDs, and pregnancy, as equal-opportunity plagues without reference to gender or homosexuality. Representative Rowland of Georgia used his credibility as a physician to state that, in spite of his discomfort at the questions, the information was essential because AIDS threatened the welfare and health of Americans. Representative McDermott of Washington noted that "children may be embarrassed by such discussion—but they will not die from embarrassment," as they might from AIDS. Representative Miller of California argued that it was the very normality of teens' risk-taking that put them at risk: "We are talking about the most vulnerable people in the United States, the next big class of people that troubles us deeply with respect to AIDS. You do not have to engage in sexually deviant behavior. You do not have to engage in high risk. You may just be a normal child who experiments with sex against the wishes of your parents, against the counseling of your parents. Your partner may be high risk and you may then get AIDS." And, in case anyone missed the message, he added that "these are not the children of bad parents . . . They are all of society's children."[54]

The NIH Revitalization Bill then went to the Senate Labor and Human Resources Committee, chaired by Edward Kennedy of Massachusetts. Although Senator Kennedy was supportive, his personal history made it politically awkward for him to lead debate on the surveys, so Senator Brock Adams of Washington assumed this role. The bill included other controversial topics, including funding for research using fetal tissue and research on women's health. Much wrangling went on in committee, and before the bill came before the full Senate the HHS budget bill provided an opportunity, on September 12, for a Senate debate on sex surveys. By this time Senate conservatives knew that Laumann and his colleagues had received funding for the two-city study, so they attacked this and ATS simultaneously.

The pro-survey lobbyists were focused on the NIH revitalization, so Senator Jesse Helms of North Carolina surprised them when he introduced an amendment to the budget bill to take money targeted for the surveys and reallocate it to abstinence education under Title XX of the Adolescent Family Life Act. In presenting his amendment Helms skillfully combined possible questions from the teen questionnaire with controversial descriptions of some SHARP researchers. The conflation of the two surveys was politically astute: while the ATS researchers were harder to attack, their questions were more inflammatory since they were directed at youth.

Helms named as two of the three principal researchers on the adult survey Stuart Michaels, whom he described as a gay activist and therefore not objective, and John Gagnon, who, he claimed, advocated sex between children and adults. The repeated elevation of Michaels, who was a graduate student at the time, to principal investigator occurred because, to strengthen their case, conservatives intentionally confused him with NORC director Robert Michael. Michael and the unmentioned Edward Laumann were both politically conservative and appeared difficult to attack. Helms also focused on homosexuality and teenage pregnancy, particularly the former. He claimed that a sexual liberation cabal had deliberately sexualized the nation's children, using sex education and contraception to promote teenage pregnancy and abortions. This cabal now wanted to convince Americans that homosexuality was normal and acceptable, even though this would mean that AIDS could never be controlled. This was the intent, Helms claimed, of the proposed surveys, which were also flawed because about half of those contacted would refuse to participate. In fact, he argued, the scientific community was counting on a high nonresponse rate among decent people. Participants would then disproportionately represent "sexual deviates and perverts and homosexuals," leading to inflated estimates of homosexuality and a resulting argument that this was a normal lifestyle.[55] Thus Helms challenged the Senate to choose between educating the young to restrain themselves sexually and promoting sexual decadence.

Unlike Helms, the only speaker in favor of his amendment, those few who spoke against it scarcely mentioned sex. Senator Moynihan of New York gave a rambling speech about illegitimacy, assured the Senate that NORC was a reputable institution, and noted that he had talked to the SHARP researchers, who were fine men. Well briefed by his staff, Senator Adams pointed out that Helms was reading questions that had been dropped from the proposed survey two years earlier. The last speaker,

Senator Kohl of Wisconsin, showed how difficult this issue was politically. Kohl charged that Helms mischaracterized the research and argued that to ban the surveys would be embarrassing. Yet he voted with the silent majority of senators (66–34) to transfer the funding to abstinence education. Helms's rhetorical skill carried the day. He forced senators to choose between asking America's teenagers explicit questions about sexual acts and telling them to postpone sexual activity until marriage. Even if most senators did not believe such postponement possible, they found it expedient to support his agenda.

Most of those voting against Helms's amendment voted for the budget bill itself because they supported other provisions, including the suspension of the "gag rule" prohibiting federally funded clinics from providing referrals for abortion counseling. The final language banned the surveys but transferred no money to abstinence education. When the bill went to President Bush, he vetoed it because of the removal of the gag rule. The surveys, however, were in serious trouble, and Baldwin of NICHD decided not to approve the funding for the NORC team's two-city study.

In debating the NIH Revitalization Bill, the Senate had one last fight about the surveys. This time everyone had advance notice, and lobbying was fierce. By now Senator Adams was confronting his own sexual scandal, and Paul Simon of Illinois took the lead. Simon already believed in the need for sex research and, with the University of Chicago in his home state, had discussed the surveys with Laumann. But he had an even more important qualification for leadership on the issue. Unlike Kennedy or Adams, he had a reputation as "Mr. Boy Scout."[56] Only such a man could risk taking the lead in favor of a sex survey. He proposed an amendment adding the language Waxman had previously used in defeating Dannemeyer's amendment in the House, that is, to allow NIH to approve any survey of sexual behavior that after careful review was declared useful in the fight against any sexually transmitted or other infectious disease. On the Senate floor, on March 13, 1992, opposing versions of the truth were debated.

Helms was again the only speaker in favor of his amendment, which explicitly prohibited SHARP and ATS. He repeatedly evoked the image of "sexual deviants, perverts and homosexuals" to the exclusion of other topics, and he confidently claimed that most Americans knew that homosexuality was abhorrent and dangerous.[57] To taint the liberals with sexual scandal, he asked Kennedy, who spoke strongly for the surveys, to read proposed teen survey questions aloud. When Kennedy refused, pointing out that he did not even know if Helms's paper contained authentic questions, Helms stated that he could not read them himself (even though he had read some the previous November) because of their offensive nature, and he put them into the record instead.

To Helms's focus on sin liberals responded with an emphasis on illness. A number of senators spoke in support of Simon's amendment. They acknowledged that some persons might be offended by the questions Helms read aloud on the Senate floor, but they argued that the surveys would save lives and reduce the suffering caused by the three "major social ills" of unintended pregnancy, STDs, and AIDS. Reflecting the ambivalence of many, both amendments passed, Simon's 57–40 and Helms's 51–46. President Bush again vetoed the bill, this time because it ended the ban on research using fetal tissue.[58]

As these political battles demonstrated, a century after Clelia Mosher, sex remained a dangerous topic of inquiry. A writer from the *Chicago Tribune* in a November 1991 review of the whole fiasco pointed to the contradictions: "We know that Geraldo Rivera apparently had a quickie with Bette Midler before his television show, and that Fergie, the Duchess of York, sunbathed topless on the Riviera with an American lover. We know comparable gossip about the sex lives of famous people as dissimilar as Woody Allen, Bill Clinton, Wade Boggs, Liberace, and Nancy Reagan. What we don't know—and what is of immensely greater importance—is what the rest of us ordinary folks have been doing between the sheets."[59] The controversy also revealed that all the characters in this drama implicitly understood the power of surveys to create and shape seemingly objective, scientific knowledge.

Explaining the defeat of these surveys is difficult. It is true that conservatives harked back to a time when young women took responsibility for the moral standards of society. Now, they complained, young women's standards were as low as young men's. But this is not enough to explain why the surveys got into trouble. Young women's sexuality had been scrutinized for decades without raising public ire. And magazines for young women were full of advice on sexual hedonism. Helms succeeded because he focused on homosexuality, a topic liberals found so frightening they barely mentioned it, and because he spoke in a climate in which heterosexual men found their own behavior under attack.

The combined effect of gay liberation and sexual hedonism had been to make gay sexual relations with many partners seem not all that different from the general norm. This made many Americans, especially men, uneasy. Furthermore, the image of heterosexual men's sexuality as the unproblematic norm had been undermined by the masses of research showing that women were most likely to be sexually assaulted in established intimate relationships. In fact, while the debate over the surveys was under way, the nation's attention was riveted on another Senate scene. Americans watched senators who voted against the sex surveys, such as Arlen Specter of Pennsylvania, rush to defend the sexual behavior of a nominee to the Supreme Court, Clarence Thomas—behavior that had long been considered normal. Survey results suggested that men's desire for sexual variety would get them into trouble, not just from women who no longer acquiesced, but also from a deadly disease. AIDS was much less threatening to mainstream Americans if it was a metaphor for deviant sex than if it was a danger to any man with a normal sexual appetite. Those who defended the surveys tried to create their own panic about the danger of AIDS to public health without assigning blame, but in the end this proved an impossible balancing act.

While politics had never been far from sex research, as shown by, for example, the congressional investigation of Kinsey, it was not until the 1980s that the two became closely intertwined. AIDS provided survey researchers and other experts, who had little direct experience with sex research, with government funding and the opportunity to use their skills to fight a terrible disease. Many simply portrayed AIDS as threatening and frightening to all, a message to which the federal government was forced to pay attention. At the same time, the religious right and other conservative forces politicized sex for their own purposes. They played on the same fears as the researchers did but were more explicit. They treated AIDS as a sexually transmitted disease associated with sin and shame. They did so in order to argue for returning to their version of traditional and gendered morality, for blaming the victims, and for cutting federal funding.

These competing visions collided in the battle over two large surveys. It is easy to be cynical about surveys, given the often inadequate methodology and the attempts of many researchers to control the results of their research. But large surveys would have added to our understanding of AIDS transmission. The survey of teens would have provided useful insights into the true risks faced by young people. NORC's researchers were eventually able to conduct a much smaller version of their survey using private funding. Unfortunately, it was too small to answer the questions about the national incidence of HIV or the size of high-risk groups that would have been answered by the larger study. The survey of adults really did have the potential to save lives, as well as to reduce anxiety among the many who had little to fear from AIDS. Instead it was killed by the confluence of conflicting political goals.

10

The Story Continues

Since 1971, reliable, nationally representative data have been collected about young women's sexual activity and contraceptive utilization . . . Comparable information for adolescent males over time is simply not available.

—Freya Sonenstein, 1986

THE ATTACKS on government-funded sex surveys did not bring an end to such research, and several surveys appeared over the next few years. The surveyors feared their funding too might be in jeopardy. Most were trained as demographers and did not consider themselves sex researchers, so they were unused to controversy. They had obtained funding for surveys of sexual behavior by stressing the risks of AIDS. Now if they argued that a serious problem existed they might be accused, by the activists in Congress and elsewhere who had defeated the surveys, of creating the problem themselves by their nonjudgmental "scientific" attitudes, since conservatives saw "nonjudgmental" as a code for removing the restraints and punishments that were necessary to contain sexual licentiousness. And yet if they took the alternative position and argued that the problem was less serious than previously thought, they would be vulnerable to charges of wasting government money on boondoggles.

In this climate researchers became even more careful and managed their research so as not to draw attention to it. Four government-funded national surveys of sexual behavior quietly continued during the fight over SHARP and ATS. Three of these, the National Survey of Adolescent Males, the National Survey of Women, and the National Survey of Men, were funded by the National Institute of Child Health and Human Development (NICHD), and the fourth, the National AIDS Behavioral Survey, was supported by the National Institute of Mental Health. These surveys all used random sampling, trained interviewers, and pretested questionnaires, but with the troubles surrounding ATS and SHARP, their investigators did not employ the usual technique of seeking publicity so that potential respondents might hear about the survey. Instead they maintained low profiles.

The National Survey of Adolescent Males, conducted by Freya Sonenstein and Joseph Pleck, was a long-overdue survey of the reproductive behavior of young men aged 15–19. Sonenstein interviewed her respondents first in 1988 and again in 1990 and used data from Kantner and Zelnik's 1979 survey of young men as a comparison. The first round of interviews, largely about contraceptive use, was conducted about a year before the eruption of controversy over the American Teenage Survey (ATS). On the second round Sonenstein and Pleck added AIDS and other STDs to their concerns, which entailed even more explicit questions.[1] For example, on the first round they confined questions on anal intercourse to their section on homosexual behavior, but by the second round they also asked about anal intercourse with women.

By 1989 Sonenstein was aware of the need to be careful, and in her preliminary report to the Population Association of America she did not mention the forthcoming second round. Headlines about the first survey announced "Teenage Boys More Sexually Active, Survey Finds" with text describing a dramatic increase in boys' sexual activity between 1979 and 1988. No crisis developed after these headlines, but it became apparent that spin doctoring would be necessary in the future. When results from the second round of interviews appeared, the Urban Institute, where Sonenstein worked, presented them to the media so as to calm fears, and headlines reassured: "Sexual Activity Dropping among Teenage Males." The reports on the surveys pushed the theme of AIDS prevention, especially condom use. By this time the condom had been thoroughly rehabilitated as a contraceptive method. The authors of the reports portrayed young men as knowledgeable about AIDS and as taking its risks seriously. This had led to increased use of condoms and decreased use of ineffective methods of contraception. Furthermore, researchers added, popular stereotypes notwithstanding, condom use was highest among black adolescents. These were not young men who could not resist temptation.[2]

In 1990 the Center for AIDS Prevention Studies (CAPS) undertook its first nationwide probability survey, the National AIDS Behavioral Survey, entailing 13,885 telephone interviews.[3] Joseph Catania and his colleagues followed carefully laid plans and remained silent about the survey until completion of the fieldwork. They also developed a careful rationale for each question in case of attack. Catania and his colleagues were the only nondemographers among the researchers involved in the four surveys. Consistent with the CAPS position that heterosexuals risked AIDS, they took a different approach from that of Sonenstein and Pleck. They argued that previous estimates of rates of HIV infection had been based on inadequate data about heterosexuals, and they estimated that 15 percent of all adults and 20 percent of those living in "high-risk" cities were at high risk of the disease. Some of their estimates went much higher. They obtained these results by conflating disparate risks: having two or more sexual partners in the past year, having a risky primary partner, receiving a blood transfusion, having hemophilia, injecting drugs in the past five years. Some of these activities, such as injecting drugs, involved real risks, but others, such as having two partners, involved minimal risk. And with some, such as having a risky partner, the risk varied: in this case because risky partners were identified by the same disparate set of activities.

Koray Tanfer managed the other two studies at the Battelle Research Center in Seattle. The 1990 National Survey of Women consisted of follow-up interviews with women from Tanfer's earlier study (see Chapter 5) plus interviews with a new sample. As with Sonenstein's study, the original focus on fertility and contraception now had AIDS and STDs appended. The proposal title of the men's study, "Condom Use by Adult Men to Prevent AIDS," indicated a narrower focus than the women's study. When they realized SHARP and ATS were in serious trouble, Tanfer and his colleagues on the men's study, John Billy, William Grady, and Daniel Klepinger, took precautions. They were more nervous about this survey than about the women's study: "We thought, first of all, a men's study wasn't done before, and a women's study included other things, pregnancy, childrearing, breast exam . . . With men, we had nothing but sexual behavior in there, basically. Secondly, we thought that men would be more against this type of stuff. Women were always conditioned to these types of surveys . . . And . . . most congressmen are men."[4] To protect the research, Tanfer's program officer at NICHD gave Battelle all the money up front to ensure funding, and the researchers stopped talking about the surveys even to those they trusted. They did not even talk to the press in support of ATS and SHARP. Their concerns proved justified. The results of the men's study were explosive.

Results from the men's study first appeared in four articles in *Family Planning Perspectives* (FPP) in April 1993.[5] Although they disclaimed the attention the press paid to their data on homosexuality, they in fact emphasized this issue. In contrast to FPP's usual practice of illustrating reports about women with pictures of couples, the April 1993 cover showed a crowd of casually dressed men with no women in sight. Furthermore, the data on male-to-male sex appeared in the first of the four articles and was highlighted in the introduction.

The sample size (3,321) was too small to accurately measure such rare events, and the questionnaire included few questions on the topic, but the press had a field day. The *New York Times* headlined its front-page story "Sex Survey of American Men Finds 1% Are Gay." Describing the survey as the most thorough since the Kinsey report, the *Times* announced the astonishing finding that only about 2 percent of men engaged in sex with other men and only 1 percent considered themselves exclusively homosexual. *Newsweek* confirmed that gay activists were unhappy with the news: "if gays really represent such a tiny fraction of the population, will that stall the political momentum the gay-rights movement has built in recent years?" Researchers were loath to criticize one another given the political climate and commented that these results resembled those of other surveys. Instead of noting that sex research was inherently difficult or describing the design problems with the Battelle questions on homosexuality, they blamed commercial surveys as the source of problems.[6]

The publicity generated by the news that male homosexuality was rare shows how disturbing the issue was to many heterosexual men. For a century women's sexual activities had been scrutinized as researcher after researcher worried about some aspect of their sexual behavior or response, and the Battelle survey of young adult women was published with no fanfare or controversy. When the spotlight was finally turned on men, it was in the context of a terrible disease identified with a sexual group many men feared. As long as gays were the only men whose sex lives were subject to scrutiny, objections were few. And adolescent boys might also be interviewed about their behavior. But once surveys started to include all men, and to include questions about sex with other men, many felt threatened. Men often exaggerated their sexual performance with women, but were reluctant to acknowledge other types of activity or interest. Many would not admit such experiences or feelings to themselves, let alone to a stranger promising confidentiality. One barely noted finding provides some evidence of this discomfort. In 1988, when Sonenstein and Pleck asked their teenage respondents about male-to-male sexual activities, thirty respondents (about 1.5 percent of the total) reported having had anal or oral intercourse with another man. But by 1991 nineteen of these same respondents denied ever having done this. These tiny numbers should be treated with caution but suggest that men have great difficulty in admitting to such activity and may wish to forget about it afterward.[7]

None of these four studies were able to replace the two banned national surveys. With the exception of the CAPS survey, all had small sample sizes and targeted specific groups. The CAPS survey used telephone interviewing, so anyone without a telephone was missed. Since AIDS was more prevalent among the urban poor, this was a problem. Each of the banned surveys reappeared in an altered form, but before the results were published both groups of researchers wrote postmortems analyzing their experiences and proposing ways to avoid future incidents. In writing about what had happened, Edward Laumann and his colleagues rightly understood that national reticence over personal sexual histories had enabled their opponents to politicize the surveys, but they assumed that increased knowledge about the sexual behavior of others could prevent this in the future. This was a utopian assumption: conservatives did not want more data, even data that did not sensationalize sex. Richard Udry understood this point in his own postmortem account, which he wrote alone, without his co-investigator on the ATS, Ronald Rindfuss. Udry blamed the liberal politics of sex researchers for the debacle and envisioned producing true scientific findings uninfluenced by surveyors' preconceptions or wish to manage the results.[8] But this is impossible in any research, and especially in sex research.

Udry obtained funding for a version of his proposed survey by waiting for a more favorable administration in Washington. When President Clinton signed the bill revising the National Institutes of Health, it included an amendment inserted by Congresswoman Schroeder in the heat of the debate over the surveys. This amendment required a survey of adolescent health. Udry thus received support for the National Longitudinal Survey of Adolescent Health. By now both researchers and funders had learned to be careful with presentation. The new survey's goals were to measure "those behaviors that place teens at risk" as well as "positive influences and behaviors that promote good health." In announcing the funding NICHD did not mention sex. When Udry and his students began presenting their preliminary results at academic meetings in 1997, only the knowledgeable could see the earlier survey in the new one.[9]

Laumann and his colleagues took a different tack. Unwilling to sacrifice questions about sex, they received foundation support, first from the Robert Wood Johnson Foundation and subsequently from a number of others, and by 1992 began interviewing for a national sex survey. Although funding limits made the survey much smaller than originally proposed, this was the most comprehensive picture to date of the sexual behavior of American adults. To prevent media distortions and take advantage of the interest in their work, the researchers published a book for popular consumption, *Sex in America,* written with the science journalist Gina Kolata, as well as one for academic audiences, *The Social Organization of Sexuality.*[10]

Both books made it clear that the topic was sex, not some euphemism for sex. Where previous researchers had presented sexual activity as something individuals decided on alone, Laumann and his colleagues understood that sexual behavior usually involved social interaction and thus involved negotiation. This led to a number of observations not previously reported. Yet the researchers were cautious. They opened *Sex in America* by reassuring readers that "the public image of sex in America bears virtually no relation to the truth." In demonstrating this, they interspersed small amounts of data with individual voices in the manner of commercial sex surveys. But the comparison ended there. Where commercial surveys delineated a world of frequent sexual coupling, *Sex in America* portrayed Americans who usually dated and married people from backgrounds similar to their own and most of whom were sexually contented when they did so. Heterosexual marriage was alive and well in America after all. Even while acknowledging some permissive trends, such as a decline in age at first intercourse, the authors emphasized that most Americans had few sexual partners and were faithful in marriage. Only a few adults had numerous partners, and even fewer had extramarital affairs. Most never had sex with a partner they had just met. And the authors approved of this fidelity. Not everything was rosy, however. There were high rates of sexually transmitted diseases, and many women had been forced into sexual activity against their wills. But in general the book reassured.

In contrast to the paucity of data in the popular version, the academic book included numerous tables and charts and detailed descriptions of the varieties of sexual behavior among Americans. It also celebrated monogamy and emphasized the half of the sample with three or fewer lifetime partners rather than the 20 percent with five or more. The authors reported that people largely confined sex to those in their social networks and that these networks were similar by age and race. Yet most sexual networks contained both men and women, and while those of the same race and age reported more similar sexual interests and experiences, men and women appeared to differ greatly in every aspect of sex. Women had less interest in every type of sexual activity than men and reported less experience.

This finding seemed to confirm what sexologists had claimed all along—that women had a problem with sex. Unlike most of their predecessors, the authors understood that individualistic explanations for this were inadequate. Instead, in a section largely framed by Laumann and John Gagnon, they used Gagnon's sexual scripting theory to argue that women received little teaching or social support for erotic scripts. They even noted that Masters and Johnson's "discovery" of the clitoral orgasm did not seem to have helped. But, in assuming that this was a problem of and for women, they did not fully consider the role of their questionnaire in producing it. For example, they measured which sexual activities respondents found appealing by asking them to rate a list of activities: group sex, same-sex sex, forcing another sexually, being forced, watching others have sex, sex with a stranger, watching a partner undress, vaginal intercourse, using a dildo or vibrator, receiving oral sex, performing oral sex, receiving anal stimulation, performing anal stimulation, receiving anal intercourse, and (for men only) performing anal intercourse. Men found every one of these items "very appealing" at higher rates than women, seeming to make the case for women's lack of interest.

But another interpretation is possible. This list consisted of acts that often appear in pornography for men. Absent were activities that women's sexual scripts define as pleasurable, such as kissing and mutual masturbation. Women might have found these appealing at higher rates than men. While the authors noted that they had left out such items, they did not discuss the full implications of doing so. And there were other ways to measure female sexual desire. They might have asked about the appeal of longing, a staple of women's romance novels. Most important, the impersonality of the hypothetical partners was also reminiscent of pornography. Women would surely want to know who the partner was before they knew what they wanted to do with that partner. The authors, like many male researchers before them, described a world in which men owned desire and initiated sexual activity and women chose whether to respond. This was a world conservatives should have found reassuring.

In spite of these shortcomings, the survey demonstrated the important results that could be obtained from competent research. The authors were rightly proud of their questionnaire, and they reproduced it in the back of both books for all to see. Sex surveyors rarely make their questionnaires so readily available, an omission that makes it difficult to interpret results. And these results provided a lone, calm voice about AIDS. Although their survey was not specifically related to AIDS, the authors devoted considerable discussion to the risk of HIV transmission and stated that the disease had not become as prevalent in the general population as anticipated. The reason, they explained, was that most adults were monogamous and their sexual networks were not closely connected. If most people had few partners, and those with many tended to confine their sexual activities to interconnected networks, then the more partners a person had, the more rapidly AIDS would spread within a particular network. This helped explain how AIDS had spread so rapidly in some gay networks but had not spread to all segments of the population. Furthermore, the authors found little evidence that anal intercourse was practiced by most heterosexuals, and the probability of transmitting HIV through vaginal intercourse was relatively low in the United States and other Western countries.

Of their several new and enlightening ways of viewing sexual issues, a good example is their challenge to the idea of sexual orientation. In a section largely analyzed and written by Stuart Michaels, they separated sexual desire, identity, and behavior. To measure behavior they asked the total number of sexual partners and then the gender of these partners. For desire they first asked: "On a scale of 1 to 4, where one is very appealing and 4 is not at all appealing, how would you rate having sex with someone of the same sex?" And then: "In general, are you sexually attracted to only men, mostly men, both men and women, mostly women, only women?" Finally, for identity they asked: "Do you think of yourself as heterosexual, homosexual, bisexual, or something else?"

Few respondents reported having same-sex sexual experience *and* homoerotic desire *and* homosexual identity. Many more respondents reported only one of these: about 10 percent of the men indicated either homosexual experience, desire, or identity, but only 2.5 percent indicated all three. Furthermore, Michaels provided convincing evidence that homosexuality was largely an urban phenomenon: under 3 percent of the men in the total sample identified themselves as homosexual or bisexual, but almost 10 percent of those from the twelve largest central cities did. Thus for the first time a survey showed why gay men's experiences of the prevalence of gays in the population differed from the percentages reported in surveys.[11]

With Americans happily in bed with their spouses, with women long-suffering as usual, with AIDS on the back burner, and with gay men and lesbians few and far between, America seemed safe from sexual excess. While the books provided a far more nuanced picture of sex, this is essentially the story that appeared in the media. The authors and their publishers managed publicity carefully, publishing both books simultaneously and making themselves available for television, radio, and newspaper interviews. The news media still put their own spin on the results, however, playing the monogamy theme above all others with headlines like "Americans Lead Conventional Sex Lives, Contrary to Popular Notion, Survey Finds." Columnists poked fun at what they saw as Americans' puritanical and boring lives, and weekly news magazines weighed in with long accounts. Most reports described the survey as definitive although some questioned the accuracy of the answers. Many discussed the authors' earlier funding problems, and the columnist Ellen Goodman speculated that "if Jesse Helms had known it would come out this way, he might have mortgaged the state of North Carolina to come up with the research funds."[12]

The books were not only a media event. They became an important academic event also, with long reviews in social science journals and reviews by academics in the highbrow media. The Stanford University historian Paul Robinson, an expert on twentieth-century sexology, wrote a glowing review in the *New York Times,* finding the books superior to the Kinsey Reports because of their representative sample. Robinson enthusiastically summarized many of the books' sexual facts, noting in particular the massive amount of data demonstrating that women were less interested in sex than men. He was also one of few reviewers to observe that although Laumann and his coauthors stressed the essential conservatism of Americans, their data showed considerable licence in some quarters and striking changes over time. Robinson, not unreasonably, explained their caution as arising from a desire "to confound the dire expectations of their critics" as a result "of their political mauling." Most sociologists praised the surveys' great contribution to knowledge about sex, but they raised more questions than Robinson did. The survey expert Stanley Presser had methodological concerns, especially about response errors. He surmised that both deliberate misreporting and faulty recall helped explain why men, on average, reported more partners than women.[13]

The issue of gender difference in responses to questions about sexual behavior surfaced acrimoniously in a review in the *New York Review of Books* by the biologist Richard Lewontin. Lewontin took issue with the whole enterprise, stating that autobiographies, including autobiographical answers on surveys, were fictions produced to portray authors (in this case, respondents) in certain ways. This was especially likely with reports of sexual behavior that could not be verified. Accounts of what people did sexually could not be trusted because they even lied to themselves.

Lewontin dismissed the study's methodological sophistication, arguing that earlier researchers had been right to believe that how they got their samples did not matter. The central issue was the truth of the answers. His major example of lies on the survey was the gender difference in reported number of partners, a finding researchers had long had difficulty explaining. Laumann and associates had admitted that this difference probably resulted from dishonest answers by respondents, so Lewontin asked how they could believe the rest of their data. He urged sociologists to accept that many things were unknowable, to stop trying to do science, and to become more modest in their claims. Laumann and his coauthors, instead of countering with examples in which respondents appeared to have told truths they might have preferred not to reveal, such as the surprisingly high levels of STDs and of nonconsensual sex, reiterated the care they had taken in collecting their data and protested that their confidential survey could not be compared to autobiography.[14]

Lewontin's objections were disingenuous. He assumed there was a single truth to be learned, but one that could never be verified because the behavior it measured would be private. Yet there is an important question to be asked about the nature of the information obtained from sex surveys. Surveys continue to appear, in spite of conservative opposition, and researchers continue to promise urgently needed information that will help cure the nation's ills. Over the past hundred years, as the epigraphs to our chapters have illustrated, writer after writer has called for more data to solve a bewildering array of sexual problems, and yet surveys do not seem to have solved the problems. Is this because of imperfect methodology, or are there other explanations for the continued search for solutions?

11

Reforming Sex Research

Study of Sex Is Experiencing a 2d Revolution Half a Century after Kinsey

—*New York Times* headline, 1997

EXISTING on the margins of academic respectability, sex surveyors have worked hard to come into the scientific fold. Like all science, theirs has not been a strictly neutral enterprise. They have been influenced both by their culture and by the work of earlier researchers, while they have also seen new things and made new discoveries. And they have shocked. From the beginning sex researchers managed their results carefully, out of a fear of the personal consequences of their controversial work and also out of a desire to impose their views. They managed both the voices of respondents and their presentation of those voices in ways that influenced readers.

Researchers were never able to control the process completely. Respondents did not always give the answers surveyors wished to hear, and audiences wanted to know things surveys could not tell them. And over time it became more difficult for researchers to present their work in just the way they chose. From Kinsey on, the media brought the work of sex surveyors into the public arena and thus influenced the meaning attributed to findings. Researchers had to learn to take this media interest into account in reporting on their surveys. Their ability to manage respondents and audiences was further reduced by the increased political involvement in sex surveys after 1970, when the federal government began funding them and justifying doing so as in the national interest. Finally, in national debates, sex research became the occasion for battles over other issues. Teenage pregnancy, abortion, gays in the military, and the national sex surveys can all be seen as metaphors for fundamental disagreements about such issues as race, social class, and the role of government, and most particularly about gender. Because these issues stayed in the background, battles never really ended but reappeared in new incarnations each time one side claimed victory.

After one hundred years of research, two questions arise. What kind of knowledge do surveys provide, if any? And have researchers helped create trends in sexuality rather than merely reporting them? Moralists, hard scientists like Richard Lewontin, and others asserted that sex surveyors learn nothing of value and that they have a dangerous effect on sexual behavior by providing the public with insidious distortions of reality. Faced with such hostility, sex researchers ignored the limits of their knowledge and repeatedly argued that their data revealed the truth about the sexual behavior of Americans. Some questioned specific aspects of data collection, but most concluded that criticisms were unfounded or suggested relatively simple remedies.

One limitation to knowledge was technical. In a climate in which to admit uncertainty was to admit defeat, few researchers undertook the careful methodological research needed to document discrepancies and to evaluate and improve data. In his review of the survey produced by Edward Laumann and his colleagues, Stanley Presser contrasted the lack of evaluation studies on sex research with research on voting surveys.[1] When interviewed in postelection surveys, more people claim to have voted than have actually done so. Research by Presser and others has thrown light on this phenomenon and led to greater accuracy in predicting the outcomes of elections. The lack of comparable research on sex surveys has made it difficult to assess or improve them.

When AIDS appeared, accurate estimates became crucial, since small variations in findings could substantially affect projections about the spread of the disease. The methodology of sex surveys was finally treated as an important topic. In 1990 the National Academy of Sciences Committee on AIDS Research and the Behavioral, Social, and Statistical Sciences issued its second major report and devoted a chapter to survey methodology. The committee concluded that response rates were not noticeably lower in surveys of sexual behavior than in other surveys. This put to rest Kinsey's claim, repeated by subsequent researchers, that random samples were inappropriate in sex surveys. The authors of the report also demonstrated the consistency from survey to survey in answers to such questions as age at first intercourse. This reassuring finding did not necessarily indicate a lack of response bias, however, and the authors provided evidence of consistent underreporting, especially of stigmatized behaviors such as sex between men.[2]

Since research on AIDS-related behavior was the sole focus of the AIDS committee's report, many issues of importance to other kinds of sex surveys received scant attention. But the committee's recommendation that researchers concentrate on methodology helped increase interest in such issues. A group headed by Joseph Catania at the Center for AIDS Prevention Studies assessed the state of methodological knowledge relevant to AIDS surveys. They focused particularly on problems of recalling sexual events and partners. This is a concern in surveys of gay men, since some have had a great many partners and episodes. Catania and his colleagues also worried that respondents in high-risk populations might misreport changes in behavior, such as increased use of condoms, because of social pressure to seem sexually responsible.[3]

One issue of less concern to AIDS researchers but important for sex surveys was the long-noted gender difference in reported number of partners. By the early 1990s a number of researchers were working on this puzzle. Most treated it solely as a technical problem rather than as an illustration of the gendered difference in sexual meanings. Few connected it to the consistent differences between men's and women's descriptions of sexual interest. In a study published in the prestigious journal *Nature,* the sociologist Martina Morris argued that most people gave accurate answers: the problem was that respondents with many partners had difficulty remembering. Using data from the General Social Survey, she removed persons who said they had had more than twenty partners (10 percent of the sample) and, for those with twenty or fewer partners, produced a low male-to-female partner ratio of 1.2:1. This was much lower than the ratio of 3.2:1 when all respondents were included. However, Morris's analysis was flawed.[4]

In a more enlightening approach, Roger Tourangeau and Tom Smith compared responses to questions on sexual behavior from several computer-assisted interview methods. Instead of having an interviewer read the questions and record the answers, they first tried allowing respondents to answer in private by punching their answers into the computer. But this lessened response rates because some respondents had trouble reading and following the instructions on self-administered questionnaires. When they allowed the respondents to hear the questions through a headset and answer on a computer, they had greater success with response rates and with the number-of-partners dilemma. Men reduced their reported number of sex partners and women increased theirs. The resulting averages for the two genders were quite close. The potential of these new methods of ensuring respondents' privacy was demonstrated when Freya Sonenstein added a new cohort of young men to the National Survey of Adolescent Males and, with the help of Charles Turner, used the same headset-and-computer technique as Tourangeau and Smith. In her previous surveys few young men said they had had sex with other men, but with the new methodology the rate increased fourfold.[5]

While such research would seem to affirm the feasibility of sex surveys, the issue is more complex. An implicit assumption that a single truth exists underlies much methodological research. But when respondents answer questions their responses may involve more than one truth.[6] It is possible, for example, that women would exclude nonconsensual sexual encounters from their list of partners but men would not. And the difference in reporting of partners must be influenced by respondents' conceptions of what behavior is proper for men and for women. In this instance the truth is quite unclear.

Furthermore, when researchers ask about a certain topic it takes on more importance than those not mentioned. The very act of asking the questions shapes the responses, no matter how neutral the wording. For example, many more surveys have asked about number of partners than about consent. Reading accounts of sex surveys in magazines and elsewhere, women have compared themselves with the survey respondents and in doing so have counted their own number of partners and have made decisions about what constitutes a partner. In contrast, many have never asked themselves what it means to consent to sex. Even though some sex surveys now include questions about consent, findings are relegated to the back of the book, as in the Laumann survey. This topic has yet to become a methodological concern. And when answers are not open-ended but multiple choice, as is inevitable for most survey questions, the list of possible answers can alter respondents' words into those of the researchers.

How researchers view reality and attempt to reproduce it in their results is in large part shaped by their own backgrounds. Researchers' viewpoints are inevitably formed by factors such as gender, race, class, and sexual identity. If men and women report different numbers of sexual partners, the researchers' gender will surely influence their interpretations of this discrepancy. The greater the variety of researchers' backgrounds, the greater the variety of truths revealed. As long as almost all researchers were white men, this limited the topics chosen, the questions asked, and the meanings assigned to the findings. When women researchers joined this largely male enterprise, this did not automatically change the questions and the answers; as newcomers in a field shaped by men's assumptions, women often had to be content with bringing a slightly different perspective to the traditional interest of male researchers in the supposed inadequacy of female sexual response. Still, it is unlikely that research on nonconsensual sex would have appeared without the presence of female researchers influenced by feminism. And not only were women more likely to examine the topic in the first place, they asked different questions and uncovered different realities. Similarly, when gay researchers responded to the need for AIDS-related surveys of gay men, they accepted many heterosexual assumptions about monogamy, but undertook surveys more experienced researchers hesitated to conduct.

So what kind of knowledge, if any, can surveys provide? They help shape social reality, and in the competent surveys, some of the shape they give to reality is based on empirical fact. But even here the knowledge they provide is limited. Sex surveys cannot reveal the essential nature of sexuality. They can tell us how individuals understand their sexual selves and what they do sexually at particular times, and this information is worth knowing. And if this information is shaped by the researchers' views of the world, so is all knowledge. Methodological improvements can limit researchers' influence to some degree, but especially in the choice of research area, it is not possible for researchers to remove themselves from their own historical contexts.

Thus sex surveys tell us about survey researchers and their world views as well as about respondents. Surveyors' underlying assumptions and concerns always influence their choice of topics and the evidence they uncover. Over time their concerns changed, but for most of the hundred-year history of sex surveys the majority of researchers considered sexuality as inherently a property of gender, that is, they viewed women's desire for men as a natural part of being a woman and men's desire for women as a natural part of being a man. Therefore they privileged heterosexuality. This led to an obsessive interest in female sexuality and the problems it caused for men. With a few exceptions, such as the worry in the early part of the century about the effects of young men's sexual incontinence on their ability to develop into men and the later anxiety about the transmission of AIDS, male sexuality appeared uncomplicated and in little need of analysis. When men did face problems, these were deadly enemies from without, such as syphilis and HIV. In contrast, women's problems came from within themselves: inadequate sexual desire or an unfortunate tendency to get pregnant. In addition, for many years surveyors assumed that only the white middle classes could have fulfilling and mutual sex lives, so they confined their surveys to them. When other races, classes, and groups were subsequently included, assumptions about difference remained and influenced the nature of the inquiries and the outcomes.

From the beginning researchers had to justify their study of sex, and they did so by citing the urgent need for data. The data they produced fit their preconceptions about the nature of sexuality. Their reports helped solidify existing beliefs and even brought new beliefs into being. Early sex researchers strove to help young men manage their prodigious sexual urges in the interest of their own futures and the futures of those they loved. As researchers interpreted the answers to their questions, they told other experts of their evidence that the male sex drive was hard to control. Over time the Victorian message that men could learn to avoid developing an overstimulated sex drive was replaced by the assumption that raging hormones were a normal aspect of male sexuality. While surveys were not the only source of such messages, they had the stamp of authenticity and told a "truth" other sources of advice could not claim. It was the evidence from surveys that impressed upon Americans the idea that sexual longings came from inside men. And survey results were instrumental in rehabilitating this male sex drive from a threat to society into a normal aspect of male-female relationships.

Throughout the twentieth century, as Jeffrey Weeks and others have argued, panics about such topics as sexual disease, pedophilia, and pornography repeatedly gripped the nation. These were often metaphors for more generalized anxieties about such issues as the future of the family, the state of the economy, and even a sense of crisis over individual autonomy. Sometimes surveys appeared in response to sexual panics. The early surveys on young men's sexual desires were undertaken because new information about venereal disease made those desires suddenly more threatening. At other times surveys helped create sexual panics. It is hard to imagine the panic about teenage pregnancy without the surveys of Melvin Zelnik and John Kantner. In these and subsequent surveys of teenage girls, researchers' presuppositions made them view girls, depending on class and race, either as victims unable to take control of their lives or as manipulators forcing the state to pay for their irresponsible behavior. There was little discussion of the various reasons young women might have for becoming sexually active, just an agreement that their sexual activity challenged the stability of the family and was a serious problem for the nation.[7]

It was in research on women that the surveys conveyed the clearest messages. From the 1930s on, sexologists strove to liberate what they saw as the repressed sexuality of middle-class women. But even though these sexologists thought of themselves as supporters of progress battling forces of repression, they were nervous about seeming enthusiastic. They shared the general opinion that sex was powerful, uncontrollable, and dangerous, and they argued for its careful liberation within the confines of the social order. While some researchers understood that "learning had to be a major part of sexuality,"[8] they also believed in the existence of a sexual instinct.

In the 1930s surveyors focused on the sexual behavior of the married, hoping to find the key to marital stability in women's appropriate sexual enthusiasm. They interpreted their surveys as demonstrating that Victorian society had repressed normal sexuality, especially among women, and that the key to marital happiness lay in selecting the most compatible mates and adjusting to them. The writers who produced these models of marital selection and adjustment believed that science would reveal men's and women's true sexual natures, and that once these were known harmony between sexual desires and social order could be attained. They educated generations of women about their sexual obligations in marriage and taught them that achieving sexual happiness was a difficult but essential task. These male researchers were careful not to allow science to sever the link between sex and marriage, and when Kinsey appeared to do this he found himself in trouble.

During the more tolerant 1960s and 1970s surveyors became bolder, and, even though their methodology had improved, their world views continued to influence their findings. They pushed an agenda of sexual liberation while insisting that they were just reporting the facts. When social science professors suggested that sexual experimentation before marriage might help young women overcome their inhibitions, learn about their bodies, and better select their mates, the young women in their classes listened. In research on adults, surveyors used the ideas of the human potential movement to investigate every aspect of sexual activity while insisting that social context was unimportant and that practice would make women perfect. They assuaged their well-founded fear that sex was still a dangerous topic by using technical language and complicated techniques to hide respondents' voices.

At the same time, an outpouring of consumer-oriented sex surveys in magazines and popular books echoed the scientists' findings in ways the public could understand. This created new dangers for sex researchers. In telling readers what they wanted to hear, popular surveys celebrated themselves loudly, pushed the experts into the background, and appeared to let respondents speak for themselves. By asking questions and selecting voices that promoted visions of sexual joy, they placed the idea that sex surveys were a liberal and liberating activity firmly in the minds of the American public, including members of Congress. Only Shere Hite told a different story, and ultimately she was silenced.

In contrast with Hite, most women researchers used male-built frameworks for their research. But they also saw things not seen by their male colleagues. For example, they shared the men's interest in female sexual response, but their view was different from men's. And by the early 1980s feminist researchers began managing their research questions to criticize the relations between heterosexual men and women. Sexual activity brought pleasure to many women, but it also brought danger, as witnessed by the many women who reported sexual assaults. In the main, feminist researchers focused on dangers. Even they often removed women's voices, by determining the meanings of answers in advance rather than using respondents' definitions. Young women who stated that they had been coerced into sex, but that what had happened was not rape, were overruled as victims of false consciousness.

In the 1980s conservative attacks endangered sex research and prompted surveyors to manage their projects even more carefully. AIDS exacerbated this by giving conservatives new ways to attack sexual liberalism and its perceived consequences. Instead of counterattacking, surveyors, ever mindful of their vulnerability, retreated to extolling monogamous sex as the safest and most acceptable course. In AIDS-related surveys of gay men, an emphasis on the number of partners and the equation of high-risk behaviors such as anal intercourse with less risky behaviors such as oral sex helped push this theme. The view that all aspects of gay sex were in urgent need of reform was widely accepted as truth. This meant not simply that gay men must use condoms but that they must change from a deviant lifestyle to one modeled on heterosexual marriage. Lesbians in the meantime were ignored. Their sexual activity appeared to pose no risk of disease to themselves or others, so it was preferable not to acknowledge their existence. Researchers furthered their agenda by searching for innocent victims of AIDS to enumerate. When they found none, they settled for innocent *potential* victims. While not at high risk of contracting AIDS, the young had long been a focus of concern, and their innocence helped attract support for AIDS research. Research agendas helped increase sexual panic about AIDS in all segments of society.

The liberation movements of the 1960s and 1970s had enabled formerly excluded groups, particularly women and gay men, to join the ranks of researchers. Yet the surveys provoking the largest storms were proposed by heterosexual men. Only they could interrogate adult men as well as women and teens, but even they had to back down. The researchers who worked on the ill-fated survey of adults, SHARP, were unusual in acknowledging that sexuality is a social creation. But in the face of conservative criticism they hesitated to give full weight to the variety of sexual cultures revealed in their data, choosing instead to emphasize the priority accorded marriage and commitment.

Throughout the history of surveys of sexual behavior, members of the public have absorbed the information provided and used it to evaluate their own behavior. In a world where sexual normality is an important basis for general normality, this is inevitable. At first the public learned this information directly from those who collected the data or from other professionals to whom these data were presented. With the advent of intense media interest in sex surveys, information became both more accessible and less complete.

For the most part, the information provided limited the options open to individuals rather than expanding them. For example, most surveys presented heterosexual marriage as the goal and promoted the idea that sex within marriage, or at least within a monogamous heterosexual relationship, would be the most satisfying. When the government began to fund some surveys, this aspect became even more apparent and many surveys conveyed the message that sex outside of marriage caused problems.

But surveys have also had liberating effects. Many young men validated their sexual tastes by reading Kinsey's reassurances that sex between men was not only common but nothing more than another form of sexual outlet. And young women seem to have taken to heart their professors' assurances that "permissiveness with affection" was becoming the standard for premarital sexual relations. In such instances it seems likely that surveys gave people permission to follow desires they already had.

Contrary to the charges of some critics of sex research, changes in sexual behavior were not simply caused by the surveys. Human beings are not merely passive recipients of socialization, absorbing all the messages they receive. Few would argue that young women's increased sexual permissiveness has no origin other than a survey-created sexual revolution. Women appear to have resisted experts' definitions and to have made powerful changes in their own sexuality. A pattern of researchers' providing information and respondents' ensuring that some version of their own voices was heard can be seen in rape surveys. Before such surveys were undertaken, rape was thought to be a crime involving strangers. When the surveys presented definitions of sexual assault that included "date rape," a change of consciousness occurred both among victims and among prosecutors. As a result, more rapists were prosecuted. This would not have happened without the voices of the surveys' respondents: the staggering proportions of women reporting nonconsensual sexual experiences were crucial in transforming awareness.

In these and other examples, the ability of surveys to uncover versions of the truth while encouraging changes in behavior has helped large sectors of society. This is most apparent in AIDS-related surveys of gay men, which determined the transmission pattern of the disease in advance of biomedical identification of the virus and instigated behavioral changes that lessened the spread of HIV. Even AIDS-related surveys of young heterosexuals, mistaken as the researchers are in their premise that AIDS is a dire threat to this group, encouraged the use of condoms and led to decreases in unintended pregnancies and sexually transmitted diseases. Surveys have also been helpful in reassuring people that their own sexual desires and preferences are normal.

If sex surveyors would acknowledge that surveys, at best, produce only a kind of knowing and that their own preconceptions and fears influence their findings, they could lessen the impact of their biases by employing modern techniques like probability sampling. And they could reveal their biases by publishing their questionnaires, still a rare event in sex surveys. Some of this is beginning to happen, as evidenced by recent studies of the methodology of data collection, and the results can teach us a great deal about sexual meanings.[9]

These improvements will not turn surveyors into mere recorders of fact, and it will not tell Americans all they want to know about sex. Surveys cannot capture the complex negotiations and meanings involved in decisions to have sex. And they cannot capture the feelings of women and men about sex. We social scientists need to look critically not only at the quality of our surveys but at our role in creating knowledge. We are quick to blame the media or politicians for the meanings assigned to the sexual lives of research subjects such as pregnant teenagers, but we rarely assume any of the blame ourselves. Most funded research goes through the peer review process, and researchers must take responsibility for setting research priorities. For example, surveyors must not simply fault funders for not supporting a large national survey to estimate how many men have sex with other men and to document their behavior. They have to insist that, in a time of AIDS, studies of gay men have a higher priority than studies of high school students. This means no longer claiming to stand above the fray but recognizing that research choices, agendas in making those choices, and presentation of findings are political activities and not just neutral scientific endeavors. Sex researchers cannot avoid involvement in the ideological wars of the late twentieth century.

Conservatives do not fear sex surveys only because of what they might reveal. They also fear the discussions they might generate about sex. Talking about sex, thinking about it, and asking questions about it make people more comfortable with sex and its variety. Those whose political agendas are served by public discomfort over such topics as homosexuality, teenage sexuality, and sex outside of marriage will continue to see sex surveys as a political strategy of the enemy. Surveys differ from other kinds of sexology precisely because they are not simply the work of experts. Experts provide the medium for the voices of ordinary citizens. For the past hundred years these voices have been interpreted through a vision of sex as struggling for liberation against social forces of repression. To face the future, to allow experts to play a role as interpreter of voices, researchers need a new vision, new humility, and new honesty about the possibilities and limitations of their work.

Notes

1. *Asking Questions about Sex*

1. Bruce Voeller, "Some Uses and Abuses of the Kinsey Scale," in David P. McWhirter, Stephanie A. Sanders, and June Machover Reinisch, eds., *Homosexuality/Heterosexuality* (New York: Oxford University Press, 1990).

2. Interview with Robert Knight, May 24, 1993.

3. John O. G. Billy et al., "The Sexual Behavior of Men in the United States," *Family Planning Perspectives* 25, no. 2 (March/April 1993).

4. John D'Emilio, *Sexual Politics, Sexual Communities* (Chicago: University of Chicago Press, 1983).

5. Thomas Laqueur, *Making Sex* (Cambridge, Mass.: Harvard University Press, 1990).

6. Michel Foucault, *The History of Sexuality,* vol. 1 (New York: Random House, 1978).

7. Richard von Krafft-Ebing, *Psychopathia Sexualis* (New York: Physicians and Surgeons Book Co., 1931).

8. John D'Emilio and Estelle B. Freedman, *Intimate Matters: A History of Sexuality in America* (New York: Harper and Row, 1988).

9. Havelock Ellis, *Studies in the Psychology of Sex* (1899; New York: Random House, 1942).

10. Patricia Cline Cohen, *A Calculating People* (Chicago: University of Chicago Press, 1982).

11. James MaHood and Kristine Wenburg, *The Mosher Survey* (New York: Arno, 1980).

12. Bernard Lecuyer and Anthony R. Oberschall, "The Early History of Social Research: Postscript: Research in the United States at the Turn of the Century," in *International Encyclopedia of Statistics,* ed. William H. Kruskal and Judith M. Tanur (New York: Free Press, 1978).

13. Walter F. Robie, *Rational Sex Ethics* (Boston: Richard G. Badger, 1916), 30; Katharine Bement Davis, *Factors in the Sex Lives of Twenty-Two Hundred Women* (New York: Harper and Row, 1929), x.

14. Morris H. Hansen, William Hurwitz, and William G. Madow, *Sample Survey Methods and Theory*, vol. 1 (New York: Wiley, 1953). In "simple random sampling," individuals in the population have an equal chance of selection. For example, for a sample of 1,000 from a population list containing 100,000 names, the sampling fraction would be 1/100. The scientist would randomly select one case for each 100 names listed. Sometimes researchers want to ensure enough interviews with a small segment of the population. Thus, if 10 percent of the above population was black, a sample of 1,000 would produce only 100 blacks, too few to analyze. Oversampling blacks, with a sampling fraction of 3/100, would produce 900 nonblack names and 300 black ones. Different weights would then be used in generalizing to the population. Samples of large populations, while more complex and with multiple stages, are based on the same principles.

15. Gilbert V. Hamilton, *A Research in Marriage* (New York: A. C. Boni, 1929), 17–18.

16. Ronald Freedman, Pascal K. Whelpton, and Arthur A. Campbell, *Family Planning, Sterility and Population Growth* (New York: McGraw-Hill, 1959).

17. Davis, *Factors in the Sex Lives*, 96.

18. Max J. Exner, *Problems and Principles of Sex Education* (New York: Association Press, 1915), 3.

19. Edward O. Laumann et al., *The Social Organization of Sexuality* (Chicago: University of Chicago Press, 1994).

20. Davis, *Factors in the Sex Lives;* Dorothy Dunbar Bromley and Florence Haxton Britten, *Youth and Sex* (New York: Harper, 1938).

21. Jesse Helms, "Debate on Amendment no. 1757 to the 1992 NIH Revitalization Act," *Congressional Record* (April 2, 1992), S4738.

2. In Urgent Need of the Facts

1. F. S. Brockman, "A Study of Moral and Religious Life of 251 Preparatory School Students in the United States," *Pedagogical Seminary* 9 (1902): 267.

2. Dorothy Ross, *G. Stanley Hall* (Chicago: University of Chicago Press, 1972).

3. Samuel Chipman, *The Temperance Lecturer* (Albany, 1842); William W. Sanger, *The History of Prostitution* (New York: AMS Press, 1974).

4. David I. Macleod, *Building Character in the American Boy* (Madison: University of Wisconsin Press, 1983).

5. Brockman, "Study of Moral and Religious Life," 267.

6. Barbara Epstein, "Family, Sexual Morality, and Popular Movements in Turn-of-the-Century America," in *Powers of Desire,* ed. Ann Snitow, Christine Stansell, and Sharon Thompson (New York: Monthly Review Press, 1983).

7. G. Stanley Hall, "The Needs and Methods of Educating Young People in the Hygiene of Sex," *Pedagogical Seminary* 15 (March 1908).

8. Steven Seidman, *Romantic Longings: Love in America, 1830–1980* (New York: Routledge, 1991). But see Karen Lystra, *Searching the Heart: Women, Men, and Romantic Love in Nineteenth-Century America* (New York: Oxford University Press, 1989).

9. Max Exner, *Problems and Principles of Sex Education* (New York: Association Press, 1915), 3–4.

10. Ibid., 17–18.

11. Ibid., 5.

12. In 1920 Walter Hughes surveyed a cross-section of male adolescents from North Carolina to corroborate Exner: "Sex Experiences of Boyhood," *Journal of Social Hygiene* 12, no. 5 (May 1926). Our discussion of venereal disease benefited from Allen M. Brandt, *No Magic Bullet* (New York: Oxford University Press, 1987).

13. Prince A. Morrow, *Social Diseases and Marriage* (New York: Lea Brothers, 1904), 25.

14. Walter F. Robie, *Rational Sex Ethics* (Boston: Richard G. Badger, 1916), 21, 25.

15. Walter F. Robie, *The Art of Love* (Boston: Gorham Press, 1921), 354.

16. Nancy Cott, "Passionlessness: An Interpretation of Victorian Sexual Ideology, 1790–1850," *Signs* 4, no. 2 (1978).

17. Robie, *Rational Sex Ethics*, 31.

18. Robie, *Art of Love*, 354.

19. Paul Strong Achilles, *The Effectiveness of Certain Social Hygiene Literature* (New York: American Social Hygiene Association, 1915), 115–116.

20. William S. Taylor, "A Critique of Sublimation in Males," *Genetic Psychology Monographs* 13, no. 1 (Jan. 1933), 17.

21. M. W. Peck and F. L. Wells, "On the Psycho-Sexuality of College Graduate Men," *Mental Hygiene* 7 (1923): 710–711.

22. Ibid., 707.

23. M. W. Peck and F. L. Wells, "Further Studies in the Psycho-Sexuality of College Graduate Men," *Mental Hygiene* 9 (July 1925): 513–514.

24. Carl Degler discovered Mosher's survey in the Stanford University Archives. The questionnaires appear in James MaHood and Kristine Wenburg, *The Mosher Survey* (New York: Arno, 1980).

25. Clelia Duel Mosher, *Health and the Woman Movement* (New York: Woman's Press, 1918).

26. Peter Gay, *Education of the Senses* (New York: Oxford University Press, 1984); Margaret Marsh and Wanda Ronner, *The Empty Cradle* (Baltimore: Johns Hopkins University Press, 1996).

27. MaHood and Wenburg, *Mosher Survey*, 23–24.

28. Florence M. Fitch, "What Are Our Social Standards?" *Social Hygiene* 1, no. 4 (Sept. 1915): 551.

29. Katharine Bement Davis, *Factors in the Sex Lives of Twenty-Two Hundred Women* (New York: Harper and Brother, 1929).
30. W. David Lewis, "Katharine Bement Davis," in Edward T. James, ed., *Notable American Women, 1607–1950,* vol. 1 (Cambridge, Mass.: Harvard University Press, 1971), 441.
31. The task of assembling the tables was overwhelming, and they contain numerous errors.
32. Estelle B. Freedman, "The New Woman: Changing Views of Women in the 1920s," *Journal of American History* 61, no. 2 (Sept. 1974).
33. Davis, *Factors in the Sex Lives,* 19, 76.
34. Havelock Ellis, *Studies in the Psychology of Sex,* vol. 1 (1899; New York: Random House, 1942).
35. Lilburn Merrill, "A Summary of Findings in a Study of Sexualism among a Group of One Hundred Delinquent Boys," *Journal of Delinquency* 3, no. 6 (Nov. 1918): 257, 259. Merrill cites contradictory numbers; 31 may be incorrect.
36. Lillian Faderman, *Surpassing the Love of Men: Romantic Friendship and Love between Women from the Renaissance to the Present* (New York: William Morrow, 1981).
37. Davis, *Factors in the Sex Lives,* 246, 244–245.

3. Sex in the Service of the Conjugal Bond

1. Ernest R. Groves, *Social Problems of the Family* (Philadelphia: Lippincott, 1927).
2. Ernest R. Groves, *The Drifting Home* (Boston: Houghton Mifflin, 1926), 94.
3. Linda Gordon, *Woman's Body, Woman's Right* (New York: Penguin, 1990), 197.
4. Phyllis Blanchard and Carolyn Manasses, *New Girls for Old* (New York: Macaulay, 1930), 32.
5. Ben B. Lindsey and Wainwright Evans, *The Revolt of Modern Youth* (New York: Boni and Liveright, 1925).
6. Gilbert Hamilton, *A Research in Marriage* (New York: A. C. Boni, 1929).
7. Ibid., 192.
8. Ibid., 442.
9. Robert Latou Dickinson and Lura Beam, *A Thousand Marriages* (Baltimore: Williams and Wilkins, 1931); idem, *The Single Woman* (Baltimore: Williams and Wilkins, 1934).
10. Dickinson and Beam, *A Thousand Marriages,* 129–130.
11. More conservative groups included the American Social Hygiene Association, which added family life education to its concerns about prostitution and venereal disease, and the American Home Economics Association.

12. Ernest R. Groves and William F. Ogburn, *American Marriage and Family Relationships* (New York: Henry Holt, 1929), 13–14.

13. Willard Waller, *The Family* (New York: Dryden Press, 1938), 5.

14. Henry A. Bowman, "Marriage Education in the Colleges," *Journal of Social Hygiene* 35 (1949).

15. Ernest W. Burgess and Leonard S. Cottrell, *Predicting Success and Failure in Marriage* (New York: Prentice-Hall, 1939), 15; Ernest W. Burgess and Paul Wallin, *Engagement and Marriage* (Chicago: Lippincott, 1953); Lewis Terman, *Psychological Factors in Marital Happiness* (New York: McGraw-Hill, 1938).

16. Lewis M. Terman and Catharine Cox Miles, *Sex and Personality* (New York: McGraw-Hill, 1936).

17. Burgess and Wallin, *Engagement and Marriage,* 673.

18. Burgess and Cottrell, *Predicting Success and Failure,* 226.

19. Terman, *Psychological Factors,* 375.

20. Burgess and Cottrell, *Predicting Success and Failure,* 219.

21. Lewis M. Terman and Melissa H. Oden, *The Gifted Child Grows Up* (Stanford: Stanford University Press, 1947).

22. Terman, *Psychological Factors,* 320.

23. An example of this argument appears in Waller, *The Family.*

24. Terman, *Psychological Factors,* 304–305.

25. Although the Rockefeller Foundation gave over $1 million between 1925 and 1950 to support sex research, its official history devotes only a single paragraph to it: Raymond B. Fosdick, *The Story of the Rockefeller Foundation* (New York: Harper and Row, 1952).

26. When Hamilton circulated his message more widely in a popular book written with Kenneth Macgowan, *What Is Wrong with Marriage?* (New York: A. C. Boni, 1930), and with reports in *Redbook, Harpers,* and the *Woman's Home Companion,* the Bureau of Social Hygiene told him to take its name off his study. See Vern L. Bullough, "The Rockefellers and Sex Research," *Journal of Sex Research* 21, no. 2 (1985).

27. Alfred C. Kinsey, Wardell B. Pomeroy, and Clyde E. Martin, *Sexual Behavior in the Human Male* (Philadelphia: W. B. Saunders, 1948), 544.

28. Ibid., 5.

29. Speech to Phi Beta Kappa, 1939, rpt. in Cornelia V. Christenson, *Kinsey: A Biography* (Bloomington: Indiana University Press, 1971), 8–9.

30. Kinsey insisted that only white married "non-ethnic" men could conduct his interviews. He eventually used one woman, Cornelia Christenson, but argued that married women could not leave their husbands for the long periods of time required to collect data.

31. Interview with Paul Gebhard, Feb. 18, 1994.

32. Janice Irvine, *Disorders of Desire* (Philadelphia: Temple University Press, 1990).

33. Alfred C. Kinsey et al., *Sexual Behavior in the Human Female* (Philadelphia: W. B. Saunders, 1953), 538–539.

34. Interview with Wardell Pomeroy, May 20, 1993. James H. Jones, in *Alfred C. Kinsey* (New York: Norton, 1997), argues that Kinsey's sexual predilections greatly influenced his research. While Jones adduces considerable evidence of Kinsey's complex sexual desires, he does not present convincing evidence that Kinsey appeared radical to his neighbors or to other than his closest academic colleagues.

35. George Henry, *Sex Variants* (New York: Paul B. Hoeber, 1941), xii.

36. Ibid., 1023.

37. Estelle B. Freedman, "'Uncontrolled Desires': The Response to the Sexual Psychopath, 1920–1960," *Journal of American History* 74 (June 1987).

38. Carney Landis, *Sex in Development* (New York: Paul B. Hoeber, 1940); Carney Landis and M. Marjorie Bolles, *Personality and Sexuality of the Physically Handicapped Woman* (New York: Paul B. Hoeber, 1942).

39. Kinsey et al., *Sexual Behavior in the Human Male*, 614–615.

40. Kinsey et al., *Sexual Behavior in the Human Female*, 446.

41. Gebhard interview.

42. Christenson, *Kinsey*; James H. Jones, "The Origins of The Institute for Sex Research: A History" (Ph.D. diss., Indiana University, 1972).

43. Pomeroy interview.

44. Gebhard interview.

45. Gebhard described the procedure: they would approach a group and start with the most willing. For resistant individuals they used high-pressure tactics, suggesting that others might wonder what they were hiding if they refused. Gebhard interview.

46. William G. Cochran, Frederick Mosteller, and John W. Tukey, "Statistical Problems of the Kinsey Report," *Journal of the American Statistical Association* 48 (Dec. 1953).

47. Gebhard interview.

48. Christenson, *Kinsey*, 103.

49. A. H. Hobbs and Richard. D. Lambert, "An Evaluation of 'Sexual Behavior in the Human Male,'" *American Journal of Psychiatry* 104 (1948).

50. Gebhard interview.

51. William Simon examined the press responses to the research and found that the first press reports became the source for subsequent references to Kinsey's work. Interview with William Simon, March 18, 1994.

52. Bruce Thomason, "Marital Sexual Behavior and Total Marital Adjustment: A Research Report," in *Sexual Behavior in American Society*, ed. Jerome Himelhoch (New York: Norton, 1955); Clifford R. Adams, "An Informal Preliminary Report on Some Factors Relating to Sexual Responsiveness of Certain College Wives," in Manfred F. DeMartino, *Sexual Behavior and Personality Characteristics* (New York: Citadel Press, 1963); George Levinger, "Task and Social Behavior in Marriage," *Sociometry* 27, no.4 (Dec. 1964).

53. E.g., R. W. Reevy, "Premarital Petting Behavior and Marital Happiness Predic-

tion," *Journal of Marriage and the Family* 21 (1959); Paul Popenoe, "Premarital Experience No Help in Sexual Adjustment after Marriage: A Preliminary Report from the Department of Research, AIFR," *Family Life* 21, no. 8 (1962).

54. John W. Riley and Matilda White Riley, "The Uses of Various Methods of Contraception," *American Sociological Review* 5, no. 6 (Dec. 1940).

55. Clyde V. Kiser and Pascal K. Whelpton, "Resume of the Indianapolis Study of Social and Psychological Factors Affecting Fertility," *Population Studies* 7, no. 2 (Nov. 1953).

56. Interview with Ronald Freedman, April 3, 1993.

57. Ronald Freedman, Pascal K. Whelpton, and Arthur A. Campbell, *Family Planning, Sterility and Population Growth* (New York: McGraw-Hill, 1959), 8.

58. Pascal K. Whelpton, Arthur A. Campbell, and John E. Patterson, *Fertility and Family Planning in the United States* (Princeton: Princeton University Press, 1966).

59. Norman B. Ryder and Charles F. Westoff, *Reproduction in the United States, 1965* (Princeton: Princeton University Press, 1971), 387.

60. Norman B. Ryder and Charles F. Westoff, *The Contraceptive Revolution* (Princeton: Princeton University Press, 1977); Charles F. Westoff and Norman B. Ryder, "The Predictive Validity of Fertility Intentions," *Demography* 14 (1977).

61. Charles F. Westoff, "Coital Frequency and Contraception," *Family Planning Perspectives* 6, no. 3 (1974).

62. Both views found expression in Daniel Patrick Moynihan's controversial report for the U.S. Department of Labor, *The Negro Family: The Case for National Action*, rpt. in Lee Rainwater and William L. Yancey, *The Moynihan Report and the Politics of Controversy* (Cambridge, Mass.: MIT Press, 1967).

63. Lee Rainwater, *And the Poor Get Children* (Chicago: Quadrangle, 1960).

64. Udry wrote a series of papers with the biologist Naomi Morris on the periodicity of sexual intercourse. It is not clear which are separate studies and which report on the same data. E.g., "Distribution of Coitus in the Menstrual Cycle," *Nature* 220 (1968); "A Method for Validation of Reporting Sexual Data," *Journal of Marriage and the Family* 29, no. 3 (Aug. 1967); "Frequency of Intercourse by Day of the Week," *Journal of Sex Research* 6, no 3 (Aug. 1970).

65. Two studies appear to have the same name; the second may be of a subset of the first. Reports are too numerous to list and are cited only where specifically discussed.

66. J. Richard Udry, "Differential Fertility by Intelligence: The Role of Birth Planning," *Social Biology* 25, no. 1 (Spring 1978): 14.

4. Sex before Marriage

1. Lester A. Kirkendall, "Values and Premarital Intercourse: Implications for Parent Education," *Marriage and Family Living* 22 (Nov. 1960): 319.

2. J. T. Landis, "The Teaching of Marriage and Family Courses in Colleges," *Marriage and Family Living* 21, no. 1 (1959).

3. Thomas Poffenberger et al., "Premarital Sexual Behavior: A Symposium," *Marriage and Family Living* 24 (1962).

4. This was the position of an influential book: James S. Coleman, *The Adolescent Society: The Social Life of the Teenager and Its Impact on Education* (New York: Free Press, 1961).

5. Dorothy Dunbar Bromley and Florence Haxton Britten, *Youth and Sex* (New York: Harper, 1938), 83–86.

6. Ibid., 56.

7. Winston Ehrmann, *Premarital Dating Behavior* (New York: Henry Holt, 1959).

8. Lester A. Kirkendall, *Sex Education as Human Relations* (New York: Inor, 1950).

9. Irving B. Tebor, "Male Virgins: Conflicts and Group Support in American Culture," *Family Life Coordinator* 9, nos. 3–4 (March–June 1961).

10. Leslie Hohman and Bertram Schaffner, "The Sex Lives of Unmarried Men," *American Journal of Sociology* 52, no. 6 (1947): 503.

11. Eugene J. Kanin, "Male Aggression in Dating-Courtship Relationships," *American Journal of Sociology* 63, no. 2 (1957): 200. See also Clifford Kirkpatrick and Eugene Kanin, "Male Sex Aggression on a University Campus," *American Sociological Review* 22, no. 1 (Feb. 1957). Kanin was to repeat these studies during the 1960s and 1970s.

12. Ehrmann, *Premarital Dating Behavior*, 2.

13. Lawrence Podell and John C. Perkins, "A Guttman Scale for Sexual Experience: A Methodological Note," *Journal of Abnormal and Social Psychology* 54 (Jan.–May 1957).

14. Lester A. Kirkendall, *Premarital Intercourse and Interpersonal Relationships* (New York: Julian Press, 1961); Ira L. Reiss, *The Social Context of Premarital Sexual Permissiveness* (New York: Holt, Rinehart and Winston, 1967). Reiss had preliminary reports as early as 1963 and had articulated his position in *Premarital Sexual Standards in America* (Glencoe, Ill.: Free Press, 1960).

15. Ira L. Reiss, "The Double Standard in Premarital Sexual Intercourse: A Neglected Concept," *Social Forces* 34, no. 3 (March 1956): 229.

16. Reiss, *Social Context*, 202–203.

17. Interview with Ira Reiss, Oct. 10, 1994.

18. Ira L. Reiss, "Sociological Studies of Sexual Standards," in *Determinants of Human Sexual Behavior*, ed. George Winokur (Springfield, Ill.: Charles C. Thomas, 1963), 117.

19. E.g., Harold Christensen and George Carpenter, "Value-Behavior Discrepancies Regarding Pre-Marital Coitus in Three Western Cultures," *American Sociological Review* 27, no. 1 (1962); and Robert L. Karen, "Some Variables Affecting Sexual Attitudes, Behavior, and Inconsistency," *Journal of Marriage and Family Living* 21, no. 3 (Aug. 1959).

20. Reiss interview. Most researchers of premarital sexuality received no funding.

21. Judson T. Landis and Mary G. Landis, *Building a Successful Marriage* (Englewood Cliffs, N.J.: Prentice-Hall, 1963), 188.

22. Harrop A. Freeman and Ruth S. Freeman, "Senior College Women: Their Sexual Standards and Activity," *Journal of the National Association of Women Deans and Counselors,* pt. 1 (Winter 1966); pt. 2 (Spring 1966).

23. Vance Packard, *The Sexual Wilderness: The Contemporary Upheaval in Male-Female Relationships* (New York: David McKay, 1968).

24. *Newsweek,* April 6, 1964, 52.

25. John P. Clark and Larry L. Tifft, "Polygraph and Interview Validation of Self-Reported Deviant Behavior," *American Sociological Review* 34, no. 4 (Aug. 1966).

26. "Campus '65," *Newsweek,* March 22, 1965.

27. Robert H. Walsh, Mary Z. Ferrell, and William L. Tolone, "Selection of Reference Group, Perceived Reference Group Permissiveness, and Personal Permissiveness Attitudes and Behavior: A Study of Two Consecutive Panels (1967–1971; 1970–1974)," *Journal of Marriage and the Family* 38, no. 3 (Aug. 1976).

28. Robert A. Lewis, "Parents and Peers: Socialization Agents in the Coital Behavior of Young Adults," *Journal of Sex Research* 9, no. 2 (May 1973): 164; Gerald H. Wiechmann and Altis L. Ellis, "A Study of the Effects of 'Sex Education' on Premarital Petting and Coital Behavior," *Family Coordinator* 18, no. 3 (July 1969); Richard R. Clayton, "Religious Orthodoxy and Premarital Sex," *Social Forces* 47, no. 4 (June 1969); Barbara Schulz et al., "Explaining Premarital Sexual Intercourse among College Students: A Causal Model," *Social Forces* 56, no. 1 (Sept. 1977).

29. Schulz et al., "Explaining Premarital Sexual Intercourse."

30. Interview with John Gagnon, Nov. 2, 1993. Interview with William Simon, March 18, 1994.

31. John H. Gagnon and William Simon, *Sexual Conduct: The Social Sources of Human Sexuality* (Chicago: Aldine, 1973). Their other federally funded projects were an NIMH-funded pilot study of homosexuals, the precursor of a larger study undertaken by Alan Bell and Martin Weinberg, and a never-completed study of the effects of sex education at a school in Chicago where Kinsey had conducted a number of interviews.

32. John H. Gagnon, William Simon, and Alan S. Berger, "Some Aspects of Sexual Adjustment in Early and Later Adolescence," in Joseph Zubin and Alfred Freedman, eds., *The Psychopathology of Adolescence* (New York: Grune and Stratton, 1970), 279.

33. John H. Gagnon and William Simon, "The Sexual Scripting of Oral-Genital Contacts," *Archives of Sexual Behavior* 16, no. 1 (1987): 21.

34. William Simon, Alan S. Berger, and John H. Gagnon, "Beyond Anxiety and Fantasy: The Coital Experiences of College Youth," *Journal of Youth and Adolescence* 1, no. 3 (1972): 204.

35. Quoted in "The Campus Mood: From Rage to Reform," *Time,* Nov. 30, 1970.
36. Harold S. Bernard and Allan J. Schwartz, "Impact of a Human Sexuality Program on Sex Related Knowledge, Attitudes, Behavior and Guilt of College Undergraduates," *Journal of the American College Health Association* 25 (1977).
37. E.g., Donald L. Mosher and Herbert J. Cross, "Sex Guilt and Premarital Sexual Experiences of College Students," *Journal of Consulting and Clinical Psychology* 36, no. 1 (1971); Donald L. Mosher, "Sex Differences, Sex Experience, Sex Guilt, and Explicitly Sexual Films," *Journal of Social Issues* 29, no. 3 (1973); Paul R. Abramson and Donald L. Mosher, "Development of a Measure of Negative Attitudes toward Masturbation," *Journal of Consulting and Clinical Psychology* 43, no. 4 (1975).
38. Karl King, Jack O. Balswick, and Ira E. Robinson, "The Continuing Premarital Sexual Revolution among College Females," *Journal of Marriage and the Family* 39 (Aug. 1977): 458.
39. James P. Curran, Steven Neff, and Steven Lippold, "Correlates of Sexual Experience among University Students," *Journal of Sex Research* 9, no. 2 (1973): 131; Lee H. Bukstel et al., "Projected Extramarital Sexual Involvement in Unmarried College Students," *Journal of Marriage and the Family* 40, no. 2 (May 1978).
40. Alan S. Berger, John H. Gagnon, and William Simon, "Urban Working-Class Adolescents and Sexually Explicit Media," *Technical Report of the Commission on Pornography* 9 (1971); Patricia Y. Miller and William Simon, "Adolescent Sexual Behavior: Context and Change," *Social Problems* 22, no. 1 (1974). Richard Jessor and Shirley L. Jessor, *Problem Behavior and Psychosocial Development: A Longitudinal Study of Youth* (New York: Academic Press, 1977), xiii.
41. John DeLamater and Patricia MacCorquodale, *Premarital Sexuality: Attitudes, Relationships, Behavior* (Madison: University of Wisconsin Press, 1979). John D. DeLamater, "Methodological Issues in the Study of Premarital Sexuality," *Sociological Methods and Research* 3, no. 1 (Aug. 1974).

5. Adolescent Fertility

1. John F. Kantner and Melvin Zelnik, "Sexual Experience of Young Unmarried Women in the United States," *Family Planning Perspectives* 4, no. 4 (Oct. 1972).
2. Much of the historical information in this chapter is from Constance A. Nathanson, *Dangerous Passage: The Social Control of Sexuality in Women's Adolescence* (Philadelphia: Temple University Press, 1991), and Maris A. Vinovskis, *An "Epidemic" of Adolescent Pregnancy? Some Historical and Policy Considerations* (New York: Oxford University Press, 1988).
3. Ronald Freedman and Lolagene Coombs, "Childspacing and Family Economic Position," *American Sociological Review* 31, no. 5 (Oct. 1966). Arthur A. Campbell, "The Role of Family Planning in the Reduction of Poverty," *Journal of Marriage and the Family* 30, no. 2 (May 1968): 238.

4. Interview with John Kantner, Nov. 30, 1993.

5. Kantner and Zelnik, "Sexual Experience"; John F. Kantner and Melvin Zelnik, "Contraception and Pregnancy: Experience of Young Unmarried Women in the United States," *Family Planning Perspectives* 5, no. 1 (Winter 1973).

6. The *New York Times*, for example, published at least seven articles on the 1965 NFS, paying particular attention to the declines in the overall birth rate and in fertility among Catholics.

7. "Sex: 46% of Teen Girls Do It," *St. Petersburg Times*, May 10, 1972; "Outmoded Virginity," *Time*, May 22, 1972; "Sex and the Teen-Age Girl," *Newsweek*, May 22, 1972. "Sex and the Teenager," *Time*, Aug. 21, 1972.

8. Melvin Zelnik, John F. Kantner, and Kathleen Ford, *Sex and Pregnancy in Adolescence* (Beverly Hills: Sage, 1981), 16.

9. Phillips Cutright, "The Teenage Sexual Revolution and the Myth of an Abstinent Past," *Family Planning Perspectives* 4, no. 1 (Jan. 1972): 31.

10. Sandra L. Hofferth, "Teenage Pregnancy and Its Resolution," in Sandra L. Hofferth and Cheryl D. Hayes, eds., *Risking the Future: Adolescent Sexuality, Pregnancy, and Childbearing*, vol. II (Washington: National Academy Press, 1987), 80. Nathanson, *Dangerous Passage*.

11. Commission on Population Growth and the American Future, *Final Report: Population and the American Future* (Washington: U.S. Government Printing Office, 1972).

12. E.g., Madelon Lubin Finkel and David J. Finkel, "Sexual and Contraceptive Knowledge, Attitudes and Behavior of Male Adolescents," *Family Planning Perspectives* 7, no. 6 (Nov./Dec. 1975); Diane S. Fordney Settlage, Sheldon Baroff, and Donna Cooper, "Sexual Experience of Younger Teenage Girls Seeking Contraceptive Assistance for the First Time," *Family Planning Perspectives* 5, no. 4 (Fall 1973): 6.

13. Julian Roebuck and Marsha M. McGee, "Attitudes toward Premarital Sex and Sexual Behavior among Black High School Girls," *Journal of Sex Research* 13, no. 2 (May 1977): 104–105; George Cvetkovich and Barbara Grote, "Psychosexual Development and the Social Problem of Teenage Illegitimacy," in Catherine Chilman, ed., *Adolescent Pregnancy and Childbearing: Findings from Research* (Washington: U.S. Department of Health and Human Services, 1980).

14. E.g., Douglas Kirby, *Sexuality Education: An Evaluation of Programs and Their Effects* (Santa Cruz: Network Publications, 1984); William L. Yarber and Tim Anno, "Changes in Sex Guilt, Premarital Intimacy Attitudes, and Sexual Behavior during a Human Sexuality Course," *Health Education* 12, no. 5 (1981).

15. Melvin Zelnik and John F. Kantner, "Sexual and Contraceptive Experience of Young Unmarried Women in the United States, 1976 and 1971," *Family Planning Perspectives* 9, no. 2 (1977)

16. Interview with Wendy Baldwin, Jan. 15, 1993.

17. Kristin Luker, *Dubious Conceptions: The Politics of Teenage Pregnancy* (Cambridge, Mass.: Harvard University Press, 1996).

18. This research is summarized in Hofferth and Hayes, eds., *Risking the Future.*
19. Baldwin interview.
20. Alan Guttmacher Institute, *11 Million Teenagers* (New York: Planned Parenthood Federation of America, 1976), 9.
21. Bill Peterson, "Abortion Alternatives Cited in HEW Memo; Task Force Head Lists 'Abortion, Motherhood and . . . Madness,'" *Washington Post,* Nov. 27, 1977.
22. "Inter-agency Task Force Report on Adolescent Pregnancy," memo, Department of Health, Education and Welfare, Aug. 4, 1977, 1. Congressional Record (April 13, 1978), S10035.
23. Senate Committee on Human Resources, *Hearings to Consider S.2910, the Adolescent Health, Services, and Pregnancy Prevention and Care Act of 1978,* June 14, July 12, 1978, 100, 89.
24. Baldwin interview.
25. Shelby H. Miller, *Children as Parents: A Final Report on a Study of Childbearing and Child Rearing among 12–15-Year-Olds* (New York: Child Welfare League of America, 1983); Dennis P. Hogan and Evelyn M. Kitagawa, "The Impact of Social Status, Family Structure, and Neighborhood on the Fertility of Black Adolescents," *American Journal of Sociology* 90, no. 4 (Jan. 1985); Greer Litton Fox and Judith K. Inazu, "Mother-Daughter Communication about Sex," *Family Relations* 29 (July 1980).
26. Joseph Lee Rodgers, John O. G. Billy, and J. Richard Udry, "The Rescission of Behaviors: Inconsistent Responses in Adolescent Sexuality Data," *Social Science Research* 11, no. 3 (Sept. 1982). Howard Schuman and Stanley Presser, *Questions and Answers in Attitude Surveys: Experiments on Question Form, Wording, and Context* (Orlando: Academic Press, 1981).
27. Edward A. Smith, J. Richard Udry, and Naomi M. Morris, "Pubertal Development and Friends: A Biosocial Explanation of Adolescent Sexual Behavior," *Journal of Health and Social Behavior* 26 (Sept. 1985): 187.
28. Interview with J. Richard Udry, Dec. 4, 1992.
29. J. Richard Udry, Luther M. Talbert, and Naomi M. Morris, "Biosocial Foundations for Adolescent Female Sexuality," *Demography* 23, no. 2 (May 1986). Susan F. Newcomer and J. Richard Udry, "Mothers' Influence on the Sexual Behavior of Their Teenage Children," *Journal of Marriage and the Family* 46, no. 2 (May 1984): 483. J. Richard Udry and John O. G. Billy, "Initiation of Coitus in Early Adolescence," *American Sociological Review* 52 (Dec. 1987).
30. Melvin Zelnik and John F. Kantner, "Sexual Activity, Contraceptive Use, and Pregnancy among Metropolitan-Area Teenagers: 1971–1979," *Family Planning Perspectives* 12, no. 5 (Sept./Oct. 1980). Melvin Zelnik, "Sexual Activity among Adolescents: Perspectives of a Decade," in Elizabeth R. McAnarney, ed., *Premature Adolescent Pregnancy and Parenthood* (New York: Grune and Stratton, 1983), 27.
31. E.g., George Cvetkovich and Barbara Grote, "Psychosocial Maturity and Teen-

age Contraceptive Use: An Investigation of Decision Making and Communication Skills," *Population and Environment* 4, no. 4 (Winter 1981); Laurie Schwab Zabin and Samuel D. Clark Jr., "Institutional Factors Affecting Teenagers' Choice and Reasons for Delay in Attending a Family Planning Clinic," *Family Planning Perspectives* 15, no. 1 (Jan./Feb. 1983).

32. Alan R. Sack, Robert E. Billingham, and Richard D. Howard, "Premarital Contraceptive Use: A Discriminant Analysis Approach," *Archives of Sexual Behavior* 14, no. 2 (1985): 165.

33. Myra MacPherson, "The Militant Morality of Jeremiah Denton," *Washington Post*, Dec. 7, 1980, L1. Congressional Record (May 4, 1981), S8266.

34. Frank F. Furstenburg Jr. et al., "Race Difference in the Timing of Adolescent Intercourse," *American Sociological Review* 52 (Aug. 1987); William Marsiglio and Frank L. Mott, "The Impact of Sex Education on Sexual Activity, Contraceptive Use and Premarital Pregnancy among American Teenagers," *Family Planning Perspectives* 18, no. 4 (July/Aug. 1986); William D. Mosher, "Fertility and Family Planning in the United States: Insights from the National Survey of Family Growth," *Family Planning Perspectives* 20, no. 5 (Sept./Oct. 1988). William F. Pratt, William D. Mosher, and Christine A. Bachrach, "Understanding U.S. Fertility: Findings from the National Survey of Family Growth, Cycle III," *Population Bulletin* 39, no. 5 (1984): 5.

35. Among these were surveys of previously ignored groups like Latinos, foster children, and those living in rural areas: e.g., John W. Gibson and Judith Kempf, "Attitudinal Predictors of Sexual Activity in Hispanic Adolescent Females," *Journal of Adolescent Research* 5, no. 4 (Oct. 1990); Denise F. Polit, Thomas D. Morton, and Cozette Morrow White, "Sex, Contraception, and Pregnancy among Adolescents in Foster Care," *Family Planning Perspectives* 21, no. 5 (Sept./Oct. 1989); Cheryl S. Alexander et al., "Early Sexual Activity among Adolescents in Small Towns and Rural Areas: Race and Gender Patterns," *Family Planning Perspectives* 21, no. 6 (Nov./Dec. 1989).

36. Deborah Anne Dawson, "The Effects of Sex Education on Adolescent Behavior," *Family Planning Perspectives* 18, no. 4 (July/Aug. 1986).

37. Koray Tanfer and Marjorie C. Horn, "Contraceptive Use, Pregnancy, and Fertility Patterns among Single Women in Their 20s," *Family Planning Perspectives* 17, no. 1 (Jan./Feb. 1985).

38. Frank L. Mott and R. Jean Haurin, "Linkages between Sexual Activity and Alcohol and Drug Use among American Adolescents," *Family Planning Perspectives* 20, no. 3 (May/June 1988); Marsiglio and Mott, "Impact of Sex Education." Denise F. Polit, "Effects of a Comprehensive Program for Teenage Parents: Five Years after Project Redirection," *Family Planning Perspectives* 21, no. 4 (July/Aug. 1989); Frank F. Furstenburg Jr., J. Brooks-Gunn, and S. Philip Morgan, "Adolescent Mothers and Their Children in Later Life," *Family Planning Perspectives* 19, no. 4 (July/Aug. 1987).

39. Baldwin interview.

40. Marvin Eisen and Gail L. Zellman, "Changes in Incidence of Sexual Intercourse of Unmarried Teenagers Following a Community-Based Sex Education Program," *Journal of Sex Research* 23, no. 4 (Nov. 1987). Mark W. Roosa and F. Scott Christopher, "Evaluation of an Abstinence-Only Pregnancy Prevention Program: A Replication," *Family Relations* 39, no. 4 (Oct. 1990): 367.

41. Marion Howard and Judith B. McCabe, "Helping Teenagers Postpone Sexual Involvement," *Family Planning Perspectives* 22, no. 1 (Jan./Feb. 1990). Terrance D. Olsen, Christopher M. Wallace, and Brent C. Miller, "Primary Prevention of Adolescent Pregnancy: Promoting Family Involvement through a School Curriculum," *Journal of Primary Prevention* 5 (1984).

42. Kristin Anderson Moore, Christine Winquist Nord, and James L. Peterson, "Nonvoluntary Sexual Activity among Adolescents," *Family Planning Perspectives* 21, no. 3 (May/June 1989): 111.

43. Planned Parenthood Federation, *The Planned Parenthood Poll: American Teens Speak: Sex, Myths, TV, and Birth Control* (New York: Louis Harris and Associates, 1986), 5.

44. Cheryl D. Hayes, ed., *Risking the Future: Adolescent Sexuality, Pregnancy, and Childbearing*, vol. 1 (Washington: National Academy Press, 1987), ix.

45. Ibid., xiii, 1.

6. *Coupling and Uncoupling*

1. Leon Jaroff, "A Weekend Encounter: Strength from the Group," *Time*, Nov. 9, 1970, 56–57. "Human Potential: The Revolution in Feeling," *Time*, Nov. 9, 1970, 54.

2. Ann Swidler, "Love and Adulthood in American Culture," in Neil J. Smelser and Erik H. Erikson, eds., *Themes of Work and Love in Adulthood* (Cambridge, Mass., Harvard University Press, 1980).

3. Abraham H. Maslow, *Toward a Psychology of Being*, 2nd ed. (New York: Van Nostrand, 1988), 28.

4. Barbara Ehrenreich and Deirdre English, *For Her Own Good* (New York: Anchor/Doubleday, 1979).

5. Abraham H. Maslow, "Self-Esteem (Dominance-Feeling) and Sexuality in Women," *Journal of Social Psychology* 16 (1942): 260, 283, 278.

6. Manfred F. DeMartino, "Dominance-Feeling, Security-Insecurity, and Sexuality in Women," in Manfred F. DeMartino, ed., *Sexual Behavior and Personality Characteristics* (New York: Citadel Press, 1963); Manfred F. DeMartino, *Sex and the Intelligent Woman* (New York: Springer, 1974); Manfred F. DeMartino, *The New Female Sexuality* (New York: Julian Press, 1969). Robert R. Bell, "Some Emerging Sexual Expectations among Women," in Robert R. Bell and Michael Gordon, eds., *The Social Dimension of Human Sexuality* (Boston: Little, Brown, 1972), 164.

7. Seymour Fisher and Howard Osofsky, "Sexual Responsiveness in Women," *Archives of General Psychiatry* 17 (Aug. 1967): 215.

8. Joseph T. Freeman, "Sexual Capacities in the Aging Male," *Geriatrics* (Jan. 1961): 43. Clyde E. Martin, "Factors Affecting Sexual Functioning in 60-79-Year-Old Married Males," *Archives of Sexual Behavior* 10, no. 5 (1981).

9. Steven Seidman, *Romantic Longings* (New York: Routledge, 1991).

10. Barbara Ehrenreich, *The Hearts of Men* (Garden City, N.Y.: Anchor, 1983).

11. Janice M. Irvine, *Disorders of Desire* (Philadelphia: Temple University Press, 1990).

12. Marilyn Peddicord Whitley and Susan B. Poulsen, "Assertiveness and Sexual Satisfaction in Employed Professional Women," *Journal of Marriage and the Family* 37, no. 3 (Aug. 1975); Dana Wilcox and Ruth Hager, "Toward Realistic Expectations for Orgasmic Response in Women," *Journal of Sex Research* 16, no. 2 (May 1980); Linda J. Beckman, "Reported Effects of Alcohol on the Sexual Feelings and Behavior of Women Alcoholics and Non-Alcoholics," *Journal of Studies on Alcohol* 40, no. 3 (1979).

13. Emily Franck Hoon, Peter W. Hoon, and John P. Wincze, "An Inventory for the Measurement of Female Sexual Arousability: The SAI," *Archives of Sexual Behavior* 5, no. 4 (1976): 299.

14. Ibid., 294–295.

15. David Sue, "Erotic Fantasies of College Students during Coitus," *Journal of Sex Research* 15, no. 4 (Nov. 1979).

16. Ron Harris, Sergio Yulis, and Diane Lacoste, "Relationships among Sexual Arousability, Imagery Ability, and Introversion-Extraversion," *Journal of Sex Research* 16, no. 1 (Feb. 1980): 83. Douglas T. Kenrick et al., "Sex Differences, Androgyny, and Approach Responses to Erotica: A New Variation on the Old Volunteer Problem," *Journal of Personality and Social Psychology* 38, no. 3 (1980).

17. Of over forty studies of couples undertaken in the 1970s, only three involved only married couples.

18. Caroline K. Waterman, Emil Chiauzzi, and Mindy Gruenbaum, "The Relationship between Sexual Enjoyment and Actualization of Self and Sexual Partner," *Journal of Sex Research* 15, no. 4 (Nov. 1979): 260.

19. Robert R. Bell and Dorthyann A. Peltz, "Extramarital Sex among Women," *Medical Aspects of Human Sexuality* 8 (March 1974).

20. Joseph LoPiccolo and Jeffrey C. Steger, "The Sexual Interaction Inventory: A New Instrument for Assessment of Sexual Dysfunction," *Archives of Sexual Behavior* 3, no. 6 (1974).

21. Philip Blumstein and Pepper Schwartz, *American Couples* (New York: William Morrow, 1983).

22. They defended their sample by asserting that representativeness became less problematic as the size of the sample increased. This would be true only with a sample large enough to include a very large proportion of the total target

population, something that was not the case here. Kinsey had made the same error thirty years earlier.

23. This debate is summarized in Steven Seidman, *Embattled Eros* (New York: Routledge, 1992).

24. Susan Brownmiller, *Against Our Will* (New York: Simon and Schuster, 1975); Diane Russell, *The Politics of Rape* (New York: Stein and Day, 1975); Susan Griffin, *Rape* (New York: Harper and Row, 1979).

25. Mary P. Koss, "The Hidden Rape Victim: Personality, Attitudinal, and Situational Characteristics," *Psychology of Women Quarterly* 9, no. 2 (1985); Mary P. Koss and Cheryl J. Oros, "Sexual Experiences Survey: A Research Instrument Investigating Sexual Aggression and Victimization," *Journal of Consulting and Clinical Psychology* 50, no. 3 (1982); Mary P. Koss and Mary R. Harvey, *The Rape Victim: Clinical and Community Interventions* (Newbury Park, Calif.: Sage, 1991).

26. Koss and Oros, "Sexual Experiences Survey," 456.

27. Dean G. Kilpatrick, Christine N. Edmunds, and Ann Seymour, *Rape in America: A Report to the Nation* (Arlington, Va.: National Victim Center, 1992). David Johnston, "Survey Shows Number of Rapes Far Higher than Official Figures," *New York Times,* April 24, 1992.

28. F. Scott Christopher, "An Initial Investigation into a Continuum of Premarital Sexual Pressure," *Journal of Sex Research* 25, no. 2 (May 1988); Sarah K. Murnen, Annette Perot, and Donn Byrne, "Coping with Unwanted Sexual Activity: Normative Responses, Situational Determinants, and Individual Differences," *Journal of Sex Research* 26, no. 1 (Feb. 1989).

29. Eugene J. Kanin, "Date Rapists: Differential Sexual Socialization and Relative Deprivation," *Archives of Sexual Behavior* 14, no. 3 (1985); Neil M. Malamuth, "Rape Proclivity among Males," *Journal of Social Issues* 37, no. 4 (1981).

30. Neil M. Malamuth, "Aggression against Women: Cultural and Individual Causes," in Neil M. Malamuth and Edward Donnerstein, eds., *Pornography and Sexual Aggression* (Orlando: Academic Press, 1984).

31. Malamuth rarely described data collection procedures and did not give dates of data collection, so it is unclear whether two articles report on the same study. The studies were repetitive, so we treat them together. See Neil M. Malamuth, Christopher L. Heavey, and Daniel Linz, "Predicting Men's Antisocial Behavior against Women: The Interaction Model of Sexual Aggression," in Gordon C. Nagayama Hall et al., eds., *Sexual Aggression: Issues in Etiology, Assessment, and Treatment* (Washington: Hemisphere, 1993).

32. Mary Koss et al., "Nonstranger Sexual Aggression: A Discriminant Analysis of the Psychological Characteristics of Undetected Offenders," *Sex Roles* 12, nos. 9–10 (1985): 991.

33. E.g., Donald L. Mosher and Mark Sirkin, "Measuring a Macho Personality Constellation," *Journal of Research in Personality* 18 (1984); Terrel L. Tem-

pleman and Ray D. Stinnett, "Patterns of Sexual Arousal and History in a 'Normal' Sample of Young Men," *Archives of Sexual Behavior* 20, no. 2 (1991).

34. Mary P. Koss, Christine H. Gidycz, and Nadine Wisniewski, "The Scope of Rape: Incidence and Prevalence of Sexual Aggression and Victimization in a National Sample of Higher Education Students," *Journal of Consulting and Clinical Psychology* 55, no. 2 (1987); Mary P. Koss and Thomas E. Dinero, "Predictors of Sexual Aggression among a National Sample of Male College Students," *Annals of the New York Academy of Sciences* 528 (1988).

35. E.g., Cindy Struckman-Johnson, "Forced Sex on Dates: It Happens to Men Too," *Journal of Sex Research* 24 (1988); Charlene L. Muehlenhard and Stephen W. Cook, "Men's Self-Reports of Unwanted Sexual Activity," *Journal of Sex Research* 24 (1988).

36. E.g., Judith Lewis Herman, *Father-Daughter Incest* (Cambridge, Mass.: Harvard University Press, 1981); Pamela C. Alexander and Shirley L. Lupfer, "Family Characteristics and Long-Term Consequences Associated with Sexual Abuse," *Archives of Sexual Behavior* 16, no. 3 (1987); Sylvia Robbins Condy et al., "Parameters of Sexual Contact of Boys with Women," *Archives of Sexual Behavior* 16, no. 5 (1987).

37. Robert L. Flewelling and Karl E. Bauman, "Family Structure as a Predictor of Initial Substance Use and Sexual Intercourse in Early Adolescence," *Journal of Marriage and the Family* 52, no. 1 (1990): 175; Terri D. Fisher, "A Comparison of Various Measures of Family Sexual Communication: Psychometric Properties, Validity, and Behavioral Correlates," *Journal of Sex Research* 30, no. 3 (Aug. 1993); Richard H. Fabes and Jeremiah Strouse, "Perceptions of Responsible and Irresponsible Models of Sexuality: A Correlational Study," *Journal of Sex Research* 23, no. 1 (Feb. 1987); Arthur P. Jacoby and John D. Williams, "Effects of Premarital Sexual Standards and Behavior on Dating and Marriage Desirability," *Journal of Marriage and the Family* 47, no. 4 (Nov. 1985).

38. Lynn White and Bruce Keith, "The Effect of Shift Work on the Quality and Stability of Marital Relations," *Journal of Marriage and the Family* 52, no 2 (1990): 455; Patricia J. Morokoff and Ruth Gillilland, "Stress, Sexual Functioning, and Marital Satisfaction," *Journal of Sex Research* 30, no. 1 (1993); Cathy Stein Greenblat, "The Salience of Sexuality in the Early Years of Marriage," *Journal of Marriage and the Family* 45, no. 2 (May 1983).

39. Lillian B. Rubin, *Intimate Strangers: Men and Women Together* (New York: Harper and Row, 1983); Denise A. Donnelly, "Sexually Inactive Marriages," *Journal of Sex Research* 30, no. 2 (May 1993).

40. Edward W. Eichel, Joanne De Simone Eichel, and Sheldon Kule, "The Technique of Coital Alignment and Its Relation to Female Orgasmic Response and Simultaneous Orgasm," *Journal of Sex and Marriage Therapy* 14, no. 2 (Summer 1988). Gary L. Hansen, "Extradyadic Relations during Courtship," *Journal of Sex Research* 22, no. 3 (Aug. 1986); David Charles Frauman, "The Relation-

ship between Physical Exercise, Sexual Activity, and Desire for Sexual Activity," *Journal of Sex Research* 18, no. 1 (Feb. 1982); Suzana Cado and Harold Leitenberg, "Guilt Reaction to Sexual Fantasies during Intercourse," *Archives of Sexual Behavior* 19, no. 1 (1990).

41. Paula S. Nurius and Walter W. Hudson, "Sexual Activity and Preference: Six Quantifiable Dimensions," *Journal of Sex Research* 24 (1988): 34–35.

42. Janell Lucille Carroll, Kari Doray Volk, and Janet Shibley Hyde, "Differences between Males and Females in Motives for Engaging in Sexual Intercourse," *Archives of Sexual Behavior* 14, no. 2 (1985); Naomi B. McCormick, Gary G. Brannigan, and Marcia N. LaPlante, "Social Desirability in the Bedroom: Role of Approval Motivation in Sexual Relationships," *Sex Roles* 11, nos. 3–4 (1984). Elaine Hatfield et al., "Gender Differences in What Is Desired in the Sexual Relationship," *Journal of Psychology and Human Sexuality* 1, no. 2 (1988): 49–50.

43. Frances E. Purifoy, Alicia Grodsky, and Leonard M. Giambra, "The Relationship of Sexual Daydreaming to Sexual Activity, Sexual Drive, and Sexual Attitudes for Women across the Life-Span," *Archives of Sexual Behavior* 21, no. 4 (1992): 372. Barbara L. Wells, "Predictors of Female Nocturnal Orgasms: A Multivariate Analysis," *Journal of Sex Research* 22, no. 4 (Nov. 1986): 427.

44. E.g., Thomas Mulligan and C. Renee Moss, "Sexuality and Aging in Male Veterans: A Cross-Sectional Study of Interests, Ability, and Activity," *Archives of Sexual Behavior* 20, no. 1 (1991).

45. Myers deRosset et al., "Dimensions of Female Sexuality: A Factor Analysis," *Archives of Sexual Behavior* 12, no. 2 (1983).

46. Victor E. Loos, Charles F. Bridges, and Joseph W. Critelli, "Weiner's Attribution Theory and Female Orgasmic Consistency," *Journal of Sex Research* 23, no. 3 (Aug. 1987).

47. J. Kenneth Davidson Sr. and Linda E. Hoffman, "Sexual Fantasies and Sexual Satisfaction: An Empirical Analysis of Erotic Thought," *Journal of Sex Research* 22, no. 2 (May 1986).

48. Purifoy, Grodsky, and Giambra, "Relationship of Sexual Daydreaming."

49. Claire D. Coles and M. Johnna Shamp, "Some Sexual, Personality, and Demographic Characteristics of Readers of Erotic Romances," *Archives of Sexual Behavior* 13, no. 3 (1984).

50. David L. Weis, "The Experience of Pain during Women's First Sexual Intercourse: Cultural Mythology about Female Sexual Initiation," *Archives of Sexual Behavior* 14, no. 5 (1985).

51. Israel M. Schwartz, "Affective Reactions of American and Swedish Women to Their First Premarital Coitus: A Cross-Cultural Comparison," *Journal of Sex Research* 30, no. 1 (1993).

52. Charles F. Bridges, Joseph W. Critelli, and Victor E. Loos, "Hypnotic Susceptibility, Inhibitory Control, and Orgasmic Consistency," *Archives of Sexual Behavior* 14, no. 4 (1985).

53. Albert D. Klassen and Sharon C. Wilsnack, "Sexual Experience and Drinking among Women in a U.S. National Survey," *Archives of Sexual Behavior* 15, no. 5 (1986).

54. Christine B. DeHaan and Jan L. Wallander, "Self-Concept, Sexual Knowledge and Attitudes, and Parental Support in the Sexual Adjustment of Women with Early- and Late-Onset Physical Disability," *Archives of Sexual Behavior* 17, no. 2 (1988).

55. Wells, "Predictors of Female Nocturnal Orgasms."

56. Samuel Juni and Phyliss Cohen, "Partial Impulse Erogeneity as a Function of Fixation and Object Relations," *Journal of Sex Research* 21, no. 3 (Aug. 1985).

57. Sharon Propper and Robert A. Brown, "Moral Reasoning, Parental Sex Attitudes, and Sex Guilt in Female College Students," *Archives Of Sexual Behavior* 15, no. 4 (1986).

58. J. Kenneth Davidson Sr. and Carol A. Darling, "The Sexually Experienced Woman: Multiple Sex Partners and Sexual Satisfaction," *Journal of Sex Research* 24 (1988).

59. Carol A. Darling, J. Kenneth Davidson Sr., and Coleen Conway-Welch, "Female Ejaculation: Perceived Origins, the Grafenberg Spot/Area, and Sexual Responsiveness," *Archives of Sexual Behavior* 19, no. 1 (1990): 38–39.

60. Lillian B. Rubin, *Erotic Wars* (New York: Harper, 1990), 189.

7. Excising the Experts

1. Gael Greene, *Sex and the College Girl* (New York: Dial, 1964), 19–20, 96.

2. Alice Lake, "Teenagers and Sex: A Student Report," *Seventeen* (July 1967): 88.

3. "A Research Questionnaire on Sex," *Psychology Today* 3 (July 1969).

4. Robert Athanasiou, Phillip Shaver, and Carol Tavris, "Sex," *Psychology Today* 4 (July 1970): 39.

5. "Student Survey," *Playboy* 17, no. 9 (1970): 182.

6. "Student Survey: 1971," *Playboy* 18 (Sept. 1971).

7. "What's Really Happening on Campus?" *Playboy* 23 (Oct. 10, 1976): 128, 161.

8. Robert C. Sorensen, *Adolescent Sexuality in Contemporary America* (New York: World Publishing, 1973), 4.

9. Ibid., 189–190.

10. Aaron Hass, *Teenage Sexuality* (New York: Macmillan, 1979), 1, 189.

11. Interview with Morton Hunt, Aug. 19, 1993.

12. Morton Hunt, *Sexual Behavior in the 1970's* (Chicago: Playboy Press, 1974), 298.

13. Ibid., 178.

14. Interview with Shere Hite, Jan. 27, 1993.

15. Shere Hite, *The Hite Report* (New York: Macmillan, 1976), xiii–xiv. Hite interview.

16. Hite, *Hite Report*, 171, 170, 174, 308, 309.

17. Linda Gordon, "The Hite Report: The Myths Keep Coming," *Seven Days,* Feb. 14, 1977, 35.

18. Carol Tavris and Susan Sadd, *The Redbook Report on Female Sexuality* (New York: Delacorte, 1977), 2.

19. Ibid., 144.

20. Shere Hite, *The Hite Report on Male Sexuality* (New York: Knopf, 1981), xxii–xxiii.

21. Robert Asahina, "Reading and Writing: Social Science Fiction," *New York Times,* Aug. 2, 1981, sec. 7, 35. Shere Hite, "Letter to the Editor," *New York Times,* Nov. 29, 1981, sec. 7, 51.

22. Anthony Pietropinto and Jacqueline Simenauer, *Beyond the Male Myth* (New York: Times Books, 1977), 49.

23. Shere Hite, *Women and Love* (New York: Knopf, 1987).

24. Elizabeth Mehren, "Hite Report Finds Gloomy View of Love," *Los Angeles Times,* Oct. 6, 1987; Robert L. Miller, "A Letter from the Publisher," *Time,* Oct. 12, 1987, 4; Claudia Wallis, "Back Off, Buddy," *Time,* Oct. 12, 1987, 71.

25. Farrell quoted in Elizabeth Mehren, "The War over Love Heats up Again: Author Shere Hite's Third Report on Sexuality Fuels an Old Debate over Her Methodology," *Los Angeles Times,* Oct. 29, 1987, pt. 5, 1. William Robertson, "Hite of Folly: Shere Hite's Latest Is Insipid, Infantile, and Altogether Insulting to the Women It Purports to 'Study,'" *Chicago Tribune,* Dec. 2, 1987; "The Shere Hite Report: Sheer Hype?" *U.S. News and World Report,* Nov. 23, 1987. Rubin quoted in David Streitfeld, "Shere Hite and the Trouble with Numbers: For the Famed Sex Researcher, Questions and Controversy over 'Women and Love,'" *Washington Post,* Nov. 10, 1987, B1; Groves quoted in Fox Butterfield, "Hite's New Book Is under Rising Attack," *New York Times,* Nov. 13, 1987, B4.

26. James R. Peterson, "The Hate Report; None Dare Call It Science; Survey Methodology Used in 'Women and Love' Book by Shere Hite Criticized," *Playboy* 35, no. 2 (Feb. 1988): 41.

27. Arlie Russell Hochschild, "Why Can't a Man Be More Like a Woman?" *New York Times Book Review,* Nov. 15, 1987, 34.

28. Linda Wolfe, *The Cosmo Report* (New York: Cosmopolitan Magazine, 1981), 22.

29. "The Cosmo Sex Survey," *Cosmopolitan,* Jan. 1980, 175.

30. "The Lovelife of the American Wife: Take Part in a Landmark Survey," *Ladies' Home Journal* 99, no. 6 (June 1982); Ellen Frank and Sandra Enos Forsyth, "The Lovelife of the American Wife," *Ladies' Home Journal* 100, no. 2 (Feb. 1983): 72.

31. Frank and Forsyth, "Lovelife of the American Wife," 118.

32. James R. Petersen et al., "The Playboy Readers' Sex Survey, Part 1," *Playboy* 30 (Jan. 1983): 112.

33. James R. Petersen et al., "The Playboy Readers' Sex Survey, Part 3," *Playboy* 30 (May 1983): 126–127.

34. Kevin Cook, "The Playboy Readers' Sex Survey, Part 5: When You Get Right Down to It, You'll Find Sexual Synchronization the Key to Sexual Success," *Playboy* 30 (Sept. 1983): 189.

35. "What Are Men Like Today?" *Cosmopolitan* 199, no. 8 (Aug. 1985); Claudia Bowe, "What Are Men Like Today?" *Cosmopolitan* 200, no. 5 (May 1986); James Gilbaugh Jr., "What Men Do, or *Want* to Do in Bed," *Cosmopolitan* 206, no. 5 (May 1989).

36. Carin Rubenstein and Carol Tavris, "Special Survey Results: 26,000 Women Reveal the Secrets of Intimacy," *Redbook* 169, no. 5 (Sept. 1987).

37. Curtis Pesman, "Love and Sex in the '90s," *Seventeen* 50, no. 11 (Nov. 1991): 63–64.

38. "Who, What, Where, and How, Do You Love?" *Redbook* 176, no. 6 (Oct. 1989): 134–135.

39. Carin Rubenstein, "Generation Sex," *Mademoiselle* (June 1993): 130, 132, 134, 135.

40. George Smith, "How Sexy Are You?" *Cosmopolitan* 214, no. 4 (April 1993); Priscilla Donovan, "Are You a Right-Brained or Left-Brained Lover?" *Redbook* 175, no. 3 (July 1990); "What's Your Love-Making IQ?" *Cosmopolitan* 201, no. 7 (July 1986).

8. Gay Men and AIDS

1. David M. Auerbach et al., "Cluster of Cases of the Acquired Immune Deficiency Syndrome: Patients Linked by Sexual Contact," *American Journal of Medicine* 76 (March 1984): 490. See also Harold W. Jaffe et al., "National Case-Control Study of Kaposi's Sarcoma and *Pneumocystis carinii* Pneumonia in Homosexual Men: Part 1, Epidemiologic Results," *Annals of Internal Medicine* 99, no. 2 (Aug. 1983).

2. Bruce Voeller, "Some Uses and Abuses of the Kinsey Scale," in David P. McWhirter, Stephanie A. Sanders, and June Machover Reinisch, eds., *Homosexuality/Heterosexuality* (New York: Oxford University Press, 1990), 34.

3. Martin S. Weinberg and Colin J. Williams, *Male Homosexuals* (New York: Oxford University Press, 1974).

4. Alan P. Bell and Martin S. Weinberg, *Homosexualities* (New York: Simon and Schuster, 1978).

5. E.g., Stephen N. Haynes and L. Jerome Oziel, "Homosexuality: Behaviors and Attitudes," *Archives of Sexual Behavior* 5, no. 4 (1976); Martin Manosevitz, "Early Sexual Behavior in Adult Homosexual and Heterosexual Males," *Journal of Abnormal Psychology* 76, no. 3 (1970); Letitia Anne Peplau et al., "Loving Women: Attachment and Autonomy in Lesbian Relationships," *Journal of Social Issues* 34, no. 3 (1978).

6. Bruce Voeller and James Walter, "Gay Fathers," *Family Coordinator* 27, no. 2

(1978). Karla Jay and Allen Young, *The Gay Report* (New York: Summit Books, 1979).

7. Interview with William W. Darrow, Aug. 26, 1993. William W. Darrow, "Changes in Sexual Behavior and Venereal Diseases," *Clinical Obstetrics and Gynecology* 18, no. 1 (March 1975).

8. Wolf Szmuness et al., "On the Role of Sexual Behavior in the Spread of Hepatitis B Infection," *Annals of Internal Medicine* 83 (1975): 494.

9. William W. Darrow et al., "The Gay Report on Sexually Transmitted Diseases," *American Journal of Public Health* 71, no. 9 (Sept. 1981).

10. M. T. Schreeder et al.,"Hepatitis B in Homosexual Men: Prevalence of Infection and Factors Related to Transmission," *Journal of Infectious Diseases* 146, no. 1 (July 1982): 11. Donald P. Francis et al., "The Prevention of Hepatitis B with Vaccine: Report of the Center for Disease Control Multi-Center Efficacy Trial among Homosexual Men," *Annals of Internal Medicine* 97 (1982).

11. Darrow interview.

12. We use the term *gay* here in the sense in which the CDC and other researchers used it: to refer to men with sexual experience involving other men.

13. Harold W. Jaffe et al., "The Acquired Immunodeficiency Syndrome in a Cohort of Homosexual Men: A Six-Year Follow-Up Study," *Annals of Internal Medicine* 103 (1985); D. Echenberg et al., "Update: Acquired Immunodeficiency Syndrome in the San Francisco Cohort Study, 1978–1985," *Morbidity and Mortality Weekly Report* 34, no. 38 (Sept. 27, 1985).

14. Lynda S. Doll et al., "Sexual Behavior before AIDS: The Hepatitis B Studies of Homosexual and Bisexual Men," *AIDS* 4, no. 11 (1990).

15. William W. Darrow et al., "Risk Factors for Human Immunodeficiency Virus (HIV) Infections in Homosexual Men," *American Journal of Public Health* 77, no. 4 (April 1987).

16. One of the earliest of many articles is Leon McKusick, William Horstman, and Thomas J. Coates, "AIDS and Sexual Behavior Reported by Gay Men in San Francisco," *American Journal of Public Health* 75, no. 5 (May 1985).

17. Interview with Thomas Coates, June 16, 1993.

18. E.g., Warren Winkelstein Jr. et al., "Sexual Practices and the Risk of Infection by the Human Immunodeficiency Virus: The San Francisco Men's Health Study," *Journal of the American Medical Association* 257, no. 3 (Jan. 1987).

19. Cindy Patton, *Sex and Germs* (Boston: South End Press, 1985).

20. Research and Decisions Corporation, *Designing an Effective AIDS Prevention Campaign Strategy for San Francisco* (San Francisco AIDS Foundation, 1984), appendix, 2.

21. Ibid., 66–68.

22. Karolynn Siegel et al., "Patterns of Change in Sexual Behavior among Gay Men in New York City," *Archives of Sexual Behavior* 17, no. 6 (1988): 493.

23. Jane McCusker et al., "Behavioral Risk Factors for HIV Infection among Ho-

mosexual Men at a Boston Community Health Center," *American Journal of Public Health* 78, no. 1 (Jan. 1988).

24. Lawrence A. Kingsley et al., "Risk Factors for Seroconversion to Human Immunodeficiency Virus among Male Homosexuals," *Lancet* 8529 (Feb. 1987).

25. Susan M. Rogers and Charles Turner, "Male-Male Sexual Contact in the U.S.A.: Findings from Five Sample Surveys, 1970–1990," *Journal of Sex Research* 28, no. 4 (Nov. 1991).

9. *Politics and Sex Surveys*

1. Institute of Medicine, *Confronting AIDS: Directions for Public Health, Health Care, and Research* (Washington: National Academy Press, 1986), 9.

2. Victor De Gruttola, Kenneth Mayer, and William Bennett, "AIDS: Has the Problem Been Adequately Assessed?" *Reviews of Infectious Diseases* 8, no. 2 (March/April 1986): 303.

3. Nancy Padian, "Sexual Histories of Heterosexual Couples with One HIV-Infected Partner," *American Journal of Public Health* 80, no. 8 (Aug. 1990); Diane K. Lewis, John K. Watters, and Patricia Case, "The Prevalence of High-Risk Sexual Behavior in Male Intravenous Drug Users with Steady Female Partners," *American Journal of Public Health* 80, no. 4 (April 1990).

4. Paul D. Cleary et al., "Behavior Changes after Notification of HIV Infection," *American Journal of Public Health* 81, no. 12 (Dec. 1991).

5. William Darrow and the Centers for Disease Control Collaborative Group for the Study of HIV-1 in Selected Women, "Prostitution, Intravenous Drug Use, and HIV-1 in Selected Women," in Martin A. Plant, ed., *AIDS, Drugs, and Prostitution* (London: Routledge, 1990).

6. Ron Stall et al., "Sexual Risk for HIV Transmission among Singles-Bar Patrons in San Francisco," *Medical Anthropology Quarterly* (n.s.) 4, no. 1 (March 1990).

7. David R. Bolling and Bruce Voeller, "Letter to the Editor," *Journal of the American Medical Association* 258, no. 4 (July 1987).

8. Interview with Robert T. Michael, Jan. 8, 1993.

9. Norman Bradburn, *Improving Interview Method and Questionnaire Design* (San Francisco: Jossey-Bass, 1979); Seymour Sudman and Norman Bradburn, *Asking Questions* (San Francisco: Jossey-Bass, 1982).

10. Interview with Robert Knight, May 24, 1993.

11. NORC, "A Proposal to Conduct the Pretest of a Questionnaire on the Social and Behavioral Aspects of Health and Fertility-Related Behavior in a Population of 2,000 Adult Men and Women" (Proposal Submitted to NICHD, Aug. 1988).

12. William Booth, "The Long, Lost Survey on Sex," *Science* 239 (March 1988). Robert E. Fay et al., "Prevalence and Patterns of Same-Gender Sexual Contact among Men," *Science* 243, no. 4889 (Jan. 1989).

13. Judith A. Reisman and Edward W. Eichel, *Kinsey, Sex, and Fraud: The Indoctrination of a People* (Lafayette, La.: Lochinvar/Huntingdon House, 1990).

Reisman's charges resurfaced in 1995 when the new director of the Kinsey Institute, John Bancroft, acknowledged that much of Kinsey's data on adolescent boys came from one pedophile who kept notes on sexual activities with 317 boys, instead of from several trained observers as Kinsey had claimed. Marc Fisher, "Kinsey Report, Fast and Loose?" *Washington Post,* Nov. 8, 1995.

14. Charles F. Turner, Heather G. Miller, and Lincoln E. Moses, eds., *AIDS: Sexual Behavior and Intravenous Drug Use* (Washington: National Academy Press, 1989); William Dannemeyer, "The Sex Study That Almost Was . . . and Probably Will Be" (manuscript, Feb. 1987). Office of William E. Dannemeyer, "Backgrounder on National Institute of Child Health and Human Development Contract Award: 'Social and Behavioral Aspects of Health and Fertility Related Behavior,'" (manuscript, March 28, 1989), 10.

15. NORC, "The National Survey of Health and Sexual Behavior: Background and Developments through January 1989" (manuscript, undated).

16. James Davison Hunter, *Culture Wars: The Struggle to Define America* (New York: Basic Books, 1991).

17. Suzanne Fields, "Get Set to Lie—New Sex Survey Is Coming," *Chicago Sun-Times,* Jan. 30, 1989; Deborah Mesce, "Uncle Sam Wants to Probe Your Sex Life," *Journal News* (Hamilton, Oh.), March 31, 1989; "Who Loves Ya Baby? And How?" *Frederick* (Maryland) *Post,* March 31, 1989.

18. Bill Bailey, "Memo to Selected Hill Staff," Feb. 21, 1989 (memo, American Psychological Association).

19. Letter from Richard D. Darmon, Director of OMB, to Louis Sullivan, Secretary of HHS, April 6, 1989. William Dannemeyer, "Dear Colleague" (April 11, 1989).

20. Interview with Paul Mero, April 30, 1993.

21. Letter from Edward O. Laumann to Louis W. Sullivan, Secretary of HHS, April 17, 1989.

22. McGraw-Hill's *Medicine and Health* 43, no. 32 (Aug. 14, 1989), quoted Mason as planning to "placate conservative critics with a new design for the survey" and pledging to "take it personally to members of Congress" if Sullivan approved it. Laumann interview. Robert Pear, "Profile: Nabers Cabaniss: 'The Last Job a Normal Person Would Want,'" *New York Times,* Sept. 16, 1987, B6.

23. Edward O. Laumann, John H. Gagnon, and Robert T. Michael, "The National Study of Health and Sexual Behavior Design Report" (NORC, submitted to NICHD, April 1989).

24. There were occasional fights over funding in the House and Senate from 1989 to 1991, but these were moot as long as the surveys were moribund.

25. NICHD had invited proposals on STDs, but this produced no response from researchers until AIDS (Baldwin interview); we located a few isolated studies, mostly under the auspices of the CDC: e.g., Sevgi O. Aral, Willard Cates Jr., and William C. Jenkins, "Genital Herpes: Does Knowledge Lead to Action?" *American Journal of Public Health* 75, no. 1 (Jan. 1985).

26. C. Lindan et al., "Heterosexual Behaviors and Factors That Influence Condom Use among Patients Attending a Sexually Transmitted Disease Clinic—San Francisco," *Morbidity and Mortality Weekly Report* 39, no. 39 (Oct. 1990); G. Steven Bowen et al., "Risk Behaviors for HIV Infection in Clients of Pennsylvania Family Planning Clinics," *Family Planning Perspectives* 22, no. 2 (March/April 1990).

27. Ralph Hingson, Lee Strunin, and Beth Berlin, "Acquired Immunodeficiency Syndrome Transmission: Changes in Knowledge and Behaviors among Teenagers, Massachusetts Statewide Surveys, 1986 to 1988," *Pediatrics* 85, no. 1 (Jan. 1990): 24.

28. Ralph W. Hingson et al., "Beliefs about AIDS, Use of Alcohol and Drugs, and Unprotected Sex among Massachusetts Adolescents," *American Journal of Public Health* 80, no. 3 (March 1990): 295.

29. Susan M. Kegeles, Nancy E. Adler, and Charles Irwin Jr., "Sexually Active Adolescents and Condoms: Changes in One Year in Knowledge, Attitudes and Use," *American Journal of Public Health* 78, no. 4 (April 1988).

30. Heather J. Walter et al., "Factors Associated with AIDS Risk Behaviors among High School Students in an AIDS Epicenter," *American Journal of Public Health* 82, no. 4 (April 1992).

31. Laura Kann et al., "Establishing a System of Complementary School-Based Surveys to Annually Assess HIV-Related Knowledge, Beliefs, and Behaviors among Adolescents," *Journal of School Health* 59, no. 2 (Feb. 1989). It is difficult to be sure how many state and local authorities participated, since CDC reports gave different numbers. For the national survey see John E. Anderson et al., "HIV/AIDS Knowledge and Sexual Behavior among High School Students," *Family Planning Perspectives* 22, no. 6 (Nov./Dec 1990).

32. Lloyd J. Kolbe, "An Epidemiological Surveillance System to Monitor the Prevalence of Youth Behaviors That Most Affect Health," *Health Education* 21, no. 6 (Nov./Dec. 1990); Leo Morris, Charles W. Warren, and Sevgi O. Aral, "Measuring Adolescent Sexual Behaviors and Related Health Outcomes," *Public Health Reports* 108, supp. 1 (1993).

33. Ralph J. DiClemente et al., "College Students' Knowledge and Attitudes about AIDS and Changes in HIV-Prevention Behaviors," *AIDS Education and Prevention* 2, no. 3 (1990): 205.

34. Ralph J. DiClemente et al., "Comparison of AIDS Knowledge, Attitudes, and Behaviors among Incarcerated Adolescents and a Public School Sample in San Francisco," *American Journal of Public Health* 81, no. 4 (May 1991); Robert E. Fullilove et al., "Risk of Sexually Transmitted Disease among Black Adolescent Crack Users in Oakland and San Francisco, Calif.," *JAMA* 263, no. 6 (Feb. 1990).

35. John E. Anderson, Thomas E. Freese, and Julia N. Pennbridge, "Sexual Risk Behavior and Condom Use among Street Youth in Hollywood," *Family Planning Perspectives* 26, no. 1 (Jan./Feb. 1994): 23.

36. Ann F. Brunswick et al., "HIV-1 Seroprevalence and Risk Behaviors in an

Urban African-American Community Cohort," *American Journal of Public Health* 83, no. 10 (Oct. 1993); Mindy Thompson Fullilove et al., "Risk for AIDS in Multiethnic Neighborhoods in San Francisco, California: The Population-Based AMEN Study," *Western Journal of Medicine* 157, no. 1 (July 1992): 39.

37. Joseph A. Catania et al., "Issues in AIDS Primary Prevention for Late-Middle-Aged and Elderly Americans," *Generations* (Fall 1989).

38. Maria L. Ekstrand et al., "Are Bisexually Identified Men in San Francisco a Common Vector for Spreading HIV Infection to Women?" *American Journal of Public Health* 84, no. 6 (June 1994); Stephanie Tortu et al., "The Risk of HIV Infection in a National Sample of Women with Injection Drug-Using Partners," *American Journal of Public Health* 84, no. 8 (Aug. 1994).

39. Charles F. Turner, Heather G. Miller, and Lewellys F. Barker, "AIDS Research in the Behavioral and Social Sciences," in Ruth Kulstad, ed., *AIDS 1988* (Washington: AAAS Papers, 1988); Tom W. Smith, "Adult Sexual Behavior in 1989: Number of Partners, Frequency of Intercourse, and Risk of AIDS," *Family Planning Perspectives* 23, no. 3 (May/June 1991); Tom W. Smith, "A Methodological Analysis of the Sexual Behavior Questions on the General Social Surveys," *Journal of Official Statistics* 8, no. 3 (1992).

40. Public Health Service, "Coolfont Report: A PHS Plan for the Prevention and Control of AIDS and AIDS Virus," *Public Health Reports* 101 (1986); E. O. Laumann et al., "Monitoring the AIDS Epidemic in the United States: A Network Approach," *Science* 244, no. 4909 (June 1989).

41. Charles F. Turner and Robert E. Fay, "Monitoring the Spread of HIV Infection," in Turner, Miller, and Moses, *AIDS.*

42. *Report of the Presidential Commission on the Human Immunodeficiency Virus Epidemic* (Washington: U.S. Government Printing Office, June 1988).

43. Peter Hurley and Glen Pinder, "Ethics, Social Forces, and Politics in AIDS-Related Research: Experience in Planning and Implementing a Household HIV Seroprevalence Survey," *Milbank Quarterly* 70, no. 4 (1992): 605. Stephen B. Thomas and Sandra Crouse Quinn, "The Tuskegee Syphilis Study, 1932 to 1972: Implications for HIV Education and AIDS Risk Education Programs in the Black Community," *American Journal of Public Health* 81, no. 11 (Nov. 1981).

44. "National Household Seroprevalence Survey: Feasibility Study Final Report" (prepared for the National Center for Health Statistics by Research Triangle Institute, North Carolina, 1990). The large 95 percent confidence interval of between 2,200 and 7,500 was still more accurate than others.

45. With the survey quashed, NCHS administered an HIV test to a sample of the respondents in the National Health and Nutrition Examination Survey conducted from 1988 to 1991. This small sample produced an HIV infection estimate of 550,000 with an interval of from 299,000 to 1.02 million, lower than the CDC interval estimate of from 800,000 to 1.2 million. See Lawrence K. Altman, "U.S. Survey Finds 550,000 Infected with H.I.V. Outside Risk Groups," *New York Times,* Dec. 14, 1995.

46. NORC, "Social Demography of Interpersonal Relations" (Unsolicited Proposal to NICHD, Sept. 1990). Unlike SHARP, this unsolicited proposal went through a peer review in competition with proposals on a variety of topics.
47. Ronald R. Rindfuss, "The American Teenage Study: The Contraceptive Behavior of Teenage Women and Their Partners" (University of North Carolina: Final report to NICHD, contract no. NO1-HD-7–2924, 1989). This was a working document describing the researchers' recommendations. Its series of proposed questionnaires had undergone pretesting, and modifications were made during the proposal and approval stages of the study. There would have been further modification of the questionnaires had the survey been undertaken.
48. Ibid., 36.
49. Peter G. Gosselin, "Is American Science Ready for Bernadine Healy?" *Boston Globe,* July 7, 1991.
50. Paul Brown, "Teen Sex Survey Not on Ice Yet," *Chapel Hill Newspaper,* July 22, 1991, A1.
51. "Silencing Teenagers about Sex," *New York Times,* July 23, 1991, A20.
52. In an interview, May Kennedy, on the staff of Pat Schroeder's Select Committee on Children, Youth, and the Family, said Schroeder realized that "nobody communicates clearly with teens about sexual matters . . . She is committed to openness; she acknowledges that parents would prefer that kids wait, but that is as far as she'll go." Kennedy added that "only good girls get elected to Congress," so congresswomen do not have the tarnished reputations that make their male colleagues hesitant to discuss sex. Derrick Z. Jackson, "A Health Gag by Political Quacks," *Boston Globe,* July 28, 1991, 73.
53. National Institutes of Mental Health Revitalization Amendments of 1991, Congressional Record (July 25, 1991), H5869, H5872.
54. Ibid., H5872, H5873.
55. Health and Human Services Budget 1991, Congressional Record (Sept. 12, 1991), S12862.
56. Interview with Victoria Otten, Sept. 11, 1992.
57. National Institutes of Health Revitalization Amendments, April 2, 1992, Congressional Record—Senate.
58. It finally passed, with the two amendments intact, as President Clinton's first piece of legislation.
59. Jeff Lyon, "Keeping Score: A University of Chicago Team Is Exploring Sexual America," *Chicago Tribune Magazine,* Nov. 29, 1991, sec. 10, 16.

10. The Story Continues

1. Freya L. Sonenstein, "Determinants of Contraceptive Use by Adolescent Males" (Grant Application to NICHD, RO1 HD22255–01, May 1986); Freya L. Sonenstein, "1990 Follow-Up Survey of Young Men" (Grant Application to NICHD, RFA 88-HD-16, Jan. 1989).

2. Rob Stein, "Teenage Boys More Sexually Active, Survey Finds," UPI, March 30, 1989; Rebecca Kolberg, "Sex Activity Dropping among Teenage Males," UPI, Feb. 19, 1990. E.g., Freya Sonenstein, Joseph H. Pleck, and Leighton C. Ku, "Sexual Activity, Condom Use and AIDS Awareness among Adolescent Males," *Family Planning Perspectives* 21, no. 4 (July/Aug. 1989).

3. Joseph A. Catania et al., "Prevalence of AIDS-Related Risk Factors and Condom Use in the United States," *Science* 258 (Nov. 13, 1992).

4. Interview with Koray Tanfer, April 2, 1993.

5. John O. G. Billy et al., "The Sexual Behavior of Men in the United States"; Koray Tanfer et al., "Condom Use among U.S. Men, 1991"; William R. Grady et al., "Condom Characteristics: The Perceptions and Preferences of Men in the United States"; Daniel H. Klepinger et al., "Perceptions of AIDS Risk and Severity and Their Association with Risk-Related Behavior among U.S. Men," *Family Planning Perspectives* 25, no. 2 (March/April 1993).

6. Felicity Barringer, "Sex Survey of American Men Finds 1% Are Gay," *New York Times,* April 15, 1993. Melinda Beck, "The Impact on Gay Political Power," *Newsweek,* April 26, 1993, 57. Robert Knight of the conservative Family Research Council took credit for the attention paid to the survey, since whenever a newspaper had cited the Kinsey 10 percent he had pointed out problems with Kinsey's data. Interview with Robert Knight, May 24, 1993.

7. Koray Tanfer, "Knowledge, Attitudes, and Intentions of American Women Regarding the Hormonal Implant," *Family Planning Perspectives* 36, no. 2 (March/April 1994). Leighton Ku, Freya L. Sonenstein, and Joseph H. Pleck, "Young Men's Risk Behaviors for HIV Infection and Sexually Transmitted Diseases," *American Journal of Public Health* 83, no. 11 (Nov. 1993).

8. Edward O. Laumann, John H. Gagnon, and Robert T. Michael, "A Political History of the National Sex Survey of Adults" (paper delivered at the Annual Meetings of the American Sociological Association, Pittsburgh, 1992); J. Richard Udry, "The Politics of Sex Research," *Journal of Sex Research* 30, no. 2 (May 1993).

9. "New Adolescent Health Study Successfully Completes First Stage," Health and Science Briefs from the National Institute of Child Health and Human Development, undated flyer.

10. Robert T. Michael et al., *Sex in America: A Definitive Survey* (Boston: Little, Brown, 1994). Edward O. Laumann et al., *The Social Organization of Sexuality* (Chicago: University of Chicago Press, 1994).

11. The number of men who reported any homosexual sexual behavior was small (75), so to estimate the proportion of men in the population who engaged in this behavior Gagnon and Michaels combined these data with those from the General Social Survey and the CAPS National AIDS Behavioral Survey. They estimated that 2.6 percent of men had engaged in sex with other men in the previous year and 5.3 percent had done so since age 18. This was the most accurate estimate of male-to-male sex to date and was lower than Kinsey's.

Diane Binson et al., "Prevalence and Social Distribution of Men Who Have Sex with Men: United States and Its Urban Centers," *Journal of Sex Research* 32, no. 3 (1995).

12. Laurie McGinley, "Americans Lead Conventional Sex Lives Contrary to Popular Notion, Survey Finds," *Wall Street Journal,* Oct. 7, 1994; Art Buchwald, "The Other Six Are Hobby Nights," *Los Angeles Times,* Oct. 20, 1994; Philip Elmer-Dewitt, "Now for the Truth about Americans and Sex," *Time,* Oct. 17, 1994; Ellen Goodman, "A Nation of Teakettles—On a Nice, Slow Simmer," *Los Angeles Times,* Oct. 14, 1994, B7. Goodman misinterpreted Helms's objections.

13. Paul Robinson, "The Way We Do the Things We Do," *New York Times Book Review,* Oct. 30, 1994. Stanley Presser, "Sex, Samples, and Response Errors," *Contemporary Sociology* 24, no. 4 (July 1995).

14. R. C. Lewontin, "Sex, Lies and Social Science," *New York Review of Books,* April 20, 1995. Edward O. Laumann et al., "Letter to the Editor," *New York Review of Books,* April 20, 1995.

11. Reforming Sex Research

1. Stanley Presser, "Sex, Samples, and Response Errors," *Contemporary Sociology* 24, no. 4 (July 1995).

2. Heather G. Miller, Charles F. Turner, and Lincoln E. Moses, eds., *AIDS: The Second Decade* (Washington: National Academy Press, 1990).

3. On the lack of attention to other types of sex research see John H. Gagnon, "Sex Research and Sexual Conduct in the Era of AIDS," *Journal of Acquired Immunodeficiency Syndromes* 1, no. 6 (1989). Joseph A. Catania et al., "Methodological Problems in AIDS Behavioral Research: Influences on Measurement Error and Participation Bias in Studies of Sexual Behavior," *Psychological Bulletin* 108, no. 3 (1990).

4. M. Morris, "Telling Tails Explain the Discrepancy in Sexual Partner Reports," *Nature* 365, no. 6445 (Sept. 1993). Since most of those reporting more than twenty partners were men, Morris excluded many more men than women. With more women than men remaining in her sample, she compared the total partners of fewer men with those of more women. She should have computed within-group averages for number of partners and then computed ratios of those averages; among those with fewer than twenty partners, each man averaged 1.6 times as many partners as each woman, and among those with more than twenty partners, each man averaged 1.7 times as many partners as each woman.

5. Roger Tourangeau and Tom W. Smith, "Asking Sensitive Questions: The Impact of Data Collection Mode, Question Format, and Question Context," *Public Opinion Quarterly* 60, no. 2 (Summer 1996); Charles F. Turner, "Reducing Bias in Measurement of Drug Use, Sexual and Other AIDS-Related

Behaviors" (paper presented at The Science of Self-Report, NIH, Bethesda, Md., 1996).

6. This point was made by the survey expert Howard Schuman in a letter to the *New York Review of Books*, Aug. 10, 1995, during the Lewontin affair.

7. Jeffrey Weeks, *Sexuality and Its Discontents* (New York: Routledge, 1985). It was not until the journalist Sharon Thompson asked young women how they first became sexually involved that young women's many motives for having sex began to emerge: Thompson, *Going All the Way* (New York: Hill and Wang, 1995).

8. Interview with Ira Reiss, Oct. 24, 1994.

9. We attempted to obtain the questionnaires for all surveys undertaken after 1975. Many researchers complied promptly, but others did not reply or offered a variety of excuses, some even claiming that their questionnaires no longer existed. Joseph A. Catania et al., "Effects of Interviewer Gender, Interviewer Choice, and Item Wording on Responses to Questions Concerning Sexual Behavior" (manuscript, 1996).

Index

Abortion, 61, 64, 89, 91–92, 94, 104, 108, 204
Abstinence. *See* Sexual abstinence
Achilles, Paul Strong, 25–26
Acquired immune deficiency syndrome. *See* AIDS
Adams, Brock, 204–206
Adolescence: development in, 9, 14–20, 25, 27, 80–81; early attitudes toward, 14–20; and pregnancy, 87–109, 190, 228; and commercial sex surveys, 136, 140–141, 155–157; and AIDS, 190–194, 199–207
Adolescent Family Life Act (1983), 102, 105, 107, 182, 189, 205
Adolescent Health Services and Pregnancy Prevention and Care Act (1978), 96
African Americans, 64, 70, 89–95, 98–99, 101, 104–106, 193–195, 198, 200, 210. *See also* Race
Aging, 115, 132
AIDS (acquired immune deficiency syndrome), 130, 157, 158–159, 163–175, 176–201, 204–205, 207–208, 209–211, 213, 215–216, 220–221, 223; and gay men, 158–175, 176–208, 226, 228; through blood transfusions, 159, 211; through intravenous drug use, 159, 173–174, 176–178, 180, 191–198, 211; and bisexuals, 161, 166, 170–171, 176–177, 180, 194–197, 216; and lesbians, 164, 182, 226; and heterosexuals, 175, 176–208, 228; and adolescents, 190–194, 199–207
AIDS Behavioral Research Project, 168–169, 171
Alan Guttmacher Institute, 90–92, 95–98, 102, 107, 189
Alcohol use, 83, 167, 191, 193
American Social Hygiene Association, 234n11
American Statistical Association, 58
American Teenage Study, 189–190, 199, 205–206, 209–211, 213
Anal intercourse, 164–165, 167, 169–175, 177, 179, 188, 200, 210; receptive, 167, 169–172, 174–175; insertive, 171–172, 174; by heterosexuals, 180, 216
Arousability. *See* Sexual arousability
Asahina, Robert, 148
Athanasiou, Robert, 137
Auerbach, Judith, 189

Baby boom, 62, 83
Bailey, Bill, 187–188
Baldwin, Wendy, 95, 98, 107, 180, 188, 206
Bancroft, John, 254n13
Bathhouses, 161, 164, 167–168, 171
Battelle Research Center, 1, 8–11, 211–212
Bauer, Gary, 201
Bauman, Carl, 65
Beam, Lura: *The Single Woman*, 40–41; *A Thousand Marriages*, 40
Bedford Hills Reformatory for Women, 30

Bell, Alan, 161–163
Bell, Robert, 114, 145
Berger, Alan, 80
Bias, 8–10, 22, 84, 122
Billy, John, 211
Biology, 3, 17, 24, 30–31, 40, 48, 50
Birth control, 8, 149, 189–190, 200, 210–211; early attitudes toward, 20, 22–23; and marriage, 40, 61–66; and adolescents, 88–94, 96–97, 104–108
Birth Control Federation of America, 61
Birth rate, 36, 61, 96
Bisexuality, 161, 166, 170–171, 176–177, 180, 194–197, 216
Blacks. *See* African Americans
Blood transfusions, 159, 211
Blumstein, Philip, 121–122; *American Couples*, 122
Bob and Carol and Ted and Alice, 184–185
Bolling, David, 179
Booth, William, 184
Boston Psychopathic Hospital, 26
Bradburn, Norman, 181
Britten, Florence Haxton, 69–70
Brockman, F. S., 14–17, 29
Bromley, Dorothy Dunbar, 68–70
Brown, Helen Gurley, 152
Bukstel, Lee, 83
Bureau of the Census, 7, 36, 62, 197
Bureau of Social Hygiene, 30, 48
Burgess, Ernest, 43–49, 113, 155; *Predicting Success or Failure in Marriage*, 43
Bush, George, 186, 190, 201, 206–207
Bye, Larry, 172

Cabaniss, Nabers, 189
Califano, Joseph, 96, 98
Campbell, Arthur, 62, 88–89
Carnegie Corporation, 62
Case-control survey, 159, 166
Catania, Joseph, 210–211, 221
Center for AIDS Prevention Studies, 179, 193, 195, 210–211, 213, 221, 258n11
Center for Clinical and Behavioral Studies, 191
Centers for Disease Control, 158–159, 163–170, 174, 178, 180, 189, 192–194, 197–199
Chastity. *See* Virginity
Chen, Jin-Yi, 158

Child Trends, 106
Child Welfare League of America, 98
Christ, Grace, 158
Christenson, Cornelia, 235n30
Christian right, 3, 182, 185–186, 203
Christopher, F. Scott, 106, 126
Civil rights movement, 64, 76, 91, 94
Clark, John, 77
Class. *See* Social class
Clitoral orgasm, 40, 52, 116, 215
Cluster survey, 159, 166
Coates, Thomas, 168–169
Cochran, William, 58
Coital alignment techniques, 131
College students, 131, 136, 193; temptations about sex, 14, 18–20, 33–34; attitudes toward marriage, 42–43, 45–47, 56–57, 66; and sex before marriage, 67–86, 87–88; and rape, 124–128; *Playboy* surveys of, 138–140
Commercial sex surveys, 135–157, 212, 214
Commission on Population Growth and the American Future, 88, 92
Committee on AIDS Research and the Behavioral, Social, and Statistical Sciences, 176, 180, 220
Committee for Research in Problems of Sex, 48, 54, 58
Committee for the Study of Sex Variants, 53–54
Companionate marriage, 38, 42, 47
Computer-assisted interview methods, 221–222
Condoms, 107, 169, 171–172, 174, 177, 179, 190–195, 210–211, 221, 228
Confidentiality, 8, 31, 57, 181, 186, 198, 201, 218
Congress, U. S., 48, 59, 88, 92, 97–98, 102, 105, 124, 182, 185–189, 199, 202–207, 209, 226, 257n52. *See also specific legislation*
Conservatives, 1–2, 12, 22, 59, 72, 78, 92–93, 99, 102–104, 108, 123, 129–131, 139, 142, 149, 182–183, 185–189, 199–200, 202–207, 209, 213, 215, 217–218, 226–227, 229, 234n11
Consortium of Social Science Associations, 189
Contact tracing, 163

Contraception. *See* Birth control
Convenience samples, 193
Cook, Kevin, 155
Cornell University Medical Center, 53
Cosmopolitan, 116, 135, 152–155
Cottrell, Leonard, 43, 45; *Predicting Success or Failure in Marriage,* 43
Criminals, 32–33, 51, 56, 58, 83
Culture wars, 186
Curran, James, 83, 165
Current Population Survey, 197
Cvetkovich, George, 93

Dallas Gay Alliance, 198
Dannemeyer, William, 185–188, 201, 203–204, 206
Darmon, Richard, 186–188
Darrow, William, 163–166
Data analysis, 6–10, 89, 128, 151, 157, 167
Data collection, 5, 7, 12, 15–16, 50, 79, 99, 113, 128, 141, 151, 157, 171, 209, 220, 228, 246n31
Date rape, 124–125, 149, 227
Davis, Katharine, 9, 28, 30–35, 37, 47
Decter, Midge: *The New Chastity,* 123
DeLamater, John, 84–85
DeMartino, Manfred, 113–114
Democratic party, 97, 102, 202–207
Demographic research, 61–66, 88, 105–106, 108, 121, 175, 180, 190, 209
Denton, Jeremiah, 102–103, 189
Department of Health, Education, and Welfare, 96, 98
Department of Health and Human Services, 187, 189, 201, 204
Deviance, 2–3, 5, 53, 83–84, 159, 167, 185, 208
Dickinson, Robert Latou, 40–41, 53, 57
DiClemente, Ralph, 194
Divorce, 36–38, 49, 87, 116, 200
Domestic Policy Council, 197, 199
Donnelly, Denise, 130
Double standard, 70–74, 78
Douching: postcoital, 64; rectal, 165, 170
Drug use, 83, 104, 139, 159, 167, 169, 173–174, 176–178, 180, 191–198, 211

Ehrmann, Winston, 69–71
Eichel, Edward, 131, 185

Eisen, Marvin, 105–106
11 Million Teenagers, 95–96
Ellis, Havelock, 5, 23–24, 32
Enos, Sondra Forsyth, 153
Epidemics: adolescent pregnancy, 87–109; AIDS, 158–159, 163–175, 176–208
Eugenics movement, 37, 62
Evaluation research, 220
Evans, Sylvia, 110
Evans, Wainwright: *The Revolt of Modern Youth,* 38
Exner, Max, 9–10, 18–22, 24–25, 30, 102
Extramarital intercourse, 24–25, 28, 75, 147, 149, 153, 214

Family: traditional view of, 2, 21, 23, 35, 36–38, 42, 49, 52, 54, 56, 200; and homosexuality, 2, 176, 185–187; size of, 63, 88; decline of, 97, 101–102; sexual abuse in, 129
Family life movement, 42, 67
Family Planning Perspectives, 90–91, 93, 104–105, 211–212
Family planning programs, 92–93, 96, 104–105
Family Research Council, 1–2, 182, 201
Fantasies, 119–120, 127, 131
Farrell, Warren, 150
Fay, Robert, 197
Feminism. *See* Women's movement
Ferrell, Mary, 77–78, 80
Fertility: decline in, 23; studies of, 61–66; adolescent, 87–109
Fisher, Seymour, 114–115
Fisting, 169, 172
Fitch, Florence, 30
Ford, Kathleen, 87
Ford Foundation, 106
Forrest, Jacqueline, 107
Foucault, Michel, 3, 5, 13
Foundations, 48, 54, 59, 62–63, 106–107, 122, 213
Francis, Don, 165
Frank, Ellen, 153
Freedman, Ronald, 8, 62–63, 88, 103
Freeman, Harrop, 75–76
Freeman, Ruth, 75–76
Freud, Sigmund, 4–5, 23–24, 38, 40, 111, 116

Frigidity, 41
Fundamentalism, 3, 182, 185–186, 203
Funding. See Surveys, funding of
Furstenburg, Frank, 105, 107

Gagnon, John, 1, 79–81, 85, 129, 180–182, 184–185, 188, 205, 215, 258n11
Gay activists, 162, 171, 198–199, 212
Gay liberation movement, 1, 123, 160, 162, 207, 226
Gay men, 33, 116, 154, 159–163, 252n12; and AIDS crisis, 158–175, 176–208, 226, 228; sexual identity of, 160–162; number of partners, 161, 163–167, 169–172, 174, 221; as interviewers, 171–173, 223. See also Homosexuality/homosexuals
Gay Related Immune Disease, 166
Gebhard, Paul, 48, 51, 56–57, 79
Gender differences: biological, 3, 17, 30; sexual, 4–5, 9, 11–12, 17, 23–27, 41, 43; among researchers, 8, 11–12, 28, 35, 41, 60, 84, 222–223, 225–226, 235n30
Gendered sexuality, 32
Gender equality, 29, 37–38, 82
General Social Survey, 181, 184, 196, 221, 258n11
Gestalt therapy, 110
Gilbaugh, James, Jr., 155
Gilder, George: Sexual Suicide, 123
Gillilland, Ruth, 130
Gonorrhea, 21, 27, 164, 178, 190
Goodman, Ellen, 217
Gordon, Linda, 145
Government: and morality, 4, 102; funding of surveys, 10–11, 64, 74, 79, 87–105, 114, 122, 124, 130, 160, 169, 175, 177–178, 180–208, 209–218, 219, 228; early involvement in sex surveys, 48, 59; demographic research, 61–63, 105–106, 108; intervention in sexual matters, 84; programs for adolescent pregnancy, 92, 94–98, 102, 108; and AIDS crisis, 159, 164–169, 174–175, 176–178, 180–208, 209–211, 213, 215–216
Grady, William, 211
Greenblatt, Cathy, 130
Greene, Gael, 136; Sex and the College Girl, 136
Groves, Ernest, 36–37, 42

Groves, Robert, 150–151
Growth of American Families studies, 62
Guilt, 4, 82, 123, 131
Gulick, Luther, 16–18

Hall, G. Stanley, 15–18, 20–23, 25, 43; The Pedagogical Seminary, 15
Hamilton, Gilbert, 8, 38–41, 47–48, 52
Hass, Aaron: Teenage Sexuality, 141
Hatch, Orrin, 102
Hayakawa, S. I., 97–98
Healy, Bernadine, 190, 199, 201–202
Health-risk behavior, 158, 164, 167–175, 176–182, 186, 190–196, 198, 208, 209, 211, 221
Hedonism, 82–83, 92, 116, 122–123, 207
Hefner, Hugh, 79
Helms, Jesse, 12, 100, 205–207, 217
Hemophilia, 159, 211
Henry, George, 53–56
Hepatitis B, 159, 164–166, 178
Herpes, 190
Heterosexual imperative, 38
Heterosexuality: as normal identity, 3–4, 24, 116, 159–160, 207–208, 223; and AIDS, 175, 176–208, 228
Hill, Charles, 110
Hite, Shere, 141, 143–152, 154–155, 226; The Hite Report, 141; The Hite Report on Male Sexuality, 146; Women and Love, 149–150
HIV infection, 167, 169–171, 173–175, 176–180, 186, 190–201, 208, 211, 215–216, 223, 228. See also AIDS
Hobbs, A. H., 59
Hochschild, Arlie, 151
Hogan, Dennis, 98
Hohman, Leslie, 70–71
Homophobia, 171, 182
Homosexuality/homosexuals, 166; percent of population, 1–2, 9–11, 160, 212, 216, 258n11; as normal identity, 2, 34, 122, 160, 179, 227; early attitudes toward, 32–34, 53–54; Kinsey on, 53, 55–56, 160; sex surveys about, 116, 121–122, 154, 159–163, 211–213, 216; sexual identity, 160–163, 166; sexual desire, 161–162. See also Gay men; Lesbians
Hoon, Emily, 118

Hoon, Peter, 118
Hormones, 97, 99–101, 190
Horn, Marjorie, 104
Horstman, William, 168–169
House Committee to Investigate Tax Free
   Foundations, 59
Hudson, Walter, 131
Humanistic psychology, 111–112, 115
Human potential movement, 110–117,
   120–121, 133
Human sexuality courses, 81
Hunt, Morton, 141–144, 146, 151; *Sexual
   Behavior in the 1970's*, 141
Hunter, James, 186

Identity. *See* Sexual identity
Imagined Processes Inventory, 132
Insertive anal intercourse, 171–172, 174
Institute for Sex Research, 79
Intercourse: role in marriage, 18, 24–25,
   29, 32, 37–38, 40–41, 45, 49, 66, 70, 186;
   91, 96, 100; promiscuous, 21–23, 178–
   179; extramarital, 24–25, 28, 75, 214;
   first, 47; number of partners, 91, 96, 161,
   163–167, 169–172, 174, 192, 196, 214,
   217, 221–222, 259n4; satisfaction from,
   144; anal, 164–165, 167, 169–175, 177,
   179–180, 188, 200, 210, 216
Interviewer training, 7–8, 62, 186,
   210
Interviewing techniques. *See* Surveys, methodology
Interview schedules, 7, 57, 128, 199
Intravenous drug use, 159, 173–174,
   176–178, 180, 191–198, 211

Jaroff, Leon, 110
Jay, Karla, 162–165; *The Gay Report*, 162
Jessor, Richard, 83–85, 107
Johnson, Virginia, 116, 130, 215; *Human
   Sexual Inadequacy*, 116; *Human Sexual
   Response*, 116
Jones, James H.: *Alfred C. Kinsey*, 236n34
Jong, Erica, 144
Journal of Sex Research, 117, 131

Kaiser, Lisa, 188
Kanin, Eugene, 71, 124, 126

Kantner, John F., 87–92, 94–96, 101, 140,
   210, 224
Kaposi's sarcoma, 158
Kaposi's Sarcoma and Opportunistic Infection Task Force, 158–159
Keith, Bruce, 130
Kennedy, Edward, 97, 102–103, 204, 206
Kennedy, May, 257n52
King, Karl, 82
Kinsey, Alfred C., 7–9, 36, 48–53, 55–61,
   63, 78–80, 108, 116, 137, 139, 142, 146,
   151–152, 160, 163, 165–166, 175, 179,
   184–185, 188, 197–198, 208, 219–220,
   225, 227, 235n30, 236n34, 254n13,
   258n11; *Sexual Behavior in the Human
   Female*, 1–2, 49, 217; *Sexual Behavior in
   the Human Male*, 1–2, 48–50, 55, 58–59,
   212, 217
Kinsey Institute, 79, 115, 160, 181, 184,
   254n13
Kirkendall, Lester, 67–68, 70, 72–73
Kiser, Clyde, 61–62
Kitagawa, Evelyn, 98
Klepinger, Daniel, 211
Knight, Bob, 1, 3, 182–183
Kohl, Herbert, 206
Kolata, Gina: *Sex in America*, 214
Koss, Mary, 124–129
Krafft-Ebing, Richard von, 4

Ladies' Home Journal, 153–154
Lake, Alice, 136–137
Lambert, Richard, 59
Landis, Carney, 54
Landis, Judson T., 75
Landis, Mary G., 75
Latinos, 193–195
Laumann, Edward, 1, 180–181, 188, 197,
   204–206, 213–215, 217–218, 220, 222;
   Sex in America, 214; *The Social Organiza-
   tion of Sexuality*, 214
Lesbians, 33–35, 154; sexual identity of,
   160–163; and AIDS crisis, 164, 182, 226.
   See also Homosexuality/homosexuals
Lewin, Curt, 111
Lewis, Roberet, 78
Lewontin, Richard, 217–218, 220
Liberals, 92–94, 98, 102–103, 182–183, 185,
   202–207, 213, 226

Likelihood of Rape Scale, 127
Lindsey, Ben: *The Revolt of Modern Youth,*
38
Linnaeus, Carolus, 50
Little, Joan, 124
Love, 18, 38, 68–70
Lower class, 15, 22, 27, 50–51, 70–71, 83,
94, 101, 200

MacCorquodale, Patricia, 84–85
Mademoiselle, 143, 156–157
Magazine surveys, 135–157
Malamuth, Neil, 126–128
Males: as virgins, 70; and adolescent preg-
nancy, 97, 99
Marital adjustment, 41–44, 48–49, 60–61,
66, 68, 111
Marital courses/books, 42, 47, 56–57,
60–61, 66, 67–68, 72, 74–75, 81, 115
Market Research Corporation of America,
61
Marriage: role of sex in, 18, 24–25, 29, 32,
37–38, 40–41, 45, 49, 66, 70, 80, 186,
225; companionate, 38, 42, 47; and fertil-
ity, 61–66; sex before, 67–86; human po-
tential in, 112–113
Martin, Clyde, 36, 115
Maslow, Abraham, 111–113, 120; *Toward a
Psychology of Being,* 111
Mason, James, 189, 199, 201–202
Masters, William, 116, 130, 215; *Human
Sexual Inadequacy,* 116; *Human Sexual
Response,* 116
Masturbation, 9, 172; negative attitudes toward, 16–18, 20–21, 24–26; as normal activity, 27, 31–32; as substitute for
intercourse, 35, 144–145; as aid in intercourse, 40, 52, 115
Mattachine Society, 160–161
McDermott, Jim, 204
McGee, Marsha, 93–94
McKusick, Leon, 168–169
Media, 11, 219; and homosexuality, 1, 159,
212, 216–217; and Kinsey's research,
59–60; and premarital sex, 75–77, 81, 83;
and adolescent pregnancy, 90–93, 108;
and sexual liberation, 115–116, 122–124;
and commercial sex surveys, 144–145;
and AIDS crisis, 184, 210

Menstruation, 24, 28, 32
Mero, Paul, 185–188, 201–202
Merrill, Lilburn, 32–33
Mesagno, Frances Palamara, 158
Methodology. *See* Surveys, methodology
Michael, Robert, 1, 180–182, 188, 205
Michaels, Stuart, 1, 188, 205, 216, 258n11
Middle class, 12, 18, 89–91, 111, 119, 195,
200, 224; surveys focusing on, 7, 12, 22,
84, 86, 93, 223–224; women, 9, 28, 33,
37–38, 41, 45, 70, 84, 102, 112–113, 225;
young men, 14–17, 88; self-importance,
20, 31, 36, 51, 68, 75, 223–224; men, 21,
50, 70, 72, 84, 113, 177; couples, 22–23,
41–43, 61–65, 177–178; families, 37–38,
102; young women, 88, 90–91, 93–97,
101
Milbank Memorial Fund, 62
Miller, Brent, 106
Miller, George, 204
Miller, Shelby, 98
Monogamy, 51, 122, 147, 179, 186–187, 216
Moore, Kristin, 106–107
Moore, Paul, Jr., 140
Mormons, 106, 185
Morality, 4, 14, 16, 20, 22–23, 26, 49, 61,
67, 72, 76, 83, 93, 102, 186
Morokoff, Patricia, 130
Morris, Martina, 221, 259n4
Morris, Naomi, 65
Morrow, Prince, 21
Morbidity and Mortality Weekly Report, 167
Mosher, Clelia, 6, 28–30, 207
Mosher, Donald, 82
Mosteller, Frederick, 58
Motherhood, 17–18, 92, 95, 105, 108
Moynihan, Daniel Patrick, 205
Multi-Center AIDS Study, 174–175
Murnen, Sarah, 126

National Academy of Sciences, 48, 107,
176, 180, 220
National AIDS Behavioral Survey, 210–211,
258n11
National Cancer Institute, 174, 198
National Center for Health Statistics, 88,
103, 197–199, 256n45
National Center for the Prevention and
Control of Rape, 124

National Fertility Surveys, 63–65, 89–90, 189
National Gay Task Force, 1–2, 160, 162
National Health Interview Survey, 193, 197–198
National Health and Nutrition Examination Survey, 256n45
National Institute on Aging, 130
National Institute of Alcohol Abuse and Alcoholism, 83, 174
National Institute on Allergy and Infectious Diseases, 170, 174
National Institute of Child Health and Human Development, 63, 65, 79, 84, 88–89, 94–95, 98–99, 103–105, 107, 130, 180, 182, 186–189, 199–201, 206, 210–211, 213
National Institute for Drug Abuse, 177
National Institute of Health Statistics, 65
National Institute of Mental Health, 74, 124, 130, 160, 169, 174, 210
National Institutes of Health, 169, 175, 180, 183, 185, 190, 199, 203–206, 213
National Longitudinal Survey of Adolescent Health, 213
National Longitudinal Survey of Work Experience and Youth, 103
National Opinion Research Center, 79–80, 180–184, 186–188, 196, 199, 205–206, 208
National Research Council, 48, 58, 180–181, 184–185, 196–197
National Science Foundation, 181
National Survey of Adolescent Males, 209–210, 222
National Survey of Children, 103, 106
National Survey of Families and Households, 130
National Surveys of Family Growth, 65–66, 103–104
National Survey of Men, 209–212
National Survey of Unmarried Women, 104
National Survey of Women, 209–211
National Survey of Young Men, 101
National Survey of Young Women, 89, 101
National Victim Center, 126
Newton, Isaac, 15
New York Blood Bank, 164, 178
New York City, 8, 21–22, 38–39, 160, 163, 166, 173–174, 191–192, 195

New York Review of Books, 217
Nitrite inhalants, 159
Nixon, Richard, 88, 92
Nonrespondents, 8, 113
Normality. *See* Sexual normality
Nurius, Paula, 131

Odum, Howard, 42
Office of Adolescent Pregnancy Programs, 98, 104–106
Office of Management and Budget, 180, 183, 186–187, 189
Office of Population Affairs, 88
Ogburn, William, 42
Olsen, Terrance, 106
O'Malley, Paul, 166
Oral-genital sex, 169, 172–173, 188–189, 200
Orgasm: clitoral/vaginal, 38, 40, 52, 116, 215; female, 38, 40–41, 44–48, 51–52, 60, 116, 132, 144, 153, 155, 215; multiple, 40, 52; male, 47–48
Orgasm inadequacy, 40, 45, 47, 82
Osofsky, Howard, 114–115

Packard, Vance: *The Sexual Wilderness*, 76
Padian, Nancy, 177
Paperwork Reduction Act, 184
Partners, number of, 91, 96, 161, 163–167, 169–172, 174, 192, 196, 214, 217, 221–222, 259n4
Pearl, Raymond, 58–59
Peck, M. W., 26–27
Pedophilia, 56, 185, 224, 254n13
Peplau, Letitia Anne, 110
Perkins, John, 71
Permissiveness with affection, 73–75, 77, 227
Peterson, James, 150–151
Pietropinto, Anthony, 148–149
Planned Parenthood Federation of America, 61, 90, 103, 107–108
Playboy, 116, 123, 138–144, 146, 150, 154–156
Pleck, Joseph, 210–212
Pneumocystis carinii pneumonia, 158, 165
Podell, Lawrence, 71
Polit, Denise, 105
Pomeroy, Wardell B., 36, 48, 52, 57, 60

Population Association of America, 210
Population Research Act (1970), 88
Pornography, 115, 224; and guilt, 82; as aid in intercourse, 119; gender responses to, 120, 215; and sexual abuse/assault, 123, 127–128; gay/lesbian, 161
Precocity, 15, 17, 20
Pregnancy, adolescent, 87–109, 190, 228
Premarital intercourse, 19, 25, 27, 46, 66, 67–86, 87–88, 92
Presidential Commission on AIDS, 187, 197
Presser, Stanley, 217, 220
Pretests of questionnaires, 63, 84, 93, 184, 199, 210
Prisoners, 51, 56, 58
Probability sampling, 7, 58, 62–63, 78–79, 84, 89, 93, 113, 122, 128, 130, 170, 180, 193, 196–197, 228
Problem behavior, 83–84, 190
Project Redirection, 105
Promiscuity, 10, 21–23, 49, 72–74, 76, 91, 128, 161–162, 166, 176, 178–179
Prostitution, 27; as threat to family, 21, 38; and masturbation, 24–26; causes, 25, 30; and AIDS, 164, 177–178, 192
Psychology, 15, 21–22, 25, 37, 42, 89, 95, 113, 121
Psychology Today, 137–138, 145
Public Health Service, 114, 180, 189, 196, 198

Questionnaires: self-administered, 8–9, 221; design/wording of, 9, 80, 84–85, 99–100, 122, 143, 180–182, 199–201; pretests, 63, 84, 93, 184, 199, 210; for commercial sex surveys, 137, 143; publishing of, 228

Race, 98–99, 200; of interviewer, 8; and sexual behavior, 64, 210, 223–224; and adolescent pregnancy, 89–101, 104–106; and HIV transmission, 193–195, 200
Rainwater, Lee, 65
Rand Corporation, 105
Random sampling, 7–8, 22, 63, 72, 75, 79, 128, 130, 170, 210, 232n14
Rape, 56, 124–129, 149, 226–228
Reagan, Ronald, 186–187, 197
Receptive anal intercourse, 167, 169–172, 174–175

Rectal douching, 165, 170
Redbook, 145–146, 148, 153, 155–156
Reece, B. Carroll, 59
Reich, Charles: *The Greening of America*, 81
Reisman, Judith: *Kinsey, Sex and Fraud*, 185
Reiss, Ira, 67, 72–76, 78, 84–85
Religion: and sexual attitudes, 3, 14, 16–18, 78–79, 182, 185–186, 203; and family size, 63
Republican party, 97, 102, 182, 185–186, 202–207
Research and Decision Corporation, 171
Research Triangle Institute, 197–199, 202
Respondents: voices, 59, 140, 143, 146, 219, 225–229; honesty of, 77, 217–218
Response rates, 8, 63, 80, 84, 122, 143, 168
Richardson, Michaela, 201–202
Riley, John, 61
Rindfuss, Ronald, 189, 199–202, 213
Risking the Future, 107–108
Robert Wood Johnson Foundation, 213
Robie, Walter, 14, 22–25, 27–28, 32, 37
Robinson, Paul, 217
Rockefeller, John D., Jr., 30, 48
Rockefeller Foundation, 48, 54, 59, 63, 107
Roebuck, Julian, 93–94
Rogers, Carl, 110–111
Roosa, Mark, 106
Rowland, Representative, 204
Rubin, Donald, 150–151
Rubin, Lillian, 130; *Erotic Wars*, 133–134
Rubin, Zick, 110
Rusk, Dean, 59
Ryder, Norman, 63–64

Sadd, Susan, 145–146
Sampling techniques, 168, 171, 175, 184, 200–201, 245n22. *See also* Probability sampling; Random sampling
San Francisco, Calif., 160–161, 166–173, 179, 190, 194
San Francisco AIDS Foundation, 171–172
San Francisco Men's Health Study, 170–171, 195–196
Scales, 43, 45, 55, 73–74, 82, 118–119, 121, 127, 131–132
Schaffner, Bertram, 70–71
Schroeder, Patricia, 202–203, 213, 257n52

Schwartz, Pepper, 121–122; *American Couples*, 122
Science, 184
Scientific sexology, 117, 131
Self-abuse. *See* Masturbation
Self-actualization, 113–115, 120–121, 131
Seropositivity, 167, 175
Seventeen, 136–137, 140, 155–156
Sex education, 18–23, 25, 30–31, 45, 56, 78, 82, 92–94, 105–106, 189, 206
Sex fantasies, 119–120, 127, 131
Sexological surveys, 113–134
Sexology, 5, 117, 121, 129, 131, 134, 214–215, 229
Sex therapy, 116, 131
Sexual abstinence, 18, 20–21, 26–27, 105–106, 186, 189, 206
Sexual adjustment. *See* Marital adjustment
Sexual aggression, 126–128
Sexual arousability, 24, 41, 44, 69, 82, 117–121, 127, 132
Sexual Arousability Inventory, 118–119, 132
Sexual assault. *See* Rape
Sexual Daydreaming Scale, 132
Sexual desire, 4, 9, 26–27, 120, 228; of females, 12, 17, 23–25, 29–35, 37–38, 41, 44–45, 51–52, 64, 68–69, 74, 123, 225; of males, 12, 23–24, 29–30, 38, 44–45, 51, 68, 70–71, 73, 123, 224; homosexual, 161–162
Sexual development, 9, 14–20, 25, 27, 31, 80–81
Sexual hygiene, 10, 18, 21–24
Sexual identity, 3–4, 160–163, 166
Sexual Interaction Inventory, 121
Sexual intercourse. *See* Intercourse
Sexuality, 11, 20, 25, 29, 31–32, 79, 129–130, 223–224
Sexual liberation, 5, 21, 33, 37, 76–77, 93, 114–117, 121–123, 129, 132–133, 186, 224–227
Sexually transmitted diseases (STDs), 21, 23, 25–27, 158–159, 163–174, 176–208, 210–211, 218, 224, 226, 228. *See also specific diseases*
Sexual networks, 181–182, 192, 214, 216
Sexual normality, 9, 228; homosexuality as, 2, 34, 122, 160, 179, 207, 227; hetero-

sexuality as, 3–4, 24, 116, 159–160, 207–208, 223; early attitudes toward, 22, 24, 30, 32, 34, 49; Kinsey's view of, 49–50, 160, 227
Sexual repression, 23, 112, 117, 225
Sexual revolution, 64, 68, 74, 76–81, 85, 91, 138, 142, 146, 227
Sexual scripts, 129, 215
Sexual variation, 4, 43, 53, 56
Sexual victimization, 124–129
Shaver, Phillip, 137
Siegel, Karolynn, 158
Simenauer, Jacqueline, 148–149
Simon, Paul, 206–207
Simon, William, 79–81, 83, 85, 129
Smith, Tom, 196, 221–223
Social class: and sexual relations, 27–28, 50–51, 70–71, 223–224; and population growth, 61–65; and adolescent pregnancy, 90, 93–96, 98–99; and HIV transmission, 195, 200
Social hygiene movement, 21–24, 94
Social networks, 181–182, 196, 214
Society for the Scientific Study of Sex, 117
Sociology, 42–43, 67, 79, 113, 121, 130, 217–218
Sociometrics, 105
Sonenstein, Freya, 209–212, 222
Sorenson, Robert, 140–141
Specter, Arlen, 208
Spencer, Herbert, 15
Stall, Ron, 179
Statistical methods, 5, 58–59, 175
STDs. *See* Sexually transmitted diseases
Stonewall riots, 161
Student activism, 77, 81–83, 88
Student Non-Violent Coordinating Committee, 76
Students. *See* College students
Success Express Program, 106
Sudman, Seymour, 181
Sue, David, 119–120
Sullivan, Louis, 187–189, 201–203
Summary of Health and AIDS-Related Practices, 184–189, 196, 199–200, 205–206, 209–211, 227
Supreme Court, U. S., 92, 208
Syphilis, 21, 159, 163–164, 178, 198
Szmuness, Wolf, 164

Tanfer, Koray, 104, 211
Tavris, Carol, 137, 145–146
Taylor, William Sentman, 26
Tebor, Irving, 70
Teenagers. *See* Adolescence
Terman, Lewis, 43–49, 52–53, 56, 113, 155;
    Genetic Studies of Genius, 45–46
Thomas, Clarence, 208
Thomas, W. I., 30
Thompson, Sharon, 260n7
Tifft, Larry, 77
Title IX, 92
Tolone, William, 77–78, 80
Tortu, Stephanie, 196
Tourangeau, Roger, 221–222
Tukey, John, 58, 175
Turner, Charles, 184–185, 197, 222
Tuskegee Institute syphilis experiment, 198

Udry, J. Richard, 65, 99–102, 189, 199–201,
    213
Upper class, 22, 197
Urban Institute, 210

Vaginal orgasm, 38, 40, 52, 116
Venereal disease. *See* Sexually transmitted
    diseases
Victorians, 4, 17–18, 29, 38, 40, 48, 69,
    224–225
Vietnam war, 88, 139
Virginity, 46, 69–70, 76, 83–84, 104–106,
    140
Voeller, Bruce, 1–2, 160, 162, 179
Volunteer bias, 122

Waller, Willard: *The Family*, 42
Wallin, Paul, 43–47

Wallis, Claudia, 150
Walsh, Robert, 77–78, 80
Walter, Heather, 191
Washington Times, 185, 201
Waterman, Caroline, 120–121
Waxman, Henry, 103, 202–204, 206
Weeks, Jeffrey, 224
Weeks, Michael, 198
Weinberg, Martin, 160–163
Wells, Frederick Lyman, 26–27
Westoff, Charles, 63–64
Whelpton, Pascal, 61–62
White, Lynn, 130
White, Matilda, 61
Whites. *See* European Americans
Williams, Colin, 160
Wincze, John, 118
Winkelstein, Warren, Jr., 170–171
Wolfe, Linda, 152
Women researchers, 12, 28, 117, 222–223,
    225–226, 235n30
Women's movement, 70, 120, 123,
    143–144, 148–149, 151, 226
Working class. *See* Lower class
World War I, 21, 25–26, 31, 33
World War II, 62, 68, 70, 94, 160

Young, Allen, 162–165; *The Gay Report*, 162
Young Men's Christian Association, 14,
    16–18, 20–21
Youth Risk Behavior Surveillance System,
    192–193

Zellman, Gail, 105–106
Zelnik, Melvin, 87–92, 94–96, 101–102,
    140, 210, 224